Frak You!

Published by ECW Press
2120 Queen Street East, Suite 200, Toronto, Ontario, Canada M4E 1E2

LIBRARY AND ARCHIVES CANADA CATALOGUING IN PUBLICATION

Storm, Jo, 1972–
Frak you! : the ultimate unauthorized guide to Battlestar Galactica / Jo Storm.

ISBN 978-1-55022-789-5

1. Battlestar Galactica (Television program). I. Title

PN1992.77.B38S76 2007   791.45'72   C2007-903576-0

Developing editor: Jennifer Hale
Front cover image: Getty Images
Back cover photo: Christina Radish
Typesetting: Gail Nina
Production: Rachel Brooks
Printed by Webcom

DISTRIBUTION

CANADA: Jaguar Book Group, 100 Armstrong Avenue, Georgetown, ON, L7G 5S4
UNITED STATES: Independent Publishers Group, 814 North Franklin Street, Chicago, Illinois 60610

PRINTED AND BOUND IN CANADA

ECW PRESS
ecwpress.com

Table of Contents

Acknowledgments

When I started writing this book, I had no idea how huge the *BSG* universe would be, and I never thought I would have so many people to thank. I would like to thank ECW Press for picking up on my vision and encouraging me while I wrote the book, and supporting my choices. I'd especially like to thank my editor, Jen Hale, without whom this would be a much messier book, and whose weekly e-mails raving or ranting about the latest episode kept me galvanized throughout the process. Thanks very much to Professor Allan Weiss at York University for his humor and insights. To the fans, who discussed and argued and made lists and parallels and rode the same waves of emotion that I did with each new episode, thank you. To my readers, Zoë and Laurel, thank you for your encouragement and criticism, both of which helped make this book more thoughtful and streamlined. Finally, my overwhelming gratitude to JEP and EB, without whom this book could never have been written.

DRADIS Contact: Reading This Book

Science fiction conventions are a great way to meet new people, talk to old friends, and indulge completely in all things sci-fi. You can see stars, get autographs, and attend costume parties, and there are also informal get-togethers called "panels" in which participants cordon off a particular theme or subject or show and then talk exhaustively about it. In recent years, there have been more and more panels on the new kid in town, the reimagined *Battlestar Galactica*.

And they are packed. I mean, to the walls packed. Standing room only packed. Out the door packed. Why? Because for many viewers of the show, this is what they've been waiting for since those words "These are the voyages of the Starship *Enterprise*" were first heard on television sets across North America. A show with a clearly different, clearly important, clearly realistic look at a postapocalyptic society, that asks all the big questions, answers them, and then stares defiantly back into televisionland, *daring* us to disagree.

Battlestar Galactica's stories and subjects hit hard, and the media has noticed. Mainstream publications like *Time*, *Rolling Stone*, and *TV Guide* have featured the cast on their covers and run interviews and discussions about the show in their pages. National newspapers like the *Toronto Star* and the *Chicago Tribune* feature the series — and not only in their entertainment section. *The David Letterman Show* snags its stars, and its cult status is ensured as cast members lend their voices to characters on the online spoof-fest *Robot Chicken*.

For new viewers who have never even heard of Skiffy (the SciFi channel) much less watch it, there's a sense that they *finally* understand some of the appeal of that "sci-fi geeky stuff"; not because they're science fiction fans, but because *BSG* transcends its own conventions — it's much more than what most people think of when they think of science fiction. It's a way to talk about *now*, and when that's not enough, to ask even bigger questions about the future, about our responsibilities for the past and for each other. It's not filled with technobabble and physics lessons; it's filled with swearing and political arguments and easily understood dialogue. It's not about space pirates or space aliens, or even its titular spaceship; it's about ground crews and grunts and students and prostitutes. When someone says "engage," they mean it militarily, not in a transportation sense.

I have yet to meet a person who doesn't at least grudgingly admit that *BSG*, whatever they don't like about it, tells a good story. This book's purpose is to shed some light on that good story, and on why this show makes us sit up and take notice (take notes, even!) while we're watching it. Hopefully, it will give you a deeper understanding of why you enjoy it, and why it's one of the most important fictional television shows on right now.

This is not a book that tells you *what happened next*: it's a book that explores what has happened, and what those events might mean for later, and why. To get the most out of this compendium you need to watch the show first, because I won't be rehashing plots. Since *BSG* is still a newish show, I don't give away information earlier than it happens, so spoiler-free folks can breathe easy (please note: this does not apply to sidebars, which may contain some small spoilers). But, if you want to be sure, then stick to the guide only until at least the end of season 1. Each episode has its own entry that discusses in depth what it's trying to achieve and tries to connect some of the series' dots. At the end of each analysis there's some extra material that's broken out in handy little chunks for you:

Headcount: Starting out with the 47,973 survivors of a nuclear holocaust, I track the number of survivors as they are listed on the white board or stated by a character in a particular episode. Starting in season 2 that number is listed in the opening credits as well, but it's nice to have it at a glance after you've watched the episode.

Are You There, God? It's Me, Gaius. Follows the tortured footsteps of Dr. Gaius Baltar from staunch atheist scientist to radical religious convert and his many, many shades of gray in between. Gaius's journey is not just a one-way trip from geek to guru, and since his story line is often convoluted and can seem confusing, it'll be broken out separately. We'll also discuss other human and Cylons as "gods."

All of This Has Happened Before: Some of the stories in the series are rewritings or reimaginings of ancient myths, so I'll look at those here, exploring how they've been incorporated or updated for the show.

Numbers: Numbers are an essential part of the *BSG* universe, and we'll look at the important ones that come up throughout the series. For more on numbers and their importance check out "Apocalypse, Now?"

Interesting Fact: Information that isn't directly tied to the episode's story line but gives a behind-the-scenes flavor. You know, gossipy stuff.

What's In a Name? Many characters' names are important both to their personal journey and to the overall story, and this is where we'll track where these names came from in history, and what it could mean for them — and us.

Did You Notice? A sort of catch-all place for trivia, goofs, and the occasional nitpick.

Classic *Battlestar Galactica*: Many of the episodes are directly inspired by or incorporate story lines from the original *Battlestar Galactica* of 1979, and they'll be mentioned here.

So Say We All: A summation from that particular episode — sometimes it's funny, and sometimes it's a line that really gets to the heart of what I think the episode is trying to say.

Frak You!

The World of *Battlestar Galactica*

"Here lies a slumbering giant, its name known to many, its voice remembered by but a few. For a brief moment, it strode the Earth, telling tall tales of things that never were, then stumbled over a rating point and fell into a deep sleep." — Ronald Moore, 2003

I n 1978, at a time when science fiction was becoming an increasingly popular genre thanks in large part to the massive 1977 hit *Star Wars*, a cult television series was born. *Battlestar Galactica* told the story of the 12 Colonies, which waged war on the robotic Cylons for a thousand years before finally being defeated in a sneak attack during peace talks. A ragtag fleet of civilian ships survived, led by the battlestar *Galactica*, and embarked on a season-long search for the lost 13th Colony — Earth. Starring Lorne Greene as William Adama, Richard Hatch as Adama's son Apollo, and Dirk Benedict as the womanizing, cigar-smoking Starbuck, the two-hour pilot episode aired in theaters in July 1978 (although only in Canada, Europe, and Japan), and was televised in September of the same year in the United States. The most expensive TV pilot ever at the time, the episode was hugely popular, garnering spectacular Nielsen ratings.

BattlestaR GALACTICA ™ *

ATTACKING OUR HEROES!

© 1978 Universal City Studios, Inc. All Rights Reserved
* a trademark of and licensed by Universal City Studios, Inc.

99

BattlestaR GALACTICA ™ *

RICHARD HATCH IS CAPTAIN APOLLO   3

1978 Universal City Studios, Inc. All Rights Reserved
trademark of and licensed by Universal City Studios, Inc.

The show's creator, Glen Larson, said in an interview, "It's Genesis. It's about the origins of man. And our whole theme and the subtle influences on the costuming, a lot of these things bear a strong resemblance to *The Ten Commandments*, or things of that sort. It's basically the concept of all the human cultures in space having evolved from a mother planet culture." In fact, Larson has said that he originally conceived of the idea for the series back in the 1960s, but was never able to get the project, which he had called *Adam's Ark*, off the ground.

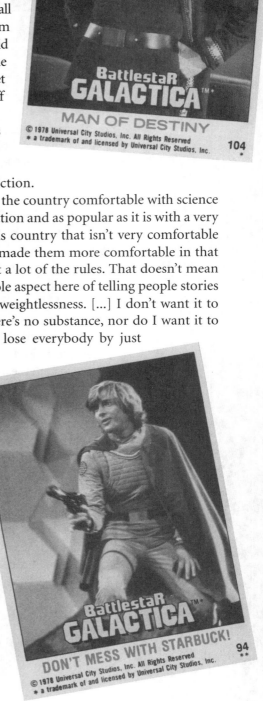

From the beginning, the show's aims were nothing short of ambitious: Larson was determined that *Battlestar Galactica* should be a portal to the world of science fiction.

"It's very important to us to try and make the country comfortable with science fiction. As successful as *Star Trek* is in syndication and as popular as it is with a very avid group, there's still a large section of this country that isn't very comfortable with science fiction. I think [George] Lucas made them more comfortable in that he didn't spend a lot of time worrying about a lot of the rules. That doesn't mean you have to ignore science, but there is a whole aspect here of telling people stories and not worrying about umbilical cords or weightlessness. [...] I don't want it to get to be just an action-adventure where there's no substance, nor do I want it to get to be so wholly philosophical that we lose everybody by just standing around talking about everything."

Later in 1978, Twentieth Century Fox sued Universal Studios, the series' production studio, for plagiarism, claiming that *Battlestar Galactica* had stolen 34 different ideas from *Star Wars*; Universal sued right back, saying that *Star Wars* had stolen ideas from previous studio productions such as *Silent Running*. The lawsuit ended up being dismissed in 1980: neither side came out a decisive winner.

Despite high hopes held by both the creators and the network, *Battlestar Galactica* ultimately proved to be a short-lived success. Despite its huge budget of

U.S. $1 million per episode — gargantuan for the time — its ratings dropped steadily over its one-season run, and in 1979, the series was dropped. Ironically enough, the show won the People's Choice Award for Best New TV Drama Series that year. Everyone involved — from Larson to the show's stars — was disappointed by the cancellation, feeling that it had not been given a fair chance to develop. Larson said, "I think we'll have taken a giant step backwards for science fiction. We've got a truly rare opportunity to really open up that frontier and talk about what could happen out there in space. It doesn't have to be all robots and flying machines."

Fan outrage was universal; protests were held outside ABC studios, and a fairly wide popular movement formed as fans tried to get the show back on the air. In fall of 1979, ABC executives met with Larson to discuss a relaunch, and in 1980, *Galactica 1980* took to the air. It, too, met with an untimely cancellation, after only 10 episodes, in part due to the poor production values. Despite these unfortunate events, the show's cult following remained strong, and several key figures of the original series continued to try for a revival. Chief amongst those figures was Richard Hatch, who produced a demonstration video for studio executives. The video features all key members of the cast in a state-of-the-art special effects environment. Although the video was a fan favorite — and continues to be a fan favorite to this day — the series was not renewed.

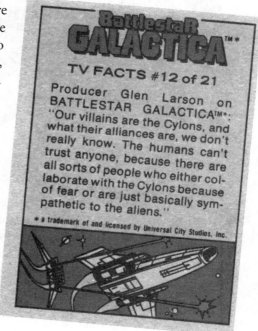

Several other attempts were made between the late 1990s and the early 2000s to revive the series, but it wasn't until Ronald D. Moore came along that *Battlestar Galactica* would rise from the ashes. A veteran of the science fiction genre, Ronald Moore had worked for many years on *Star Trek: The Next Generation*, and his production team had earned an Emmy for Outstanding Drama Series. When *TNG*, as it was affectionately known, ended, Moore had moved on to *Star Trek: Deep Space Nine*. So, when he decided to take on the defunct *Battlestar Galactica*, he knew what he was doing — and television people knew it. Once he had assembled the cast, the actors and production crew went to "boot camp," where they were shown episodes of the original series and where they forged personal bonds. This helped each person find their own sense of the mythology on which the series was based, develop their own character interpretation, and become immersed in the cult of

(ALL *BATTLESTAR GALACTICA* TRADING CARDS FROM THE COLLECTION OF DAVID CARON)

Chief reimaginer Ronald Moore
(ALBERT L. ORTEGA)

Battlestar Galactica — something that would be important if they were to maintain any connection to the series as an entity spanning decades. A huge fan of the original series, Moore went into the project with a deep love and reverence for the original premises in the material — despite the fact that he had implemented a number of more or less critical changes to the premises.

One of these — and probably the most publicly criticized by fans of the original series — was the fact that Starbuck was now a woman. Other characters and relationships underwent similar changes: Boomer became a woman, Apollo and Adama no longer enjoyed a smooth father/son bond, Adama now no longer had a daughter. Many felt that the original Starbuck had been the heart and soul of the series and to change the character in such a way was seen as a form of blasphemy. Still, Moore defended his choices, saying that by making Starbuck a woman, he was actually able to honor the original character much more fully because, as a woman, she wouldn't be a stereotype but an interesting, layered personality. He noted in an interview, "While science fiction has postulated the fully gender-integrated military of the future for some time now, it's seldom portrayed realistically. [...] The original *Galactica* was a product of its time and was obviously sexist in the way even the notion of female pilots was considered crazy until all the men were waylaid by some virus, and then (Holy Lords of Kobol!) the women had to fly the Vipers. I wanted the new *Galactica* to fully integrate women into the equation, but not blink from it, not avoid the unpleasant fact that this won't always go smoothly and that there will be problems along the way."

Battlestar Galactica, Then and Now

Despite the fact that the miniseries aired to both critical and popular acclaim, it was a huge struggle for Moore to get the networks to agree to produce a series. Weighed down by its own history and deemed too expensive for the SciFi Channel, it wasn't until the UK network Sky One decided to pitch in and added their funding to SciFi's that the series was given the green light. Production began in 2004, and Season 1 aired

starting in October of that same year. It was not immediately popular with fans of the original series, as it was considered GINO — *Galactica* In Name Only — with vastly different feel, tone, characters,

mythology, and style. However, those differences only served to emphasize the fact that Moore was engaging in a *reimagining* of the series and not a revival in the traditional sense. A reimagining is similar to what is known as a "reboot" in the comic book world: it means that issues of continuity written before the reboot are considered to not have happened — the story starts over from scratch. Moore's *Battlestar Galactica* is based on the original premise; many of the same characters populate the story; but the story and the way it is told is not the same as the original. In some ways, and as others have argued, it would be nearly impossible to recreate the original *Battlestar Galactica* in today's world; the international context of political upheaval and conflict directly affects the stories that are relevant to contemporary society. As *BSG* writer David Weddle comments, "It's an anti-sci-fi show. It's reinvented the genre, much in the way Sergio Leone and Sam Peckinpah reinvented the Western in the 1960s by turning all the set pieces and iconic characters inside out. [...] Just as *The Wild Bunch* reverberated off of the Vietnam War, this show reverberates off of post-9/11 America." He continues, "We shed the [...] juvenile melodrama of space anomalies and time warps and made it a show about people grappling with the very real

Ronald Moore, Tricia Helfer, Katee Sackhoff, Jamie Bamber, and David Eick: the faces of the new *BSG*
(ALBERT L. ORTEGA)

problems of survival, faith, or the loss of faith, love or the inability to sustain love."

Several high-profile publications have commented on the parallels between the show and current events. *Time* even wrote that *Battlestar Galactica* was, "a ripping sci-fi allegory of the war on terror, complete with religious fundamentalists (here, genocidal robots called Cylons), sleeper cells, civil-liberties crackdowns and even a prisoner-torture scandal." However, Moore rejects the idea of an outright allegory of current issues, saying, "It's about an apocalyptic attack, a group of survivors on the run and they're dealing with issues that are inherently about freedom and security. There's the civilian and the military, and lots of issues it seems very natural for them to grapple with that mirror events in the real world. We talk about it at length in the writers' room and with the cast and directors, trying to figure out where the lines are for us. We never want to go into direct allegory for today's events because there's nothing really interesting about that."

The main differences between the original series and the reinvented one lie primarily in issues of feel and style: while the original series targeted a science fiction audience — and aimed to encourage more people to enjoy science fiction — the reimagined show is much more based in reality than in fantasy. Politics, economics, gender, sexuality, and war tactics are all emphasized in this new version.

Gone are the different alien species to befriend or struggle against; gone is the high-tech gadgetry. In its place is a beaten-up battlestar with less than up-to-snuff equipment. The story remains central in both cases, but the tricks with which the story is told are not the same.

Other changing issues involved gender and ethnicity (aside from Starbuck, the original Boomer was an African American man, compared to the Asian American Boomer of the new series) but there were also differences in the very mythology of the show. In the original, the Cylons were a group of robots (the Centurions in the new show), created not by humans but by a long-extinct race of reptilian aliens. In the new series, the Cylons were created by humankind to "do the hard and dangerous work man no longer wished to do" (this dialogue is from some deleted text of the miniseries). One of the major differences between the two versions lies in the character of Gaius Baltar: originally a willing traitor to the human race, Moore decided to make him a more ambiguous character, because he himself had never really understood why Gaius would turn against the humans. In the reimagined series, Gaius is one of the most finely layered personalities on TV, an unwilling traitor at first, and yet time after time proving himself untrustworthy — to the Cylons and the humans.

One of the new *BSG*'s main concerns is the portrayal of war. Stories of war had been changing dramatically since the mid-1970s, in large part due to the Vietnam War. War is often predicated on the idea that the enemy is *not like us*, somehow dehumanized, and this is partly in order to make killing less difficult for soldiers. But Vietnam saw a large and popular uprising against this practice in the U.S., and it was reflected in science fiction as well, with stories like Ursula K. Le Guin's *The Word for World Is Forest*, or *The Dispossessed*. The enemy was again and again portrayed as being *like* us, prone to the same emotions and fears, and having the same rights as we had. In addition, it was becoming increasingly hypocritical in a multicultural environment to call another culture an "enemy" since many Western countries were lands of opportunity, home to members of that same "enemy" — only they were citizens now, who participated in their new country's life. The new *BSG* continues to wrestle with these questions through the reimagining of the Cylons as human look-alikes, as well as through characters such as Gaius, who until now has been seen as a human enemy of humanity.

Internally, the new *BSG*'s "art of war" holds its subject together visually as well as thematically. The computer-generated imagery is seamless, thanks to new technologies (which, ironically, are part of the themes of the show itself!), and color, too, plays a big part in the reimagined *BSG*. The Cylons, with their red glowing eyes and — in the first season, anyway — glowing spines, bring to mind a host of meaning, from blood, to anger, to danger Will Robinson!

The new *Battlestar Galactica* is a perfect example of using science fiction ideas to talk about present-day anxieties and problems. Contradictory points of view and ethics abound: on the one hand, we're told to be tolerant of people with different beliefs ("Bastille Day") and to practice compassionate views ("A Measure of Salvation"). On the other hand, we live in unjust societies ("Black Market"), and our beliefs are not all the same ("Epiphanies"). These differences are further complicated by the fact that we are encouraged to live communally ("The Passage"), and yet all around us are messages that say "take care of yourself first, screw everyone else" ("Black Market"); but when we do that, we are branded as evil. We want certain liberties protected ("Colonial Day"), but we also want unlimited freedom ("The Captain's Hand").

The new *BSG* is stretching and reimagining both conventions of gender — as when significant characters were made female — and genre conventions, that is, the little signals that tell us what we're watching, like a laugh track tells us we're watching comedy.

Thanks to *BSG*'s premise destruction, almost every issue that we face today can be looked at and still feel fresh, like it's a problem we've never encountered before. The stories that we see every day in the news — about human rights, wartime tactics, the use of force, civil liberties, social responsibility — are compressed into a very small population of less than 50,000 souls. And because there is no time lapse between the apocalypse and its aftermath — a device many apocalyptic texts use — the current concerns of the populace continue: no one has forgotten about Tom Zarek, no one has forgotten what liquor tastes like, and people still remember what it was like to have all the freedoms of a lawful society. The burden of futurity is taken away in *Battlestar Galactica*, which leaves room for current, contemporary settings and questions, but still makes it seem far away and fictional. It's the transition now that is intensely interesting to us.

When the reimagined *Battlestar Galactica* miniseries aired in 2003, it was the highest rated cable miniseries of the year. When the first episode aired in the UK in 2004 (before it aired in the U.S., as part of Moore's contract with Sky One), it drew approximately 850,000 viewers, and it has remained the highest rated original program in the history of the SciFi Channel. The show has received acclaim from critics — it was named one of *Time*'s six best new drama series in 2005, *Time*'s best program of the year in 2005, and a number of other renowned publications, both popular and newsy, have sung *BSG*'s praises.

A contingent of fans of the original series remains skeptical about the reimagined show. Nonetheless, *BSG* was renewed for both a second and a third season. Season 1 concentrated on the immediate aftermath of a postapocalyptic world, as well as establishing the main characters and their relationships. It tackled many science fiction questions such as how we define humanity, and our responsibility to our creations, as well as incorporating apocalyptic subjects such as the scarcity of resources, the dissemination of information, knowledge retrieval, and the role of authority in a decimated society where normal channels have ceased to exist.

Season 1 focused heavily on these issues. But as the series moved into season 2 the focus shifted to the more personal stories of the characters in a science fiction context, as they evolved both within them-

Katee, Jamie, Mary McDonnell, Ronald, and Grace Park smile for the camera (ALBERT L. ORTEGA)

selves and within the plotline, all of which was juxtaposed against a new, larger political arena that began with "Lay Down Your Burdens." Brave, light moments of happiness and levity were beacons in the darkness of this dramatic storytelling, and they somehow made the never-ending chase and pressure seem bearable.

Near the end of the third season, however, things got a bit sketchy, and drooping ratings caused some concern among the show's fans that it would not be renewed. Although the season continued to tackle difficult issues and revel in a unique cinematic style, people began to complain on online forums that the middle of the season was flagging in terms of storytelling, and opinions on exactly which aspect of the plot was at fault varied widely. Some people continued to resent that the original premise had been abandoned, claiming that *BSG* was dragging a perfectly great series through the mud and into an ugly parody of itself. Others thought that certain characters were overused, while still others thought that the third season had lost the hope that had helped the first two seasons gel, leading to a dismal, unending grind of depressing and hopeless story lines. After tense weeks of waiting, a fourth season was announced, but it wasn't until more than a month later that fans learned it would be a twenty-two-episode season rather than a shorter, thirteen-episode run.

Despite the differences between the original series and Moore's reimagined show, one thing's for sure: both versions of *Battlestar Galactica* reflect the culture of their time. In 1978, people wanted to look into the future. Space travel was a relatively recent development, the potential of humankind seemed limitless, and people wanted to explore that limitlessness. The reimagined *BSG* is airing in a context of reality television (a fact that is echoed by the series' documentary-style camerawork and use of color), a context of accountability and responsibility. As a revival of the original instead of a reboot, *BSG* would probably not have made it through the first season — as evidenced by the fact that it hadn't done so in the twenty years since the original aired. As a reimagining, it's the best thing on television, as it says something about both who we are as a people and who we want to be. Moore notes, "I like the show best when you get to a place where you're not sure who you're rooting for anymore, you're not sure whose side you're on. And you're confused and you might even be angry about what we're doing but at least it's forced you to a place of trying to define your own point of view on something."

Apocalypse, Now?

The two things people have always been interested in are how things start, and how things end. Stories, myths, and accounts of how things start are often called "creation" stories, while things that deal with how the world will ultimately end are often referred to as "end time" stories. The fancy name for these stories that talk about end times is called "eschatology." Stories about end times cover lots of ground; the term "apocalypse" is actually only one *kind* of end time story, but it's basically the template that *Battlestar Galactica* follows.

So what is an apocalypse? "It's actually one of the first questions that I ask my students," says Allan Weiss, who teaches a course on apocalyptic and post-apocalyptic science fiction at York University in Toronto. "They invariably start talking about the end of the world and mass destruction and that sort of thing." Weiss's approach to the subject is cheery, upbeat, and friendly, an odd approach to such a dire subject. "It's actually based on a Greek word meaning 'revelation,'" he continues. "The last book of the Bible, for instance, what we know as the Book of Revelation, is actually titled 'Apocalypse.' In its original understanding, 'apocalypse' meant that at an end point in time, God's purpose would be revealed."

Tales of apocalypse are more interested in where we are in time, rather than in space (if you'll forgive the bad pun). And although they tend to be thrown into the science fiction bin with *Star Wars* and *Astro Boy*, apocalyptic scenarios aren't necessarily "scientific" — they can cover a large range of topics that science today won't even go near: immortality, the resurrection of the soul, transmigration and rebirth — everything that's connected to what happens after we die. But today, most people think "science fiction" when they think "apocalypse," because somewhere along the way the two things got yoked together. Movies like *The Day After Tomorrow*, *The Sum of All Fears* and *Chain Reaction* all place their end-of-the-world scenarios firmly within the realm of science.

Television science fiction, from *Dr. Who* to *Star Trek: The Next Generation* to *Stargate: Atlantis*, doesn't fare any better, getting booed or booted around for being "just sci-fi." Into the mix comes *Battlestar Galactica*. But in order to figure out why

BSG is called "postapocalyptic science fiction," we'll start with some questions about those two terms, and why this reimagined show uses them so well. That way, the next time someone says, "you watch *Battlestar Galactica*?" or even, "you watch sci-fi?" you might have a few things to say that will leave them gaping — and maybe even curious to watch some *BSG* themselves!

But hey, what about all that death-and-destruction part of an apocalypse? "Most people think that apocalypse only refers to death," cautions Weiss. Talking of the traditional role of apocalypses, he says, "It becomes difficult to explain to people that basically, death is a good thing. One of the paradoxes that we talk of in terms of the Book of Revelation is the notion that a death also means a rebirth. We no longer think that way." While destruction was a part of an apocalyptic text in its oldest forms, it also conveyed a sense of hope, because after the destruction and mayhem, the revealing of God's will would be spectacular. These days we tend to forget the *after* part of "the end of the world."

In today's global society, the issue gets further complicated because some apocalypse tales deal with single non-repeating histories, like the Christian account by St. John. Other religions, like Hinduism, assume repeated apocalypse in a cycle of creation and destruction. In fact, the whole reason for the destruction is *for* the rebirth! *Battlestar Galactica* works in both these kinds of end stories, partly because they are familiar (the end of the world), and partly because it's television: how can you have a show that's about something that ends? That would be one short show. People show up, things blow up, credits roll. It's best perhaps to leave it to the novelist D.H. Lawrence, who said simply that an apocalypse "gives us imaginative release into another vital world"; what that particular world might be depends on what we're reading or watching.

One of the main purposes of any apocalypse tale is to act as a warning. The Book of Revelation by St. John in the New Testament is often said to be the definitive apocalyptic text in Western society.

Professor Weiss says that there's a sort of "checklist for apocalypse," and it doesn't matter if it's a book or a film or a radio program: they appear in times of conflict, and they talk about current problems in society but are set in the future or in an alternate universe. Many of them use secret codes or mystic language. These end time stories usually focus on a single person who has a vision. The vision that's seen is about an end time, after which a rebirth, reboot, restart of some kind will occur, but the end time is a violent, cataclysmic upheaval, usually with lots of fire and lots of death. The visionary or prophet is instructed or feels morally obligated to tell other people about it.

Most of us in the West think that there's only one apocalypse — I mean, how many times can the world end, right? — but actually there are more than one. The Old Testament has many apocalypses in it, and there are also apocryphal (non-canonical, or not in the Bible) apocalypses such as the First Apocalypse of James.

So how come we have more than one account of the end of time? Well, because each one serves a different purpose, even though they all have similar features, and they get refined and told to different peoples at different times. "One of the purposes of my course," says Professor Weiss, "is to show how certain terms, certain ideas, certain conventions, change over time in accordance with cultural changes."

This iconic image from 9/11 was the inspiration for the unknown pilot photo we see in *BSG*

(NEVILLE ELDER/CORBIS SYGMA)

How does *Battlestar Galactica* stack up to the list as the new apocalypse on the block? Well, *BSG* is no exception to the first indicator (arriving at times of conflict), airing at a time when the Western world, in particular the United States, is grappling with political and economic upheaval — a war in Iraq, internal social and political conflicts, religious divides that seem unbridgeable. And how do you talk about current, hot-button topics like war, the treatment of prisoners, the role of democracy, and the corrupting influence of capitalism? One way is to put it in space, and put it into a story that's set right after a cataclysmic change for mankind — you get yourself some distance, in other words. Now your critiques are just part of a story, and a story that has a long tradition with roots in the Christian Bible, among other places. Ronald Moore skirts the subject by saying that it's not intended to comment directly on the U.S. — it's more of a "what if": "Laura Roslin is not going to be George W. Bush. The Cylons are not going to be Al-Qaeda, but they were going to have elements of it, and part of the opportunity of the show was to move pieces around the game board a little bit. [...] What if I move this piece over here and what if I put you over there? How do you feel about it then?"

By putting *BSG* in the future (or at least different) time and in an alternate place, Moore can avoid getting into trouble *and* allow us to see the situation without feeling necessarily guided by our own personal politics and real-life beliefs. This win-win situation has been brought to you by an apocalypse . . .

How about secret codes and mystical content? Many texts of apocalyptic fiction come out of mystical traditions where things like numerology and symbology were used to pass along information. In Hebrew, letters can be written as numbers — a codified system that allowed secret or contentious information to be transmitted and saved. Certain other numbers were seen as divine or holy — especially the numbers 1 through 4, 10 and 100, and multiples of those, like 1,000, or 12 (3 x 4). Symbols were used by early Christians for the same reason, to veil forbidden sentiments and make them "acceptable" — or at least too vague to seem threatening to the ruling class.

Another reason for using mysterious codes or symbols in stories about apocalypses was that the very ambiguity of the language illustrates how divinely inspired content is nearly inaccessible to us non-divine mortals. So, even though the language seems to be out of our reach because of how it sounds and what it's saying, it's actually more within our reach than actual divine wisdom, which is impossible for us to comprehend directly.

In *Battlestar Galactica*, both the humans and the Cylons play with this convention: the humans often feel like they are mystified by the superior intellect of the cylons, whose machinations seem very abstract and threatening, but the Cylons are just as mystified by the actions of the humans, as they adapt quickly to situations and then respond with unconventional — and to a Cylon, no doubt cryptic — solutions.

And think of the importance of numbers in the show — the 12 Lords of Kobol, 12 Cylon models, a single God for the Cylons, 3 Cylons walking in a row, Roslin's vision of 12 Vipers, the death of 13 pilots, and President Roslin keeping the exact number of survivors in the fleet on the whiteboard next to her.

One of the other major aspects of the apocalyptic text is the presence of a visionary, prophet, or seer of one kind or another. Does *BSG* have a visionary? Well, it has several, actually. In his book *Apocalyptic Literature*, Mitchell Reddish notes that, "In the ancient world, a Sibyl was an elderly woman who made ecstatic prophetic utterances, usually of a negative nature." Sound like anyone we know? Terminally ill, on chamalla, has visions, tries to communicate those visions to the rest of the fleet through her politics? Sounds like a Laura Roslin we know. She even bases an entire presidential campaign on it — "I will lead the people to salvation. It is my sole purpose." In microcosm, the character of Oracle Selloi who appears in the beginning of season 3 could also be considered sibylline, and the Cylon Leoben also seems to be very prophetic: it was he who first uttered the phrase, "All of this has happened before, and all of this will happen again." Several episodes in the first three seasons center on visions or dreams where knowledge is given: "Flesh and Bone," "Kobol's Last Gleaming," "Epiphanies," and "Maelstrom," to name a few. And, much like ambiguous language is used to help us understand divine knowledge, visionaries *need* an altered state to encompass the divine, no matter what its form. The dream or vision tells us that we are stepping outside of our everyday existence to look at a part of, or all of, a larger plan. Because we like to "know things," this convention of the dream/vision is really helpful and appealing to us — sort of like insider trading for divine knowledge.

Finally, fear of death — one of our most common fears — is a component of our need for apocalyptic texts. The fear, Weiss says, is important because it's what helps galvanize a person to do the right thing, while the hope that apocalypses promise usually comes in the form of some sort of salvation — the belief that there is a salvation, a rebirth, or whatever incarnation the religious system embraces. "For Christians, if you've done your chores, if you've done all the right things, then when you die, you'll experience something really wonderful. And the huge battle between good and evil is important because ultimately God's plan will be revealed and will culminate. The resulting mass slaughter is not a bad thing," Weiss continues with a chuckle, "it's a positive event. All will be good again. You will transcend — you will become one with God." In *Battlestar Galactica*, Leoben's quotation of the fictional scripture to Starbuck — "All of this has happened before, and all of it will happen again" — is a great example of that tension in microcosm. The statement can be seen as both a warning and as a promise of hope: a warning because Leoben seems to have some of the privileged knowledge of what will come, and a promise because whatever happens, there's a chance to make it right as events repeat themselves.

"So you see, originally, an apocalypse didn't have a negative connotation at all," says Weiss. "It had a positive connotation. Essentially the point of the exercise for St. John, for instance, was to show that at the end time, the whole purpose of existence would be revealed. And that purpose is the second coming of Jesus Christ. And so, what would happen, in this prophecy, is that all things that were not clear before would become clear as our progress, our process, reached its culminating point. The idea of a divine revelation was very appropriate to that place and time."

But advancements in civilization, especially in technology, changed our view of the world. Industrialization — machines — began to appear more and more in our lives. As man began to rely increasingly on science, our apocalyptic texts and stories change too. "I tell my students, who have all told me about the end of the world, that the fact that all people can think about is the fire and the brimstone, mass destruction — terrible things happening — the fact that they think that is what [apocalypse] means, says a lot about our culture."

And what *is* BSG saying about our culture? The beginning of each episode of *BSG* shows the line, "They have a plan," referring to the Cylons. Over the course of the series we see that their plan is based on their religion. The great struggle comes because neither side is seeing the other's vision, and neither side is willing to compromise. These two simultaneous stories also shape another common thread in apocalypse stories, the treatment of its two main subjects: fear and hope. The fear of what could happen, or has happened, or will happen, and warnings against the causes of those things, runs all through *Battlestar Galactica*. But even its treatment of that emotion is a revised one. It seems as though all the fear is on the side of the humans and the hope on the side of the Cylons, but as the series progresses we see that both sides harbor fear and hope — a choose-your-own apocalypse?

Historically, says Weiss, the rise of science and secular thinking and industrialization worked to change our end time stories. That's because what scared us before doesn't necessarily seem so scary now. Every apocalypse tale is shaped by the culture that created it. For instance, our current view of the world is influenced more by secular thinking and material values. In turn they influence the extent and degree of hope expressed in texts, which is less than it was in ancient times because we no longer share the biblical belief of hope beyond death, or if we do, it's been hit hard by recent events in our own history — nuclear wars, genocides, and radical technological improvements.

So, instead of God's judgment at the end of time, science gave us views of an end time that was merely another facet of an amoral universe. This amoral apocalypse came about as people began to talk about the sense that the world does not follow any preconceived pattern, but is in a constant state of evolution. Probably the most famous of this type of view was H.G. Wells' *The Time Machine*, where the protagonist races forward in time and ends up on a beach in the far distant future watching the heat death of planet Earth.

The most recent change in how we imagine an apocalypse came about at the end of the Second World War. And it was a whopper of a transition for humanity: the invention of the atomic bomb. Before that, most tales of apocalypse referred to an outside source — either God or fate or maybe a giant asteroid following the disinterested dictates of gravity. But when "Little Boy" hit Hiroshima in 1945 and the world saw that first, gigantic mushroom cloud and its resultant destruction, everything changed. Now we had a do-it-yourself apocalypse. "When we see some of the images," Weiss says, "that are used in the Book of Revelation and in other texts — when we see this big flash of light, for instance, we have to understand it in terms of a *revelation*, an *illumination*, exposing something really important — God speaking to us. But in the post-Hiroshima age, a flash of light can quite easily mean something different." In a nuclear and post-nuclear age, it could now just as easily mean death. This is the "new" kind of apocalypse that we're currently dealing with: from a moral judgment of God, to an amoral indifferent event, to one that we've concocted ourselves. As purveyors of our own destruction, by our own hand, we invited the new, immoral apocalypse to take center stage.

Two of the great fears of our times are nuclear and environmental/biological annihilation; another is the fear of uncontrolled artificial intelligence. *Battlestar Galactica* shows all three of these fears at work: the *Galactica* is unnetworked for fear of an AI virus; the Cylons destroy the colonies through nuclear holocaust, facilitated by a human collaborator; and a plague runs through the Cylon population.

What's interesting about *Battlestar Galactica* is that it's billed as postapocalyptic sci-fi, but it's actually both apocalyptic *and* postapocalyptic. The series proper is definitely contemporary because the survivors of the human race are not privy to the newly revealed divine plan; not only has a divine strategy not been revealed, but destruction has been brought about by humans and their own creations, not a divine being. *Battlestar Galactica* is playing with the conventions on which it's based. Perhaps the revealing of the divine strategy is that there is no divine strategy, or that it is still unlearned so it must be repeated until we learn.

Battlestar Galactica doesn't just skim along the surface of apocalyptic conventions so that it can make a kick-ass show. It's also rewriting and revising apocalyptic metaphors — by taking stock of what's been done before to figure out what can be done in the future. From "traditional" apocalypses like the world-destroying one we saw in the miniseries; personal apocalypses that cover both the destruction and revelation in episodes like "The Farm" and "Epiphanies"; and the social apocalypses like the one we see in "Lay Down Your Burdens"; there's even a sort of ironic viewer's apocalypse in episodes like "Final Cut" when we are decimated by the information of D'Anna being a Cylon operative. Whatever the case, the message is clear: my apocalypse isn't your apocalypse, but they're all trying to say the same thing — the end could be near, and after the dust has settled, something will have radically changed. *Battlestar Galactica* is a viewer's smorgasbord — you take what you want from it.

Using the changes in how we see the world, and using traditional symbols like light, fire, and color, the writers of *Battlestar Galactica* have had to make some updates and changes. Some changes are also due to the nature of the television medium. For the story to continue to be serial, the characters in this postapocalypse world have to do some stupid things, in order for us to learn from them. All those times we've thought, "[insert character of choice here]! What are you *doing*?!?" are important because unlike a traditional apocalypse story, we're watching this one as it unfolds rather than having it told to us after the fact. Right now, too, our society leans pretty heavily toward individualism: a show where people always work perfectly in groups and put the "needs of the many" over "the needs of the few" (what book about a science fiction show would be complete without a *Star Trek* reference?), would be hard for us to understand and sympathize with. Finally, the division between doing what we want and doing what's right becomes one of the stories we look for in the show itself, because it's one of the things that we wrestle with in our own society (see "Frak You!" for more on that).

It's true that most of the "apocalypses" we see these days — whether in movies, books, comics, or web media — seem to err heavily on the "death and destruction" side of things and leave little room for redemption, let alone rebirth. *Battlestar Galactica* stands above this kind of story, makes us sit there breathless, waiting for *what happens next,* and fosters some of the best debates about who we are as human beings and why we do the things we do. Right next to all the fear and loss and apocalyptic dread stands a hope that is just as large, diverse, and powerful: humanity, and what the humanist Petrarch called "the will to good." Humanity, whether flesh or machine, imagined or real, is our one hope. But this humanity can't be limited to the biological entity we call a "human," because it's also present in Boomer and Athena, in Six in all her incarnations, and in Leoben, Cavil, and Doral. Each of them demonstrates a will to good, and once that connection has been made, can we really call the Cylons just machines? Should we? Perhaps the warning part of *Battlestar Galactica* is that, unless and until we broaden our idea of what humanity is, and take responsibility for our creations by including them, for better and worse, in that great hope, we're doomed to destroy ourselves, over and over again.

Jamie Bamber
(Lee "Apollo" Adama)

(ALBERT L. ORTEGA)

On April 3, 1973, Jamie St. John Bamber Griffith was born in Hammersmith, London, to Ralph, an American management consultant, and Elizabeth, who hailed from Ireland. When Jamie was two, together with his younger brother and four older half-brothers from his father's first marriage, the family moved to Paris. Jamie attended a bilingual school, which set the scene for much of his young adult life when he would easily pick up new languages. It was in Paris that Jamie started his acting career. His mother, Liz, had trained as an actress, and she set up a theater program for children that she ran at the American Cathedral in Paris; she became Jamie's first casting director, and because his sister had not yet been born, he landed the role of the Wicked Witch of the West in her production of *The Wizard of Oz*.

Before moving back to England close to the age of eight, Jamie got a number of professional jobs as well: he dubbed an English voiceover for a French movie, and did a few TV commercials. Back in London, he pursued his love of theater at St. Paul's School, where he became school captain in grade 12. Although he was eager to study drama, his parents convinced him to attend university first, despite (or perhaps because of) the fact that his mother had long been in the business. Jamie was accepted to Cambridge, where he graduated in 1996 with the highest possible degree — a First Class Honours Degree in Modern Languages (he studied both French and Italian). On his academic success, Jamie remains humble: "I didn't deserve it — it was a fluke. [...] I lived in Paris from the age of two, because that's where my father's job took him. I went to an international bilingual school. [...] I already had a head start in French." Many of the skills he developed at Cambridge are still important to the actor today: his time at Cambridge allowed him to hone his already developed linguistic skills and develop his critical analysis — both of which have helped him keep an open mind and broad horizons — and he starred in a number of theatrical productions. He also pursued his love of athletics and playing university rugby. His studies in Italian helped cultivate in him a love of literature, and he still considers Dante's *The Divine Comedy* his favorite book (in fact, it's the one book he'd take with him to a deserted island).

While Jamie was away in Cambridge, his parents, who had gradually grown apart, divorced. The change was easier on Jamie than on his younger brother and sister, who were still living at home at the time, and he spent a lot of time on the phone with them hearing what was going on. The divorce was amicable, however, and his parents remain friendly.

After university, Jamie reached something of a crisis point, and decided that he would pursue acting, but he was not entirely committed to it. "I was considering what to do with my life, so I took the responsibility out of my hands. I said, 'I'll apply to some of the best drama schools in the country. If get into them, I'll pursue it.' If I hadn't gotten in, I honestly think I would have given up acting and pursued something else." If his parents had encouraged him to put his studies first, they also actively encouraged him to follow his heart. "When it became time to make acting a career choice, my parents weren't encouraging me to make that choice, but once I made it, they were encouraging. I think my dad was a little more skeptical about it, because he'd lived the life of an actress via my mum and he'd seen how difficult and frustrating and unrewarding it can be along the way. So I entered into the career with very real expectations."

From 1996 to 1997, Jamie attended the London Academy of Music and Dramatic Arts; shortly after graduating, he obtained his first professional role playing Archie Kennedy in the *Horatio Hornblower* miniseries, a role for which he learned to speak basic Spanish. He speaks enthusiastically about his experience on the miniseries, saying, "It was the most memorable thing I'd ever done, I was new and fresh and I met friends who became lifelong friends. I also experienced a very romantic era in history. Especially living in the UK, there's nostalgia for that Napoleonic era. It was an amazing thing to do, my eyes were open wide the whole time, the ships, the costumes, firing muskets — it was a schoolboy dream come true."

Jamie appeared in five of the *Hornblower* episodes between 1998 and 2001, and was actively involved in every part of his character's development. A hard worker, Jamie chose to do all his own stunts: "Actors always seem [...] a bit mollycoddled, don't they?" he said in an interview. "I'd hate to be seen that way. I did every stunt that was offered to me in *Hornblower*. I dived off the ship's mast into the water and I did sword fights. I'm not afraid of hard work and I wanted the crew and cast to know that I've got bottle." (Bottle is London slang for courage, or balls.) Archie Kennedy quickly became beloved by fans worldwide, and Jamie had to get used to having such a dedicated fan base. He was embarrassed at first by the attention, and didn't quite know how to handle it — "All my fans seem to know each other. It's very strange," he said in one interview in 2002 — but has since grown into his popularity.

Between bouts of playing Archie, Jamie pursued other opportunities, appearing in the television series of *The Scarlet Pimpernel* as Lord Tony Dewhurst in 1999, and in *The Murder of Roger Ackroyd* and *Lady Audley's Secret* in 2000. His next big break came when he was hired to play in *Band of Brothers*, a miniseries directed by Tom Hanks which aired in 2001. In the same year, he starred in his first big-screen movie, *The Devil's Tattoo*, also known as *Ghost Rig*.

That movie was exciting for Jamie in more ways than one as it was there that he met Kerry Norton, who would later become his wife. It took the pair two weeks to act on their feelings for one another, and Kerry said in an interview, "We had adjoining rooms. I'd go to bed at night and think all I had to do was walk through the door and there he would be. He used to wonder what I would have done if he'd let himself in, too. There was a lot of flirting going on and our characters were in love, so the chemistry was really there. It took about two weeks to get together. In the end the door was open all the time."

In 2002, Jamie fulfilled one of his fondest dreams and took to the stage to star in a Shakespeare play. As Prince Hal in *Henry IV*, Jamie was an overnight success, and a good many Archie Kennedy fans turned up to show their support of the actor. Jamie remembers it as an incredible experience, very different from his television or movie work, and a chance for him to refine the stage acting skills he had learned in school and at university. He worked hard on his body language and diction — both of which must be more emphatic in stage productions than on camera — and came away from the Bristol Old Vic theater a more confident and fulfilled actor.

On June 12, 2003, Kerry gave birth to the couple's first child, Isla Elizabeth Angela Griffith (which is Jamie's real last name — he changed it to Bamber for professional reasons, Bamber being his mother's maiden name). The birth was filmed by the British Broadcasting Corporation (BBC) as part of a documentary on what happens in the mind of a newborn baby. Kerry and Jamie were married in September 2003, and nearly a year later, on August 27, 2004, twin girls named Ava and Darcy Griffith were born.

Early in 2003, Jamie read the script for the new *Battlestar Galactica* series, and although he was initially unenthusiastic about the idea of a remake, once he had looked at the script, he was thrilled at the opportunity. He auditioned for and was offered the part of Lee "Apollo" Adama — a role that would launch him to international stardom. He wasn't at all sure he would get the part, and has been quoted as saying, "There were several other hunks in the room that were a lot hunkier than me. They were huge! The overall average physical body type in Los Angeles is completely different [than] in the UK. So I'm not used to being in a room with a bunch of guys that look like they play college football — and yet they were obviously good actors as well. They didn't want the archetypal sort of jock hero. They wanted someone a bit more, I guess, cerebral."

"It came at a key time in my life," he says of the script. "My then girlfriend was pregnant and the future was a bit scary! I went to L.A. for two weeks and it was the first script my manger gave me to read. I cringed at the idea of the remake, but the script knocked me sideways." Although they didn't audition together, Jamie and James Callis, who was hired to play the role of Gaius Baltar, already knew each other, having worked on *The Scarlet Pimpernel* together in 1999, so there was an instant sense of camaraderie between them on set.

Professional and personal lives began to get hectic, and Jamie was actually filming in Vancouver when Kerry was in the last month of her first pregnancy, but he was able to make it home in time for the birth. The whole set knew Jamie was anxious about missing the birth, and when they had filming on the last day, everyone cheered for him. He says, "It was tough. My wife was very strong in my absence, and the director and producer worked hard to get me home early. I did get home a week early — I arrived on the due date." He continues, joking, "But my daughter waited five days for me to recover from jet lag."

When *BSG* was picked up for a full season, the family tried living in London for half the year and relocating to Vancouver when *Galactica* was filming, but the schedule quickly wore on them, and, once the twins were born, Jamie and Kerry decided it was in everyone's best interest to move somewhere a little closer than London. "It is extremely stressful uprooting a family of five twice a year, which is why we have decided to settle in L.A. We need to make a home with all our books on the shelves and the kids in their own, specially decorated, bedrooms. And as long as we are filming eight months of the year in Vancouver, London can't be that." The move required Kerry to make quite a few sacrifices of her own, but she has her own semi-recurring role on *BSG* as Layne Ishay, a paramedic, and she has maintained her own very active career in both acting and recording.

As Apollo, Jamie has to portray a fascinating range of contradictory emotions: his character is both loyal and devoted, and imbued with a real need for rebellion. As one of the more experienced younger actors on the show, Jamie continues to actively develop new approaches and skills, and considers himself extremely fortunate to share so many scenes with veterans Edward James Olmos, who plays William Adama, and Mary McDonnell (Roslin). "[Olmos is] a very challenging person to work with, and doesn't take any shit," says Jamie. "He's a guy who knows what's good and what works and he knows what's true. He's a little intimidating, I must say, but I just used that natural presence that he has in the relationship between our characters. [Olmos] is a very large presence, and his CV of great work, the uncompromising nature of his approach, was all so useful to me. My character is definitely trying to rebel and is threatened by his father's self-assurance and position in the military, so Edward's natural authority made it easy for me." Emotional work aside, the role of Apollo also required a couple of physical adjustments: just as Katee Sackhoff had to cut her hair for her role as Starbuck, Jamie has had to dye his naturally blonde hair so that it more closely resembles Edward James Olmos' darker tones.

The series' popularity on both a critical and a popular level stunned everyone, Jamie included. "I think the amazingly positive press has really astounded me. What we've done I suppose is surprise people. People had expectations that were lower, what we've done is manage to surprise them with the depth and the breadth and the content of the show. It's very political, it's very social, it's all about interpersonal relationships. It's not really about technology or concepts. There's a great deal in it that comments very directly on the world and climate we live in. Sometimes if you tell a story in a parallel world, you can sometimes be a little more brazen with your commentary."

Outside of work, Jamie remains extremely active. A mix of his mother's tireless energy and his father's pragmatism, he's keenly aware of his own need to stay occupied: "I have a very hard time when I'm not working. I'm not a person who has other things I want to do. I need to work." He rides horses, plays golf and rugby (although not as actively anymore — he feels it would be irresponsible to risk the injuries), and he skis. But his favorite activity is running, which he used to do while pushing his twins' pram around! In April 2002, he completed the London Marathon, finishing in just under three hours. He's continued to take both movie and television roles when not shooting *Battlestar Galactica* — and he still dreams of taking on the biggest role of them all: Hamlet.

James Callis
(Gaius Baltar)

A British native, like his *Battlestar Galactica* costar Jamie Bamber, James Callis was born on June 4, 1971, in London. He lived in London with his two sisters and his parents, who own a bed-and-breakfast. James attended Harrow School in north-west London. In 1990, he enrolled at the University of York in England, where he received a BA in English and Related Literature three years later. His university career allowed him to participate in a number of theater productions as writer, actor, and director — including a production of Pinter's *The Birthday Party* at Cambridge.

In 1993, invigorated by his work in the acting field, James started attending the London Academy of Music and Dramatic Arts (a school that Jamie Bamber later attended). James' first big break came in 1996 when he starred in *Old Wicked Songs* as Jon Marans, a young American taking voice lessons from a professor, who was played by veteran actor Bob Hoskins. It was James' first appearance in a West End production, and he was awarded for his performance with the Jack Tinker Award for Most Promising Newcomer.

Between 1996 and 1998, James broadened his horizons and played in a variety of television series, their genres ranging from the action-military *Soldier Soldier* to the dramatic *The Scarlet Pimpernel*. On a break between projects, he met Neha, an Indian woman with whom he fell in love, and two weeks later he asked her to marry him. About the speed of their courtship, Callis says, "[Neha] was beautiful, easy to talk to and even easier to laugh with — it had all the makings of a good friendship. But I had an overwhelming feeling that if I didn't ask her out immediately I would regret it for the rest of my life. I didn't want to become 'friends' and risk losing the chance of romance between us — I wanted her to know how I felt straight away — luckily, she felt the same way."

An avid believer in being able to "do it all," James coproduced and codirected his first feature with Nick Cohen in 1999, a short film called *Surety*. The year was a busy one, and he appeared in four separate television shows: *Heat of the Sun*; *Sex, Chips, and Rock 'n' Roll*; *Arabian Nights*; and *Jason and the Argonauts*. His first directorial break came in 2001 when he produced the popular movie *Beginner's Luck*, which starred French actress Julie Delpy and was shown at the London Film Festival in 2002.

James refused to limit himself, and set about obtaining a part in a feature film — a goal which he accomplished when he was cast as Tom in the blockbuster movie *Bridget Jones's Diary* (2001), a role that he reprised in the 2004 sequel *Bridget Jones: The Edge of Reason*. He wasn't expecting to get the part, although he mentioned to one interviewer that his sister had called him a year before to tell him that she'd dreamed he was going to star in exactly that movie! On getting the part, James said, "I think it had quite a lot to do with the fact they needed somebody fast. I didn't think my audition was much cop, but then I got a call saying they liked me and wanted to meet me right away. That was on the Saturday and I started work the following Tuesday. I hadn't even seen the script at that point. But with films you only shoot a couple of scenes every day, so you usually only need to speak three or four lines at a time, which isn't taxing — even for non-actors." The character he played is gay, and, as a straight man married to a woman, James found it a little disconcerting that everyone believed he actually *was* gay. "They kept telling me to be more like myself, and I'd say, 'But I'm not gay.' I'm not sure they believed me. I did tell a few people on the set that I was married and they just looked at me as if to say, 'Yeah, right.' Then I went home and told my family that everyone on set thought I was gay and they said: 'Well that shows you're doing a really good acting job.' I had to tell them I hadn't actually been acting at the time. Which was a bit worrying."

James's education and broad professional horizons have allowed him to develop a wide open mind, and he's known for his fierce defense of equal opportunity and feminism, which would come up later when he was hired for *Battlestar Galactica*. While some were critical about the changes to the show — bringing in female pilots, for instance, and recasting Starbuck as a woman — James was enthusiastic about the more modern outlook and he expressed dismay at the criticism. "Space is not the domain of men," he commented, "and why should it be? Why should sci-fi just be our bag? There's a Sherlock Holmes story in which it's written: 'It always works better when there's a lady involved.' There are women pilots, so let's get with the program. And Katee Sackhoff, who plays Starbuck, is a very attractive spirit and — although it may be inappropriate to say so — she has balls of fire. She also manages to be gentle and feminine at the same time. These are amazing qualities. Dirk Benedict, with all his cigar-puffing antics, did not bring that to the role."

It was his role in *Bridget Jones* that launched him to international fandom, but already before that, James already had an active fan contingent — something that he was quite excited about. "I've got a small following already and I'm so excited I can't begin to tell you. Some of the people who visit the site actually met up, and now they rarely talk about me and discuss their own lives instead. Then some other people wrote in to say that this was a James Callis Web site and they shouldn't be talking about anything else. So I wrote in and said that if you're only going to be talking about me it's going to be a very boring page indeed."

The reimagined *Battlestar Galactica* changed the course of James's career: early in 2003, he went through the grueling audition process (like everyone else, he had to do five separate auditions) and was offered the role of Gaius Baltar. In other circumstances, a British accent might have been a problem, but it turned out to be an asset: "I was picked from a list of people that included Americans, Brits, Australians . . . The character brief actually read: 'Please present all ethnicities.' The Americans don't want to be seen as bad, and so it [Gaius] has to be someone else. We just now happen to come from a long line [of British characters being the villains] that probably started with Alan Rickman in *Die Hard*."

Like most of the cast (though not all), James had seen the original *Battlestar Galactica* series as a child, and was thrilled with the changes made to his character. Gaius is demanding because he has to remain somewhat sympathetic, but he's really one of the most ambiguous villains of the show — at least partially responsible for the downfall of humanity, not once, not twice, but three times. As a result, Gaius is one of the more fascinating characters to examine in depth. As Callis puts it, "Baltar in the original was wonderfully portrayed (by the late John Colicos), but he was a pretty creepy guy. He was just a downright baddie. In this one, we've gone a different way, which I think gives me some more scope, really." He continues, "He doesn't want to be involved in the wrong, but is. And it's one of those vicious circles, because it's something he can never really escape."

James Callis is not the type of actor who tries to give his character all the backstory he can; rather, he finds that method acting serves only to take him *out* of character. "I was in a play, actually, in London, and the director just sprang up one day and said, 'What [was your character] doing when you were five years old?' And the actress was like, 'When I was five I was playing with my shoes.' Fucking hell, it was like she was a robot! They came to me and said, 'What about you?' I'm not thinking about that! I'm in a play, and it's about the play. If you want to waste time chatting about that crap when you're five — maybe these things have a relevance, but oh dear. I think all of that stuff is done just to employ people. I don't get it myself. It's Method to a crazy degree and I don't have the stamina to do that."

Always eager to try everything, James took the challenge a step further in season 3 by appearing stark naked in a scene with Tricia Helfer and Lucy Lawless. "She [Tricia Helfer]'s got her clothes off and I'm wandering around in a shirt, and I thought let's reverse it this time around and I'll be in the position she is in every week. It was a testimony of my solidarity with Tricia Helfer. It was 'I will do this as well, but I don't look nearly as good as you when I have to do it.'" The problem occurred when Lucy walked into the room: "It's all written, but Lucy just lost it. She walked in and saw me naked and fell on the floor laughing. She said, 'Nobody told me you were really going to be naked!'"

In 2006, James won a Saturn award for best supporting actor, a Peabody award, and an AFI (American Film Institute) award for his work on *Battlestar Galactica*. The same year, he appeared as Haman in a cinematic retelling of the biblical story of Esther, *One Night with the King*. He has continued to be active in other projects since joining the cast of *BSG*, and has starred in the television miniseries *Helen of Troy* as Menelaus (2003) as well as the movie *Dead Cool* (2004).

Outside of work, James is busy with his family. In 2003, he and Neha had their first son, whom they named Joshua and who was followed in 2005 by a second son, Sacha. If James ever decides to stop acting, he has an eclectic mix of skill sets on which to draw. An extremely skilled musician, James has spent a lifetime developing his musical talents. As well as singing, he writes music, and plays both the piano and the guitar at a professional level. A surprising and refreshingly down-to-earth man, James manages a wonderful blend of humor and authenticity that, combined with his talent and ambition, will no doubt take him far.

Tricia Helfer
(Number Six)

(ALBERT L. ORTEGA)

Tricia Helfer was born on April 11, 1974, in the small rural community of Donalda, Alberta (Canada), where her parents owned a grain farm. She grew up on the farm, driving a tractor and participating in all aspects of farm life, and to this day, her parents still live in the same house, which she visits as often as her schedule allows. From her farm-girl upbringing, one would never have suspected that Tricia would become a top runway and magazine model: "I've hauled grain, disced, harrowed, cultivated, fixed machinery (although without my dad telling me what to do, I wouldn't know how to do it), picked rocks, mended fences, painted barns, cleaned chickens. […] I think growing up and working on a farm makes you a hard worker who kinda sees things like they are and definitely squelches any diva tendencies."

Growing up without a television, Tricia's very rare trips to the movies were a delight to be savored. When she was seventeen, she went to see *Sleeping with the Enemy*. It was an event that changed her life: while she was standing in line to get a ticket, a scout for Mode Models spotted her, and asked her if she was interested in modeling. Although she initially refused, a few weeks later, her career as a model was launched. "This girl approached me and said she was doing some modeling for this guy, and I should meet him, and could she give him my number. I said no, but she gave him my number anyway. He took pictures of me, sent them to Ford modeling agency, and two weeks later I was in New York. I made forty thousand dollars that summer." In New York, she participated in and won the Ford Supermodel of the World Contest, and was immediately signed to Elite Model Management, a huge international modeling agency.

Her career took off: Tricia worked both in print fashion — posing for such elite magazines as *Marie Claire*, *Vogue*, and *Cosmopolitan* — and in runway fashion. She was a favorite model for Christian Dior, Givenchy, and Emanuel Ungaro. August 1993 marked the first of Tricia's forays into the world of cover shoots, this time for *Elle*. Over the next few years, she graced the covers of nearly every major fashion magazine while accumulating runway shows. She was even a Victoria's Secret model — a fact that has garnered her not a small amount of fame. "One time, I was sitting next to this guy on the plane, and he kept staring at me. And finally he asked, 'Are you a Victoria's Secret model?' And I'm like, 'Yeah.' And he said, 'You were wearing a pink sweat suit, and you were sitting on the arm of a brown leather chair. It was on page. . . .' And I said to myself, Okay, just turn away. This guy knows the catalog a little too well."

Although she was thrilled with her job and success, Tricia gradually became aware that she wanted to do more than model. She became a correspondent for a Canadian fashion show, *Ooh La La*, where she discovered a passion for moving film. She also considered going into psychology, but the newly found fascination prompted her to start taking acting classes, and she enrolled at the prestigious Penny Templeton acting school. She attended classes at night while pursuing her modeling career during the day; an assiduous student — and never one to back down from an opportunity — Tricia left her New York life behind in 2002 to move to Los Angeles. She continues to have the utmost respect and fondness for the modeling industry, and, when pressed, recalls, "I think the worst a fellow model did to me was to abuse my kindness while allowing her to take over an apartment lease. She built up a huge phone bill and damaged the apartment while it was under my name although she had technically taken over the lease. Taught me to never trust anyone legally."

In Los Angeles, Tricia immediately landed a part in the short-lived television series *Jeremiah*, but it was her guest role in the hit series *CSI* later in 2002 that helped her make her mark. She starred as Ashleigh James, a bulimic model who is compelled to cut her face to cope with the pressures and pains of her life. The subject was one close to Tricia's heart — despite her occupation, she's a firm believer in the need for both the film and modelling industries to address their harsh physical standards — and the episode garnered positive reviews, both popular and critical.

After a brief appearance in the action feature *White Rush* (2003), Tricia learned about the role of Number Six in Ronald Moore's reimagined *Battlestar Galactica*. It was a fortuitous find — she knew the casting director for the series, and he got her to audition for the part. She explains, "The casting director that hired me for *CSI* got me to audition for *BSG*, and over two months and three separate auditions, a work session and a screen test, I got the part. Auditioning is a very difficult process and I know very few actors that enjoy it, unfortunately." Having grown up without a television, she knew very little about the show before signing on to the new version. She knew nothing but the basics, and, on the advice of costar Edward James Olmos, she's modeled Number Six on the replicants from the sci-fi classic movie *Blade Runner*. "I knew of it, of course," she says of the original *BSG*, "and would try to watch when I was at someone else's house. I knew what Vipers and Cylons and such were and I thought Apollo was cute, but I didn't really know the story lines."

As Six, Tricia has amazed audiences and critics alike with her versatile, subtle performances, and, like Grace Park, has faced the challenge of playing more than one embodiment of the same character. She tries to imbue each incarnation with slightly different characteristics and personalities. While her scenes as Caprica-Six require just a couple of hours in the makeup room, episodes where she plays the tortured Cylon Gina (season 2) required twice as much time to prepare for. Like many other cast members, Tricia has had to make some physical alterations to accommodate her character: she has naturally dark hair, although she's been blonde for years, but Number Six's bleached-blonde look damaged Tricia's hair so much that it started to break off in clumps. She now wears a wig on set.

In between filming *BSG*, Tricia has kept herself busy by auditioning for parts in other projects. In 2004 she played Farrah Fawcett-Majors in an unauthorized story, *Behind the Camera: The Unauthorized Story of* Charlie's Angels. In 2005, Tricia starred in the movie *Mem-o-re*, and landed a guest role in the television series *The Collector* in 2006. Her acting career is progressing easily, and Tricia has said that although she encounters some difficulty in getting jobs simply because she doesn't have the experience yet, she also feels like she gained so much from having modeled for ten years before making the move to acting that she wouldn't want to change anything. "I wouldn't have wanted to start earlier," she comments, "because I may have been too shy — ten years of modeling helped me with that — and also I had earned enough money that I could comfortably make the move and devote my time to auditioning. On the other hand, I, with a small résumé, am going up for projects against women who have been acting for fifteen years and have much more impressive résumés, which makes it very hard to get the job."

Tricia kept working hard, and in 2007 she starred in a range of productions, from movie *The Green Chain* to video game *Command & Conquer 3: Tiberium Wars*, in which she gives voice to General Kilian Qatar. It was a totally new experience for Tricia, and because she isn't a gamer in real life, she didn't know what to expect from the script, which she received just a couple of days before filming began. "It was the same as working on a television or movie set, although the pace was a little faster. I shot all of my scenes in just under two days, so we moved pretty quick. The production team and crew were great, very organized, professional, and fun." *Battlestar Galactica* costar Grace Park also provides the voice for a character in the same video game, which made the project all the more enjoyable for the actors and *BSG* fans alike.

Number Six aside, Tricia is best known in the acting world as the very popular host and joint producer for the first season of the new television series *Canada's*

Next Top Model. Despite popular acclaim, Tricia decided not to return to host the second season of the hit show due to time constraints: with her busy schedule on the set of *Battlestar Galactica* as well as her increasing number of outside projects, Tricia felt she would not have done the series justice, as she would have been unable to devote the time and energy to it that it deserved.

She's also continued to make the most of her modeling skills: she appeared in *Maxim* (she ranked number 57 on their "Hot 100 of 2007" list, and was their wall calendar girl in 2005), and in February 2007, she posed naked for *Playboy*. She has a very body-positive attitude — which serves her well on the *BSG* set given her character's generally revealing attire — and although the shoot was seen as controversial in some fan contingents, she has no regrets. She laughs, "I love to push people's buttons. I can change moods instantly. I can be in a very sexy, playful mood and then, in a second, I'm into businesswoman mode. It's kind of a shock, but it keeps men on their toes. I think it would be boring if I were one person all the time. I'm very much like a cat. Sometimes I want to roll on my back and have you rub my belly, and sometimes if you freakin' come near me, I'm gonna bite your head off."

When not working, Tricia has a quiet life with her husband of almost five years, Jonathan Marshall. Jonathan is a prominent entertainment lawyer, and they were married in 2002. They currently live in L.A., but have plans to build a house on land they own near Tricia's parents' farm. Not that they plan on settling there permanently, but they hope to use it as a retreat from the hard-and-fast L.A. world. An active, physical woman, Tricia works out six days a week — not out of any sense of duty, but out of a genuine sense of enjoyment. "I mix it up with hikes, running, pilates, yoga, tennis, weight training, and sometimes swimming." She's involved in a number of charities, especially those involving animals — and in particular cats, of which she has several. "I guess I've never really thought that I was an idol to girls. I certainly try to live my life in an honest, hardworking way, so if that inspires girls to aim for their dreams and be proud of their achievements, then I'm honored to be part of that."

Mary McDonnell
(Laura Roslin)

A very private person, Mary McDonnell was born in Wilkes-Barre, Pennsylvania, on April 28, 1952, and was raised in Ithaca, New York. There she and her three sisters and one brother attended school, and Mary graduated from the State University of New York at Fredonia where she discovered a love of acting. She performed in college productions, and soon thereafter enrolled in drama school. She joined the East Coast's prestigious Long Wharf Theatre Company, with which she would work for over twenty years, accumulating stage credits and critical and popular acclaim while also appearing in bit roles on various television and film productions. She made her New York stage premiere in Sam Shepherd's Pulitzer Prize winning *Buried Child* in the 1978–1979 season.

It was in 1981 that Mary was first truly noticed, however, when she won the coveted Off-Broadway Theater Award (more commonly known as the Obie Award) for her role in Emily Mann's *Still Life*. In it, she played the uneducated battered wife of a Vietnam War veteran. As her popularity grew and she became known for her unusual choices in diction and body language, Mary went on to star in such Broadway and Off-Broadway productions as *The Heidi Chronicles, Letters Home, O Pioneers!*, and *A Weekend Near Madison*, also by Emily Mann. "It's really important for actors to feel that they're more than something for hire. We're not encouraged to think of ourselves as having a point of view. But I realized I needed to encounter material that asked questions I needed to ask of myself, and also I had to work with people who felt the same way," she said in an interview in 1983 of her continued association with Pulitzer Prize winner Mann. She also continued to play in *Still Life* when it appeared on different stages throughout the United States. Of these runs she said, "Sometimes I feel the need to go back into *Still Life* because the confrontational aspect was so strong. It taught me the power of the theater — to confront a sea of faces and make decisions every moment, when you see resistance, whether to try to break through or move on. You got the sense of theater taking place in that moment."

In 1990, Mary rose to international stardom when she starred in Kevin Costner's blockbuster movie *Dances with Wolves*. Although she was horribly nervous about filming the revealingly intimate sex scene, she startled audiences with her subtle performance in the movie, and was rewarded with an Academy Award nomination, the first of her career, but not her last; she was nominated again two years later for her role in *Passion Fish*. Other hit films ensued: *Sneakers* (1992), *Independence Day* (1996), and *Donnie Darko* (2001). When *Donnie Darko* hit the DVD market, writer and director Richard Kelly was incensed because Mary and her costar Katherine Ross had been taken off the credit roll on the front cover. The studio thought the actresses didn't have enough teen appeal.

Mary has become known for playing strong, vibrant female characters, and attributes that in part to her own personality shining through. "The truth is that all of these roles came to me. The roles of that kind of woman seemed to find me. Perhaps it's some kind of agreement you make unconsciously and it goes out into the universe, but I think people see that in you. They see you have an organic potential to be a leader or a fighter or to be a warrior as a woman, or you don't. It's not something you can act. In my DNA I come from a very strong matriarchal family of Irish women — very, very strong. We were all raised to be very strong-willed. It's built into the DNA and people sense that, and so that will be in a role organically."

In 2003, Mary received the script for the reimagined *Battlestar Galactica* series, in which she had been offered the role of Laura Roslin. Although her first reaction was amusement (she couldn't imagine herself in a science fiction role, and didn't think anyone *else* could imagine it, either), as soon as she read the script, she was hooked. "I always read an offer. And I read it that night, and I went, 'Oh, dear. I have to do this.' I found it so compelling. And I eventually found out Ed [Edward James Olmos] was agreeing to do it, so that made a huge difference to me." Like Edward and several others of her costars, Mary came to the reimagined series without any knowledge of the original *BSG* — largely because when it was airing, she was living in New York and performing at night. She was aware that it had had a cult following, but had never seen an episode, and in fact, still hasn't. "I've still never seen an episode. I've decided not to look, because my character didn't exist in the last one. I felt it would really be more beneficial to my character and her perception to have every single one of these ideas new to her. I didn't want to have any ideas of Adama and Starbuck [characters featured in both series], because [Roslin] didn't have any connection to them at all."

She was initially drawn to the show because of its scope and because of the sheer potential of Laura Roslin's character. "I felt interested in the idea that there are a lot of women of my generation who have a great deal of savvy that's untapped because we were right on the cusp of being prepared to do or be whatever we wanted, but we weren't necessarily raised to think we could become president. [...] I wanted the opportunity to explore it . . ." She and Edward have a great deal of respect for each other — each crediting the other with being a main attraction of the project — but Mary approaches her role and working life differently than Edward does. While Edward has a hard time leaving his work and its emotional toll behind, Mary says she doesn't think about her character at all once she gets back home to her family, unless she's called upon to read a script. "The first year, though, I have to say, she permeated my dreams. The apocalyptic nature of the situation got into my dreams. I had a very hard time. I went to therapy a little bit and just did a little bit of work on it to figure out how to let her get stronger while I got further away from her."

Outside of work, Mary is a committed wife and mother. She met her husband,

Randle Mell, in 1986, and they've been married for some 20 years. They have two children, Olivia and Michael. Mary and Randle love to go to horse races together, and one *BSG* shot was infamously difficult to get because Mary collapsed in a fit of giggles about ridiculous horse names. She's apparently a huge giggler, and once she starts, everyone joins in.

She's also a hard worker, and she encourages those around her to put in their best performance as well. "I love to work. I love to have complexity. And [Roslin is] just one of an ensemble. It's phenomenally important to me that, if I'm going to be spending years on a project, I need to be interested in the whole thing. I'm not there to be on my own. And if I'm going to be with these people, I'd best be interested in their work." She's a perfectionist, and unlike some actors who avoid watching their performances, Mary watches them out of professional curiosity. "I watch them professionally to see what can be improved upon or things I would like to ask the producers about. I don't spend a lot of time watching the show. For me, if I get too absorbed as a viewer, I lose some of my innocence as a player. I don't want Laura to be invaded by Mary's ego. [...] It is better for me not to watch too much because I will say, 'I definitely need new clothes and what about this haircut?'"

A versatile, steadfastly subtle actor, Mary is active in the community, and a firm believer in the potential of television and film — and its actors — to cross boundaries and get people involved in real-life issues. "I constantly sit at home and think how do I give to this charity and to that charity, and I don't feel that I am doing enough."

Edward James Olmos
(William Adama)

Born on February 24, 1947, Edward James Olmos grew up in an ethnically diverse neighborhood of East Los Angeles with his father, Mexican immigrant Pedro Olmos, and mother, Mexican American Eleanor Huizar. His parents, neither of whom had graduated from high school, and both of whom eventually went back to complete their schooling, divorced when Edward — or Ed, or Eddie, as he's most commonly called by friends — was just eight. The boy turned to baseball to keep his mind off his family's troubles, and to avoid getting involved in his neighborhood's drug or gang wars. His dedication served him well, both in terms of his athletic ability and more personally since it allowed him to develop his patience and self-discipline. He practiced every day, and won the Golden State (that is, California) batting championship. His parents were convinced he would stay in the field, but at the age of fifteen, Edward suddenly turned his attention to music. He formed a rock 'n' roll band which he called Pacific Ocean (when asked why, he's

said, "Because it was the biggest thing on the West Coast") and for which he was the lead singer. By the time Edward had graduated from high school, Pacific Ocean was a hot commodity at L.A. nightclubs and was earning him enough money to live. "I sang terrible," Edward told *New York* in a 1986 interview. "But I could scream real good and I could dance. So I'd dance for five minutes, then come back and sing a couple more screams, then dance again." The band remained an important part of his life, and they released an album in 1968.

In between gigs at night, Edward studied and eventually earned a degree in sociology before deciding to enroll in a drama course to improve his singing technique. "I started working in theater in my first year in college out of a necessity to learn more about myself. I never thought I could make a living because I was a sociologist at heart," he says. It was a decision that changed his life, as he quickly realized that his true passion lay in acting. In 1971, however, he married Kaija Keel, and by the time he was twenty-seven, they had two sons — Mico and Bodie. (Bodie would later go into the acting business as well, appearing in *Battlestar Galactica* alongside his father as Brendan "Hotdog" Costanza.) Edward ran a furniture delivery company during the day while indulging his acting ambitions at night by working in experimental theater.

At the same time, Edward started to audition for bit parts in television shows, and he landed several roles in such classics as *Kojak* (1975), *The Blue Knight* (1976), *Starsky & Hutch* (1977), and *Hawaii Five-O* (1977). It wasn't until 1978, some ten years after Edward first became interested in acting, that his luck broke when he was offered a role in the musical dramatic play *Zoot Suit*. Edward blew audiences and critics away, and won the prestigious Tony Award for his performance; although the play was only scheduled to run for ten days, such was its success that it actually ran for eighteen months. Three years later, Edward reprised the role for the film version of the play, in an equally impressive performance. *Zoot Suit* was a turning point in Edward's life, because it gave him some serious credentials in the acting world and it allowed him to become involved in an issue that was close to his heart — that of the Mexican American community and its tensions within the larger society of the United States. It's an issue that Edward remains firmly committed to today, and he's been actively involved in awareness-raising campaigns for the community.

After *Zoot Suit*, Edward chose his roles carefully to avoid becoming stuck in a Mexican American stereotype. His next big movie was the 1982 science fiction classic *Blade Runner*, in which he played Gaff. It was *American Playhouse*, however, a project filmed in the same year, that stood out for Edward: a PBS (Public Broadcasting Service) presentation on Gregorio Cortez, who had traditionally been portrayed as a Mexican bandit. Edward's own research led him to portray Cortez significantly differently, as a misunderstood and victimized man. When no studio offered to distribute the series on film, Edward took time off from acting — turning down role after role — in order to tour and promote the show himself. This type of commitment and integrity has become part of the legend Edward carries with him to any role.

After the political activism of *American Playhouse*, Edward took on a more easy-going role as Lieutenant Martin Castillo in the television series *Miami Vice*. From 1985 to 1989, *Miami Vice* grew in popularity and Edward James Olmos became a household name for the first time. As Castillo, Edward was nominated twice for both an Emmy Award and a Golden Globe Award: he won one of each. In between seasons, he returned to the movie industry and took on one of his most popular roles to date, that of real-life math teacher Jaime Escalante in the hit film *Stand and Deliver*. His role in the 1988 movie was that of a socially conscious teacher desperate to help disadvantaged youth get the most out of their education and their lives; his performance earned him an Academy Award nomination, making him the first Chicano (Mexican American) actor ever to receive such an honor. Edward has since ensured that a copy of the uplifting movie be available in prisons, youth organizations, and schools where the importance of education and diversity is essential to helping people understand their own strengths and potential.

In 1992, Edward made his directorial debut with *American Me* (he also starred in it), a movie that examined the problem of street crime in Edward's childhood neighborhood. "The film is not for one race, one subculture, one age range," he told an interviewer in 1992. He continued, "Gangs teach a distorted discipline, a distorted familial bonding, a distorted sense of pride and power." The movie was an important one, but for many years after its release, Edward was threatened by the Mexican Mafia. In 1993, he was sued by a gang member who alleged that his life formed the basis of Edward's character in the movie, and in 1997, another gang member admitted that Edward had been targeted by the gangs for this role.

At the same time, Edward's personal life was in bad shape: in 1992, he and Kaija divorced. He married actress Lorraine Bracco two years later, and their relationship lasted three years; it was not until 2002, however, that they divorced. He's since married Puerto Rican actress Lymari Nadal. His son Mico is a Zen Buddhist monk, while his two adopted sons, Michael and Brandon, work with Bodie at Edward's production company. They are a close-knit family, and despite Edward's outward appearance as a stern patriarch, he laughs a lot and delights in his family and job.

In 2003, Edward was offered the part of William Adama in Ronald Moore's *Battlestar Galactica*. He and costar Mary McDonnell were each drawn to their respective roles in part because of the other's participation; but it was the script's inherent fierceness and political strength in a post-9/11 world that compelled Edward to take the part. "There was a story that drew me in, especially with the mind-set that one has after 9/11. You had a whole different perspective on the end of the world, that whole philosophy. What [Ronald Moore] did before you read the piece, he put three pages at the beginning. It was like a mission statement, kind of. It told you a little bit about how it was going to be shot. The script was very powerful. It was completely different. It was very much in the realm of *Blade Runner*, rather than in the realm of the kind of *Star Wars, Star Trek* opera that I was used to seeing in the genre," he said in an interview. "I said, 'I'm game to join up, but I'm going to be very honest: the first four-eyed creature I see, I'll faint. I will faint on camera, and I will be off the show.' I just didn't want to go that route. I didn't want to act against those kind of situations; I didn't have the time to do that. So we went into this with a 9/11 perspective and mind-set."

As Adama, Edward is the patriarch of the show, with Mary's Laura Roslin as the matriarch, and he's consistently known as a generous, kind, and committed actor on set. Jamie Bamber, who plays Adama's on-screen son, has this to say about him, "As a person, he's warm and generous. He's very much the heart and soul and the conscience of the show. Us younger actors look up to him as a father. I have massive respect on a personal level. As an actor, he's got an amazing presence and he is able to leave so much unsaid and communicate so much." It's a sentiment that's echoed by every person on the cast and crew, without exception, speaking to Edward's devotion to giving the best of himself — and demanding the best of those around him. A firm believer in pushing people to give everything they can, he's known for his improvisation on set, and many of his most intense scenes are those where his costars are forced by Edward's dramatic and improvisational choices to react more fully and more forcefully than anticipated.

The apocalyptic tone of the series takes its toll, however, and after three years, Edward finds it increasingly hard to leave his character and the darkness of the show behind. "I'm on the verge of emotional breakdown. I'll be watching my daughter or I'll be watching my sons or whatever, [...] boom, my emotions just come pouring; I just can't keep them down. Because I'm so in need of that to do the work that we're doing I can't just turn it off and then walk away from it, and then have to regroup to get back into that feeling. So I stay there. Not that I stay thinking about it, but emotionally I'm as vulnerable right now as I am when I'm working. It's not easy, because you're constantly emotionally taken aback by these feelings. I can't walk away from it anymore, so I don't try." It's a particularly powerful form of method acting that Edward won't apologize for: "If he [Ron Moore] didn't want to deal with the way I work, he shouldn't have hired me," he jokes.

Outside of work, Edward remains a staunch community activist. In 1998 he formed the Latino Public Broadcasting company, where he serves as chairman; the company funds programming for television shows highlighting issues of relevance to the Latino community. Edward's focus is always on youth and teenagers, as he's always believed they are the voice and action of the future. As early as the mid-1990s, the actor became deeply involved with the fate of the Chiapas, a state of southeast Mexico that suffers to an extreme many of the issues facing the Mexican and Mexican American population in general. In a 1998 interview, Edward told a reporter that, "Chiapas is probably the main concern I have right now for the planet"; at the time, he spent a lot of time in the area, bringing food and medicine to the severely malnourished and impoverished population. Edward refuses to engage in violent forms of activism, preferring instead peaceful civil disobedience, which he regards as "the only way to bring about change that allows people to enjoy the change and not get killed in the process." In the year 2001, Edward was jailed for 20 days for participating in the protests against the use of the Vieques islands as a practice bombing target. Edward has also been an ambassador for the United Nations Children's Fund (UNICEF).

Between *Battlestar Galactica*, family life, and his community involvement, Edward has still found time in the last year to produce and star in a number of important projects, including the 2007 HBO movie *Walkout*.

Edward's other humanitarian efforts include helping the Rockefeller Foundation recruit schoolteachers, aiding in the struggle against gang violence, ensuring Latino citizenship and voting registration, and playing a role in the Juvenile Diabetes Foundation and the AIDS Awareness Foundation. Awareness and education remain Edward's key priorities in whatever field it may be. "I come from a dysfunctional family," he said in an interview. "I'm a minority, I have no natural talent, but I did it. If I can do it, anybody can do it. I take away all the excuses."

Grace Park
(Sharon "Boomer" Valerii)

Born in Los Angeles on March 14, 1974, Grace Park (Jee Un Park in her native Korean) was raised in Vancouver, Canada, where her family moved when she was just under two years old. Grace's parents, both of Korean heritage, provided a rich cultural environment for Grace and her little sister, and Grace speaks fluent Korean, as well as some French and Cantonese. She sums up her childhood with good humor, saying, "I was pretty much raised with my lil' sister by my parents in Vancouver by very modest means, high expectations, heaps of love with

encouragement to learn, Korean and Western meals, and to respect my elders . . . which meant them."

After graduating from Magee Secondary School in Vancouver in 1992, Grace went on to study psychology at the University of British Columbia. Before discovering her love of acting (in fact, she's been quoted as saying, "Considering that I wanted to be a chef or research scientist, was shy, abhorred attention and would've been mortified to be on stage, the idea of stardom was somewhat non-existent"), she pursued a career in modeling, as well as appearing in a series of commercials, but once she received her BA, she decided she wanted to try acting for a year or so. "I had done a whole bunch of commercials, they were a lot of fun and I was very fun oriented. I thought I could get used to this. I was just going to do it on a trial basis for one year, and just see where it went from there," she says.

Her parents were less than overjoyed: Grace had had architectural ambitions, so acting seemed like an unstable career. "They just kind of waited for the phase to end," Grace laughed in one interview. When her father asked her how long she was planning on acting, Grace famously retorted, "You know what? I'm going to make a movie one day, and make like twenty-five million dollars!" His disbelieving laugh just pushed her to keep auditioning: "So after that I knew I really had to do it, just to prove him wrong." He realized that acting could provide a real career path for his daughter. "I think the turning point came when I did a screen test for show called *Silicon Follies* for ABC, and my dad saw the contract and saw how much I was going to get paid per episode, and his jaw just dropped. He put his arm around me and just laughed. From that day on I think he looked at me differently."

Soon after, Grace got a role in the teen series *Edgemont*, where she played Shannon Ng, one of the most complex and popular characters on the show. The five-season run allowed Grace to develop her acting skills, and she continued to expand her horizons by taking on guest star roles in both television and film. She appeared in five episodes of *The Immortal* between 2000 and 2001, and, without meaning to, accumulated parts in other science fiction shows such as *The Outer Limits*, *Dark Angel*, *Andromeda* (2004), and sci-fi mainstay *Stargate: SG-1*. She speaks enthusiastically about her guest appearance on *SG-1*, in the season 5 episode "Proving Ground" (2001). Still new to the job, however, Grace made a couple of errors in judgment — including one involving a prop gun. She says ruefully, "One time, as a joke, between takes I pointed the dummy MP5 at another actor, and Ron Blecker in charge of weapons pounced on me and chewed me out."

In between television spots, Grace started to make a name in the movie industry as well. She landed a bit part in the 2000 hit *Romeo Must Die*, and also appeared in *L.A. Law: The Movie* (2002). At a 2006 festival, Grace laughingly spoke about her interest in movies: "I've always been interested in movies but have never spoken a line in one . . . until last week. I just worked on *West 32nd* with John Cho, by Michael Kang who most recently did *The Motel*. Fantastic. Itching to explore all things Korean now." That movie is scheduled for release in 2008. In it, she plays Lila Lee, a lawyer who gets mixed up with a Korean gang in New York. The role offers Grace the opportunity to explore new boundaries, and, as it has in the past, her psychology degree will help her to delve deeper into her character's motivations and emotional landscape. "Psychology's given me a perspective on and fascination with people's behavior and what motivates us. But when it comes to performance, though psychology will help, often the best things will come up organically and my job is then to get out of my own way and let things happen. That's not so easy as it sounds!"

The reimagined *Battlestar Galactica* series, however, changed the course of her life and career. As is so often the case in the life of an actor, Grace didn't originally audition for the role of Sharon "Boomer" Valerii, but instead tried for the part of Anastasia Dualla — a role that ultimately went to Kandyse McClure. Grace sums up the auditioning experience concisely, telling an interviewer, "I worked my butt off taking classes, and when the role of Dualla on *Battlestar* came up, I did my work on it. After the audition I was told to come back for Starbuck. I did." There were four finalists for the role of Starbuck — including Grace and Katee Sackhoff. Although Katee was told she was too young for the part, she was convinced she would get it, and called her mother to say so. She remembers telling her mother about Grace, "There was this girl that I tested against [and I said] that if they don't cast her as Boomer, they're crazy. So that's what ended up happening. And I was really happy when I found out that they did cast [Grace] as Boomer. I think it worked out for the best. I can't imagine Grace and I switching roles. We talked about it."

It wasn't until after the miniseries was filmed and the series had been picked up for a full season that Grace found out that she would actually be playing two roles — Boomer and Sharon. "I hate to say it to you, but your character is the hardest on the show," costar Edward James Olmos told her when the show first started filming. Despite the difficulties inherent in playing two (and more) versions of the same character, Grace has nothing but good things to say about her *Galactica* experience. The main challenges relating to her character involve the ways in which each Sharon changes given her own unique experiences. Grace explains, "I'd have to say a lot of the challenges were actually script-based, what the writers would give

Sharon, and many of the story lines are actually quite human. [...] I think it's actually just the clarity of keeping each character unique and separate, yet the reality is that they are the same, they are clones, but each experience that each one has does shape them and change them."

Grace came to the show one of the youngest and newest in terms of acting experience, but she was determined to make that work for her. Because Sharon is a fairly new military recruit — only two years into her service — Grace's own learning curve mirrored her character's and she was able to bring to life Sharon's enthusiasm and eagerness to learn with ease. Things were not always so easy for her: one of Grace's most personally challenging moments involved the backlash from the network regarding a disturbing scene in the season 2 episode "Pegasus." In that episode, Sharon is raped by a military officer who's trying to get information from her. It wasn't decided until the last minute that the scene would be an all-out rape — the writers had been discussing having a near-rape, instead — but when the decision was made and the scene had been filmed, the network voiced concerns over the appropriateness of airing a rape scene. "What I found was [...] the more [the networks and executives] tried to shut it down, extinguish it, or hide it, I noticed that as a woman, I started getting more concerned or upset, because this is a situation that happens. Assault or rape happens to one in three women around the world. [So] how come on our show, we can have people beating each other up to a bloody pulp, and assault, even a man to a woman, killing hundreds of thousands of people, putting people out an airlock, or people just sleeping with each other, getting drunk [...] yet something that happens every single day around the world [...] is too taboo, and we have to be shameful of it. [...] I thought that was very unfair. It robs everybody of an experience, and of a story, and of a release, and also of a compassion that we missed."

Grace is an avid student of acting: the pressure of playing several characters, combined with the heavy-duty story lines given to her personae over seasons 1 and 2 started to wear the actress down, and she had to dig deep within to find a new way of working. At one point in the middle of the second season, she came to a crisis point where she wasn't sure she would be able to find the energy to perform. Her exhaustion meant that she had to find a different way of acting — and she found it to be more effective and less draining. She says, "[In the middle of the second season] I was having a tough time with the stamina, because it was just one thing after another. Plus, I think it was the method I was using for acting. It was pretty excruciating and finally I was like, 'That's it! I've got no more left. I'm not going to do anything else. I don't know how they're going to get this scene, because I'm not going to give anything. I'm not going to do what I usually do." And then I found a whole other level to play."

Whatever happens in the future, Grace is devoted to her career, and continues to train assiduously: she attends classes whenever she's not on set. Her very popular role on *BSG* has opened a great many doors for her, and she now receives more job offers than ever before. Unlike some actors who become known for science fiction roles, however, Grace has been offered a range of parts, not limited to Sharon-like scripts. "Absolutely the most important thing is the script. If the script is great, the role can be small, I don't mind. What attracts me to a role is change within the person, how do they change throughout the story line. Or, if they don't change, why, does that hurt them? I guess that's what interests me right now."

Despite her extremely hectic professional life, Grace has continued to nurture her personal one. In late 2004, she and longtime partner Phil Kim got married in a fun, casual affair in Mexico. The couple had been dating for three years before they decided to wed, and they indulged their shared love of traveling by going to India for their honeymoon. "I didn't think I'd ever want to marry a Korean person," Grace says, "in fact I was actually very adamant about it. But obviously he's very wonderful. He's a real estate developer, but when he was in college he wanted to be a director. So sometimes he talks to me about how I should play my character in a certain way, and he has very good insight on the show, so it's very enlightening."

Unlike her parents, whom she calls "conservative" (her father once asked her tremulously if she would ever pose naked, and was greatly relieved to hear her negative response), Grace has a daredevil streak that she indulges by doing a lot of traveling and participating in extreme sports. She's an avid snowboarder, and she used to work out by doing the "Grouse Grind" — a grueling 1.8 mile hike up the face of Grouse Mountain in Vancouver. She's famously known for having danced for twenty hours straight!

When not acting, training as an actor, spending time with her husband, or traveling, Grace is learning to speak Spanish. She also continues to define herself as Korean as well as Canadian: she grew up speaking half English, half Korean, and her Asian heritage is an essential part of her life. "I don't *feel* like I'm a role model, but if I am a role model that's awesome. I mean you never really know who's going to be someone that you would draw inspiration from, but if someone can draw inspiration from what I'm doing, that's really cool. I know sometimes people will look at me and say, 'Well you're doing something you love and it must've been really hard, and you're in the industry where there aren't so many Asians, so kudos to you.' And in that way, yeah, it's good, I'm proud of the fact that I did that. It's hard. You want to see in the media people that represent you and your voice, but there's not a lot of that out there."

Grace remains deeply committed to both *BSG* and the fans that form such an integral part of the experience. "It's really nice to be in an environment where everyone's cherishing the same thing together. [...] I think that when something like this happens, everyone knows that this is something quite special. And to be able to be a part of it, whether you're just witnessing it or not, is really important and it gives an energy to the project because it wouldn't survive without that."

Katee Sackhoff
(Kara "Starbuck" Thrace)

Kathryn Ann Sackhoff — better known by her shortened name, Katee — was an enthusiastic performer from an early age. By the time she was six, Katee was taking both dancing and acting classes, both of which allowed her to star in many of her high school plays — including *A Christmas Carol*, *Les Misérables*, and *A Streetcar Named Desire*. Born in Oregon, on April 8, 1980, Katee is the daughter of Mary and Dennis, an English as a Second Language coordinator and a land developer, respectively. Her television career started early: as a kid, she and her older brother Eric would routinely watch *Star Trek* with their father. She jokes, "I was addicted to the original *Star Trek* when I was growing up, because of my dad. We grew up in St. Helen, Oregon, and we weren't allowed to watch a lot of TV. I don't think we even had more than three channels, so it was basically watch *Dynasty* with my mom, watch *Star Trek* with my dad, or watch the mating rituals of beavers on OPB [Oregon Public Broadcasting]. So my brother and I watched *Star Trek*."

Katee practiced swimming throughout high school, an activity which gave her the athletic shoulders and arms that serve her *BSG* character Starbuck so well. Competitive swimming was Katee's first career choice, but when she was fifteen, she dislocated her knee and had to abandon her dream of professional athletics. The injury prompted her to take up yoga as a form of physical therapy, and she's kept that up for the last twelve years, making it a part of her regular routine.

Her athletic ambitions dashed, Katee decided on acting as an alternative career. She auditioned for a part as an extra in the 1998 television movie *Fifteen and Pregnant*, but was offered a speaking part instead. The movie starred Hollywood darling Kirsten Dunst; both Kirsten and Katee starred as teenaged mothers trying to cope with their drastically changing lives. It was Katee's first speaking part (she had previously been cast as an extra in the movie *Mr. Holland's Opus*), and it launched her career.

Shortly after graduating from high school, Katee moved to Los Angeles to pursue her career. Her parents had agreed to support her if she was attending school so she enrolled at Loyola Marymount University, but it didn't take long before she was supporting herself, so she dropped out of college. She landed a series of roles in various genres, ranging from biographies (a 1999 movie about Hugh Hefner, called *Hefner: Unauthorized*) to television series (MTV's *Undressed*, and Fox's *The Fearing Mind* and *ER* in 2002). A supporting role in the television series *The Education of Max Bickford*, which starred Richard Dreyfuss, allowed Katee to learn from veteran actors, and provided her with a lot of exposure, despite the fact the series was short-lived. Between 2001 and 2002, Katee landed two starring roles — the first in *My First Mister*, with Christine Lahti, and the second starring as Jenna Danzig in the horror movie *Halloween: Resurrection*.

In December 2002, Katee got the script for the role of Starbuck in the reimagined *BSG*, and, despite the fact that the directors were looking for someone in her mid-thirties, Katee asked to be allowed to audition anyway. Just twenty-two years old at the time, Katee went to the audition straight from another audition: she arrived in a skirt and tank top, with hair past her waist — a far cry from the tomboy the character of Starbuck called for. Her reading for the part impressed the casting director, and, a few weeks later, Katee was auditioning for the producers themselves. After the final audition — in which she was tested against fellow cast member Grace Park, who was offered the role of Sharon — Katee explained, "I walked away from that audition and I called my mom and told her, 'I'm gonna get this part, hands down!' I didn't care that they told me I was too young for it — I was gonna get it." She got the call telling her the part was hers that night, and the rest, as they say, is history.

All was not smooth sailing however. In the original series, both Starbuck and Boomer were male characters, and Katee in particular got a lot of backlash from loyal viewers of the 1970s series who were appalled at the idea of a female Starbuck. As the tough guy of the original series, Starbuck as played by Dirk Benedict was a ladies' man; he smoked cigars, played a mean game of poker, and was generally the go-to guy on the ship, and fans were upset at the drastic change. "You know, I let it bother me at first, and I took a lot of it personally. [...] I was so angry about it. And once they started attacking me as a person, that's when I stopped caring." Even Dirk Benedict, who played Starbuck on the original *Battlestar Galactica*, went on record as being opposed to the recreation of his character — he went so far as to write an article entitled "Starbuck: Lost in Castration," which was published in *Dreamwatch Magazine* in June 2004. He writes, "[The reimagined series is] bleak, miserable, despairing, angry and confused. Which is to say, it reflects, in microcosm, the complete change in the politics and mores of today's world as opposed to the world of yesterday. [...] I would guess Lorne [Greene, who played Adama] is glad he's [...] well out of it. Starbuck, alas, has not been so lucky. He's not been left to pass quietly into that trivial world of cancelled TV characters. [...] Starbuck would go the way of most men in today's society. Starbuck would become 'Stardoe.'"

In an encounter that made news reels everywhere, Katee had met with Benedict and had developed what she felt was a rapport with him. It was not until his very public derision of the show and her portrayal of Starbuck that his true feelings about the reimagined series became apparent. Although many reports accused Katee of a sharp tongue regarding Benedict, she set the record straight and clarified, "I was so misquoted . . . by saying that I said that if he ever gets put on the show, I would quit. That's not what I said. What I said was, I can't imagine [...] why, with the success that we're having and the high that we're on, would we want to bring someone in who would blatantly bash the show?"

Despite the controversy surrounding her character, Katee took the role of Starbuck and played it for all she was worth, and she says, "For the most part now [...] I would say that ninety-five percent of the people I meet are extremely supportive and I've actually had people, most people, say they like this Starbuck better than the old Starbuck. [...] At least I've stopped getting hate mail." The role demanded some sacrifices — including Katee's hair, which she was required to cut off in order to look the part. As a self-proclaimed girly girl, she was devastated, but understood that for her character to be immediately identified as the tomboyish, rowdy pilot she is, it was a necessary physical cue. "I know this sounds so ridiculous but I cried when they cut it. Grace [Park] and I were sharing a room at boot camp and I got up in the middle of the night to see if I could still put it back in these twisty bobby pin things I used to do. I barely could. With so much hairspray I couldn't stand too close to flame!"

Katee takes her job seriously, and is actively involved in her character's development. Soon after the miniseries was aired, she discovered that her version of Starbuck had made her something of a role model, and she decided to make some changes to the character when *BSG* was picked up for its first season. One of the most noticeable changes was the fact that both she and Starbuck quit smoking. "I didn't think it was a very good thing to be portraying on television, especially when most of my fans are young girls. I think everything else can be explained away by a parent, that done safe or in moderation is great, but the smoking is the only thing that she does that, hands down, will kill you. And you can't explain that away, and I didn't think it was the responsible thing to do," she explained in an interview.

Katee is unmarried, but shares her life with her two dogs: a pug/Chihuahua mix named Meatball, and a pug named Nelly B., after Katee's character on *The Education of Max Bickford*. She divides her time between her longtime home Los Angeles, and northern Washington State, which allows her to live conveniently close to the filming location for *Battlestar Galactica* in Vancouver. Her active lifestyle has allowed her to pick up a variety of skills — all of which are listed on her professional résumé: she can dance, sing, snowboard, play soccer, swim, run, snow ski, and scuba dive. "I don't really think about my job that much. [...] I guess that makes me a horrible actress. . . . As soon as the say 'action' I do my job, and as soon as they say 'cut,' I'm like, 'What's up? Who wants to go watch a movie in my trailer?' I try not to think about it too much. It's what I do for my job, but I don't want it to consume my life," she says.

Katee also sports three tattoos, which are more or less visible depending on how her character is dressed. She has the Chinese character for "choice" on the back of her neck, a black cross on her left shoulder (which covers up a tattoo of a small blue heart that she got when she was just fifteen), and her right forearm shows the Latin words "bona fiscalia" (public property) to remind her that she's in the public arena, and liable to be held up as a role model, so she should act accordingly. She notes, "In a medium like television, where anyone can just turn this on and it is basic cable, you have a bigger responsibility than you do if you are in an R-rated film."

Katee has remained active in the movie industry, despite her hectic schedule. Just before going on hiatus from *Battlestar Galactica* in 2005, Katee landed a major part in two movies: *White Noise 2*, the sequel to the Hollywood hit *White Noise*, and the low-budget action movie *The Last Sentinel*. In the first, she plays a nurse who is able to help the main character through the grieving process for his wife and son. But the grueling schedule of working on *Galactica* during the day and then going straight to the *White Noise 2* movie set took its toll on the actress: "I have never been so tired in my entire life. I was actually crying in my trailer on the last day, because I hadn't slept at all. [. . .] I would do *Battlestar* during the day; I'd work till 7:00, I'd show up at *White Noise* at 8:30, I'd work till 4:00, and then I'd be back on *Battlestar* by 5:30. My poor mom flew up to take care of me. And my intention was to have her sleep, to keep me straight when I fell apart. But she decided to stay awake with me, so she would be able to experience the pain and actually be able to relate, and she stayed awake the entire time."

Because *The Last Sentinel* had such a low budget, she performed all her own stunts and continued to expand on the skills she had picked up for *Battlestar Galactica*. "We had a million-dollar budget with 50-million-dollar stunts, and I got to do all my own stunts. [. . .] That's why I did the film. I was so excited to do my own stunts and work with Jesse [Johnson] because he is such an amazing stunt coordinator. [. . .] I know the fighting's going to be great because I had to learn to knife-fight for it. So it was pretty interesting."

Both movies hit the screens in 2007, and with the fate of Starbuck up in the air by the end of season 3, Katee is pursuing several other opportunities, including a lead role in *BSG* executive producer David Eick's remake of the *Bionic Woman* series, and a voice-over role in the animation satire *Robot Chicken*. When asked to reflect upon her career, she posits, "In the back of my mind I guess it was always like, 'It's never going to happen,' because you never really hear of anyone that makes it. You always hear horror stories of people moving to Los Angeles and coming home a year later. So I always knew I had the drive and ambition for it, but I think that this business has so many other things that go into success that you have no control over, so you never know. I wake up every day and pinch myself, and I'm so lucky to be where I am."

Battlestar Galactica Episode Guide

Miniseries, Parts 1 & 2

Original air date: December 8 and 10, 2003
Written by: Ronald D. Moore, Christopher Eric James, Glen A. Larson
Directed by: Michael Rymer

More than forty years after the end of the Cylon Wars, the Cylons reappear — in human form — and annihilate the 12 Colonies. A lone battleship survives, and, with a ragtag fleet of civilian vessels, begins a search for the lost 13th Colony — Earth.

Color, light, and sound. These are the first things we notice within five minutes of this four-hour episode. A new space is being born, a space that is dark and speaks of blood, fire, renewal, death. There is a starkness to the opening scenes of *Battlestar Galactica* that immediately signals to us that this is a very different show than what we might expect.

The term *in media res* is often used as a sort of shorthand for writers and critics: it's a phrase that means "starting in the middle." This narrative technique changed how we tell stories from "once upon a time" to "and this is what's happening now." One of the hallmarks of the new *BSG* is this sense of immediacy, and the way that immediacy works on the audience. This story begins in the middle of things, spanning decades of Colonial and Cylon history in a glance, ending — and starting — with a long, dark hallway, a solitary man, a chair, and a table. Interspersed with these "now" moments are snippets of text giving us the background of the story. It is told starkly, and further enhanced by the stripped-bare look of the text as it "tells" us what's happened — white on black. A few sheets and we understand that humanity has made machines, machines became sentient, and then there was a war. And now — well, now, things are about to change. An immediate tension is created between the text that promises clash and disaster and the utter loneliness of the Ambassador's setup. Alone in space, waiting for someone who never shows up, his was an exercise in futility, until today.

Today a woman arrives, and changes everything.

The woman we come to know as Number Six is our first introduction to the newly evolved Cylon race, and she's certainly a sharp contrast to the dull, gray, lifeless Armistice

Is *BSG* the New Epic?

One of the "trademarks" of an epic is that, although it might be written by a single person, the story itself it considered an amalgamation of many versions of the story told through the ages. In the case of *Battlestar Galactica*, it's the same thing: although authors' individual episodes are credited, the stories are often conceived and written up to a point by teams of writers who hash out the best way to begin, continue, and end an episode. Along the way they'll incorporate ideas from many different places: from the world around them, from the cast and crew, from their reading, even from their families! Even if a story comes directly from one author, it is still often based on another person's ideas. These ideas and what comes out of them (the intertextuals of the series) give the show its epic form.

An epic also tends to have national interests, traditionally telling a story of der-ring-do and long, arduous journeys that ultimately bring glory to the nation. In *BSG*, this aspect also coincides with a convention of apocalyptic science fiction – that of concealing what's really being said behind symbolism and allegory. So, while *BSG* is in a sense fostering a sense of nationalism, the nationalism it fosters is a universal one – the nationalism of humanity.

Despite the parallels, one of the big marks against *BSG* as an epic is that an epic doesn't pose questions: an epic's job is to tell the tale, to tell the deeds of heroes and how it went down and what a glorious time it was. *Battlestar Galactica* does spend time doing that, but it asks hard questions, too, reimagining the epic genre as it goes along. This new epic *BSG* believes that asking questions is as much a part of life as life itself. Asking questions is our right and our duty.

The other non-epic element of *BSG* is that it doesn't follow the exploits of one particular hero (and his various sidekicks). In that way, too, the series is reimag-ining the epic form because there is no definitive hero. Instead, the hero becomes an idea that is embodied by many people rather than a single person, and if the traditional epic hero is a single (male) figure, then the new one is not only not just male, it's not just human, either.

Station. She seems to be all color: vibrant red dress; bright, excessively blonde hair; perfectly white teeth framed by startlingly vermillion lips. She's tall and leggy, and the only thing about her that's reminiscent in any way of the robotic Cylons we — and the Colonials — know, is that the red of her body matches their glowing red eyes.

Amazingly, until now there has been no dialogue, only passive acceptance of the story as it unfolds. But the first words spoken are incredibly compressed with meaning, and a leitmotif for the whole series: "Are you alive?" asks the woman, in a reversal of what we, the viewers, expect. Were we not silently asking the same thing about *her*? That's certainly what the delegate is thinking, and there is terror, fascination, and hope reflected in his eyes. Does the woman's presence signify a new beginning or a new battle? Either way, she marks the end of an era. "It has begun," she tells the Ambassador, after giving him, quite literally, the kiss of death (ironically enough, immediately after she asks if he's alive). Then death, our oldest enemy, arrives.

In another clashing reversal, the scene changes again, to one filled with life. The faces of the people who live and work on this battlestar are mostly scarless, unseasoned, and shockingly youthful. Next to the young pilots like Starbuck and the ground crew like Chief and Cally, the presence of old-timers like Adama and Tigh could, under different circumstances, be startling, but the relationships between the different tiers of characters — older and younger, weathered and inexperienced, high-ranking officers and knuckledragger deckhands — are well developed. Commander Adama and the Viper pilot Starbuck, Adama and his son Apollo, Starbuck and the XO Tigh, Starbuck and Chief Tyrol — each character grouping adds layers to the story as well as to the different personalities that are now going to have to live together, indefinitely, in close proximity and under extremely harsh circumstances. Starbuck and the second-in-command, Saul Tigh, for example, are both hard living, hard drinking, and dedicated — a lifestyle that seems both perfectly suited to and incredibly awkward for a military career. Tigh's face tells the story of a long-time drunk: the broken blood vessels and squinty eyes aren't present in Starbuck's face, but we can see that that is a place she could go — and so does she.

The push-pull of their relationship is one of the most interesting in the series, and neither Starbuck nor the XO holds their punches — literally! — in the miniseries. Each sees in the other the best and worst of themselves, and that combines with a sense of claustrophobia afforded by their cramped quarters, a sense of impending freedom from the upcoming decommissioning, to create almost a pressure-cooker type situation.

Other characters face similar tensions in their relationships. Apollo and his father, for instance, do not share the same easy relationship that the father/son pair shared in the original series. The difference seems to stem from Zak's death: in the original *Battlestar Galactica*, Zak died while on patrol with Apollo, and Apollo blamed himself for the death. Here, Apollo blames Adama for pushing Zak to go to flight school, a move that ultimately killed him. Adama and Lee's relationship rings true because relationships fraught with this much tension and underlying grief can't be made whole in a day or a week. It takes time, effort, and consistent trust that neither Adama nor Apollo are ready to offer yet. Still, Adama's grief when he believes Lee is dead is heartbreaking; perhaps he thought that when the war was over, there'd be time for them to work their way back to a loving relationship, and to lose that hope is unbearable.

All the characters' interactions are made more interesting by the devastating backdrop to the story: their twelve home worlds have been destroyed, their families, friends, and possessions aren't just missing — they've vanished. Against this background of decimation, it's not hard to see how small tensions and interpersonal relationships could become major friction points. In a single day, they've become more than just individuals following their personal path to whatever it is they seek — happiness, glory, dental school — they're the sole survivors of the human race. It's a worldview shift that could easily make one go crazy. The situation is such that the characters must find a way to work together and overcome their differences, or the human race simply isn't going to survive. Those are some huge stakes, and the pressure Adama, Roslin, Apollo, Starbuck, Tigh, and Boomer are under must feel like it's burning a hole right through them.

In that context, then, the struggle between the personal and the universal is a major thread in the show: in the midst of personal turmoil, is it possible for human beings to rally and put the needs of the many above their own struggle? To a certain extent, Adama's decommissioning speech is an example of the intermingling of private and public. Ronald Moore says, "Commander Adama, […] in the middle of a standard-issue speech about patriotism and sacrifice and honor and the things that we have heard many, many times in the culture, […] in this moment breaks, because of what's going on with his son. It makes him take a hard look around at who they are. Why are we worth saving? Why do we deserve to survive? Who are we really? We're putting all these men and women in harm's way, and we're spending a lot of money on defense. We're doing all these things and we're telling ourselves we're the noble creation, children of the Lords of Kobol. This was a much longer speech in the script. It was a little too long, but the ideas are still there about who are we as a people, who are we as a species."

Lee faces his own uncertainty when newly sworn-in President Roslin orders him to go against his father's command and put the lives of survivors before potential victory over the Cylons. Lee doesn't know what side to choose, and it'll be a recurring arc for his character as he figures out where he stands with regards to the military, politics, and his own future.

Roslin is the first to recognize and accept the fact that the war has not only started, it's already ended, and she has an uphill battle trying to convince a slew of military people that their duty is not to fight, this time, but to admit defeat and leave. It's an impossible situation and it's made even more difficult because, for the survivors, it's not over. Hard decisions still have to be made; the needs of the remaining survivors in the fleet have to take priority over the needs of the few on the planet; people have to be left behind. And there's no time to grieve, no time to think about any of it. An unexpected attack by an even more unexpected enemy has left the space-bound Colonists in a situation where they can't begin to accept their fate because it seems surreal.

Roslin and Adama — as leaders of the fleet — have to handle a lot of sticky, detail-oriented situations, but they'll have to do that while keeping a close eye on the big picture. They're witnessing an apocalyptic upheaval of their world: what's changing isn't just the face of their world, but the face of war. A schoolteacher and an aging ship commander are suddenly the only people standing between the Cylons and the extinction of the human race, and they have some really hard times coming up. It's reassuring to see that they're able to adapt to change, to be decisive and in charge despite their personal issues. Michael Rymer, who directed the miniseries, said in an interview, "It's a war movie. It's a political film. The themes we touch on are, I feel, universal and profound and not limited to the normal conceptual scope of sci-fi. Look at the questions that Adama raises in his speech at the decommissioning: 'Who are we? Are we worth saving?' Those questions resonated for me, because they came up, quite violently, after September 11th. I think, in many ways, the show offers a very powerful allegory to our times. . . . We were going for a reality that was recognizable to people. I would sit behind the monitor going, 'My God, that's exactly what's going on today, with the war in Iraq.' Or, 'That reminds me of a situation Bush or Hillary Clinton was put in.' There is a lot of resonance that exists between this parallel universe of the 12 Colonies of Kobol and our lost planet, Earth."

One of the most striking aspects of this miniseries is the atmosphere: the use of color and the documentary-style camerawork really add to the feeling of claustrophobia. There are virtually no outdoor scenes; all the action takes place within metal starships, in small rooms, or in a space station that's dark, dismal, rank with disuse. The ambiance seeps out of the screen, cloaking the characters and the viewers alike with a sense of despondency and grimness. The only real breathing space is provided by the scenes on Caprica: in Gaius's house overlooking the ocean (a view that will become a prominent part of Gaius's inner life from here on in); or in the marketplace when Six snaps the baby's neck, symbolically killing hope and the future of humanity; or on Caprica, after the attacks, when survivors fight for the chance to leave the contaminated planet. Each scene that offers a feeling of openness is tainted in a way by the presence of the Cylon Six, and through her, death. It's strangely ironic that it is in the small, closed spaces of the space ships that humanity has its best chance to survive. And although Michael Rymer has pointed out that *BSG* is more than just science fiction, it still carries with it many recognizable science fiction, and more specifically apocalyptic fiction, ideas. Because we *are* preoccupied with how we're ruining the environment, how we're waging war, how we're accepting responsibility for the things we build, and the things we do. These are all recurring ideas that have found outlet time and again in both sci-fi and "end of the world" stories (see both "*BSG* as Science Fiction" and "Apocalypse, Now?" for more discussion on those aspects).

Are You There, God? It's Me, Gaius. Far from being the purely evil, knowing traitor from the original series, the reimagined Gaius Baltar is an unwitting betrayer of humanity, a self-styled victim of his own desires. For such a brilliant man, he's alarmingly shortsighted and egotistical. Still, Gaius's first reaction of disbelief is totally understandable. His next reaction, self-preservation, is equally understandable. In the face of his mistakes, he wants to survive. He wants to live, and that, more than anything else right now, makes him accessible as a character. Baltar is a narcissistic personality, but he's so very human in his whims and desperation. Gaius goes from genius scientist to perpetrator of the downfall of humanity in the space of a couple of minutes — it's got to be a lot for someone to come to

BSG as Science Fiction

Whether or not *BSG* is an epic in the traditional sense (see "*BSG* as epic"), it's definitely science fiction.

Or wait – is it?

There are definitely some sci-fi clichés in the new *Battlestar Galactica* – the miraculous cure of an incurable disease by foreign body; the biological ghost in the machine or cybernetic organism; the mad scientist; a computer system that spontaneously becomes aware; a ragtag group of rebels overcoming the Ultimate Evil; the Ultimate Evil turning out to be not so ultimate – or so Evil – as expected. When you string them all together like that, it's hard to imagine why some people don't think *BSG* is sci-fi.

But clichés do not a science fiction show make. And for most science fiction aficionados, there's one crucial element in *Battlestar Galactica* that puts it out of the running, strictly speaking: religion. Allan Weiss, a professor of English who teaches a course on apocalyptic science fiction, concurs: "In science fiction, the fantastic elements are given natural, scientific, technological explanations, rather than a supernatural one."

Then why is *BSG* billed as science fiction? Weiss explains that there are "two big questions in science fiction that continue to be asked, just in different ways – and the two big questions are: what is the definition of humanity, and what is our responsibility for our own creations?" And those two things *BSG* has in spades: every episode deals with different facets of those two questions.

On the one hand, *BSG* has, like *Buffy* and *Stargate* and *Quantum Leap*, used the term "science fiction" to describe itself; on the other hand, some people argue that while *BSG* is good drama, it ain't science fiction. The main point these people make is that science fiction uses one thing and one thing only as the yardstick for the universe: science. For example, a science fiction aficionado would say that *Star Wars* is not science fiction because it contains "the Force," a nebulous, undefined . . . *thing* that just floats around and helps or hinders according to how it's used. To a hardcore science fiction fan, that's just religion with a different name. If "the Force" had been explained – given laws, say, like gravity, or another system governed by scientific, quantifiable laws – it would have been science fiction. "The fantastic elements are given a natural, scientific, technological explanation rather than a supernatural one. As soon as you introduce a supernatural element you've pulled it out of the real of science fiction and you seem to contradict the other things that you've been saying," explains Weiss. When asked why he thought science fiction stories were trying to incorporate religious or fantastical elements, he said, "I think it's that science fiction wants to become entirely its own system, including religion."

So the question of whether *BSG* is science fiction is really up to the viewer to decide: how scientific do you like your fiction? How existential do you like your big, life-altering questions – served with a side of drama, bombastic like a space opera, or lean and mean "hard" science fiction? Like so many things in the *BSG* universe, it's up to you.

Adama's speech

Adama's speech at the end of the miniseries provides the emotional pivot point for the rest of the series, as well as one of the main plot ideas – the search for Earth:

ADAMA: Are they the lucky ones? That's the question you're all asking yourselves, isn't it? . . . . Maybe it would've been better if we'd all died quickly back there on Kobol with the rest of our families than to die slowly out here in the emptiness of deep space [. . .] "Life here began out there." Those are the first words of the sacred scrolls – the first words the Lords of Kobol gave us countless centuries ago. They tell us in explicit terms that we are not alone in the universe [. . .] I know where it is. Earth. This image has been one of our most guarded secrets. The location – or at least the general location – of this star system was known only to the most senior commanders in the fleet. We dared not reveal its location to the public while the Cylon threat was still out there. And thank the Lords for that, because now we have a refuge to go to, a refuge the Cylons know nothing about. It won't be easy. It will be a long and probably arduous journey to get there. But I promise you one thing: we will make it to Earth, and Earth will be our new home.

terms with and it makes for some fascinating character development. So when it's revealed that he's seeing Six in his mind, it's not exactly surprising. Is she an angel sent to protect him? We don't know; Gaius doesn't know (not even the actors knew!). What does he do to work through the guilt? Is it possible to feel no guilt about that? Can such a person be redeemed, in his own eyes as well as the eyes of the world?

All of This Has Happened Before: The fight scene between Adama and Leoben is set on Ragnar Anchorage. In Scandinavian mythology, Ragnarok is the end of the world of gods and men. According to the myth the end time will be preceded by a series of bitter winters, and humankind will fall into moral chaos. Soon after, a slew of demons and giants will attack from all four corners of the Earth, destroying the gods; the Earth will sink into the sea, but it will rise again, and the just will live on in a gilded hall.

Interesting Fact: The quote "So say we all" that's become such an intrinsic part of the series was originally ad-libbed by Edward James Olmos.

Did You Notice? The scene of Cami, the little girl on the botanical cruiser, playing with her doll as the Cylon missiles bear down on the ship is an allusion to the infamous "Daisy"

Tahmoh Penikett and James Callis join in the fun with more of the cast (CHRISTINA RADISH)

advertisement campaign that then-presidential candidate Lyndon Johnson wrought against his opponent, Barry Goldwater. In the ad, a young girl is seen plucking petals from a daisy and counting them; she looks up and sees something that is revealed to be a nuclear warhead when a mushroom cloud appears. The highly controversial campaign was pulled immediately after its first airing, but it's still credited as a factor in Johnson's electoral victory.

Roslin's swearing-in ceremony takes place on board the *Colonial One* (hastily renamed from *Colonial Heavy 798*); this parallels the swearing-in ceremony of U.S. President Lyndon Johnson on board *Air Force One* after Kennedy was assassinated.

The human ambassador at the Armistice Station displays a few family photos on his desk; one of them is a picture of Boxey, the young boy Boomer rescues from the surface of Caprica later on in the miniseries. Boxey tells Boomer he thinks his father is dead.

One of the documents handled by the Ambassador in the beginning of the miniseries is entitled the Cimtar Peace Accord — an homage to the original series. Cimtar was where the Cylons launched their attack on the five ships assembled for the peace conference.

In the museum on the *Galactica* are two displays: a Cylon centurion and a baseship from the original series.

The last line of the miniseries is a nod to the original series, where "By your command" was the Cylons' catch-all phrase to indicate obedience. The line wasn't added until the last minute, when a friend of Ronald Moore's purportedly told him it wouldn't be *BSG* without it.

Just before Adama makes his big decommissioning speech, the music that's played is a variation of Stu Phillip's theme from the original series; it's actually the Colonial anthem.

The dialogue between Adama and Starbuck in the beginning of the miniseries ("What do you hear?" Adama asks, and Starbuck replies, "Nothing but the rain") will be repeated at the end of Season 1 in "Kobol's Last Gleaming, Part 1." Same thing for the phrase "Bring in the cat."

The Cylons call themselves "humanity's children." That's a phrase that'll come up several times over the course of the series, although it takes on a different meaning as the mythology of the Cylons is explored. (Some episodes in which the phrase occurs are "Bastille Day," "Fragged," and "Lay Down Your Burdens, Part 2.")

Off-screen, Edward James Olmos and Jamie share a much less antagonistic relationship (STHANLEE MIRADOR/SHOOTING STAR)

Classic *Battlestar Galactica*: The scene in which Starbuck is seen playing cards with a group of crewmates is a reimagining of a similar scene from the original series' pilot episode, in which Starbuck (played by Dirk Benedict) is seen playing cards just before the Cylons attack.

A pilot with the call sign "Jolly" makes a brief (and unseen) appearance on the miniseries just before the Cylons totally wipe out the Colonial squadron. That's another nod to the original series, in which Jolly was one of the Viper pilots. He did not, however, die in the original.

So Say We All: SIX: Are you alive?

AMBASSADOR: Yes.

SIX: Prove it.

SEASON ONE — January–April 2005

101   33

Original air date: January 14, 2005
Written by: Ronald D. Moore
Directed by: Michael Rymer

The fleet faces sleep deprivation on top of everything else when they are forced to do faster than light jumps every thirty-three minutes to escape the Cylons.

Unlike the miniseries, which focused on the fight against the Cylons and the humans' desperate attempt to reclaim their homes, "33" is all about escaping the enemy. The sense of finiteness afforded by the episode's numerical title is precise and very calculated; like the Cylons, time is an inescapable reality. The episode starts with the ticking of a clock, setting up an atmosphere of slow, tense waiting. We don't yet know what we're waiting *for*, since, like many *BSG* episodes, "33" begins *in media res*, but everything in the first five minutes combines to create a sense of tension: the intermittent music, the haggard, exhausted faces and terrible expressions of the crew, and the sparse dialogue. Interesting camerawork throughout the episode highlights the crew's fatigue: some quick shots are blurry, mimicking how the human eye reacts when tired — the retina "zooms" too close to a person or object, and it appears out of focus. In an interview, Michael Hogan talked about Edward James Olmos's dedication to his job, saying, "['33'] was a pretty amazing episode to start season 1 with. During the cast's first read-through of the script, Eddie said 'This sleep deprivation is serious stuff; we have to work on it.' We had doctors come on set to speak with us, and we did our research. . . ."

In the episode's first few seconds, the scene quickly shifts from a close-up on Gaius's eye to his subconscious world — pre-apocalyptic Caprica. The contrast between the two worlds — the "real" one dark and grainy, the "imagined" (remembered) one bright and imbued with soft light — immediately provides context for a world in which everything has changed.

Gaius seems the closest to cracking under the strain as he rambles spacily, "There are limits to the human body, the human mind. Tolerances that you can't push beyond," but no one else is faring any better. On edge and under tremendous pressure, the relationships between the various characters start to show cracks and fissures, which adds a layer to the landscape of the relationships. We start to get a sense of how each character reacts under pressure, and we get a clearer idea of the ties that bind them.

Starbuck continues to exhibit the rebellious personality she had in the miniseries, loudly voicing her disapproval of Apollo's motivation techniques; the shouting match is offset by the camerawork, however, which shows the two in a tight, close frame that emphasizes their underlying camaraderie.

While the scenes between Apollo and Starbuck demonstrate a close bond from a military perspective, Dualla's scenes offer a very different framework with which to approach the characters. Kandyse McClure said in an interview with Galactica.tv, "I think Dualla, in many ways, forms the link between what's emotionally going on with the civilian population and what needs to be done within the military regime," and this is the aspect of her character that is highlighted in "33." In a brief but heartbreaking scene, Dee tries to find out what has happened to her family, carrying a photo like a talisman or a prayer book. She is met with empathy but ultimately helplessness, and she ends up wandering a corridor where the walls are coated with photos and mementoes of the lost.

Adama and Tigh keep as tight a ship as possible throughout the events, and it's clear how much they trust and rely on one another. They also implicitly share the idea that when all else fails, the sheer rigidity of command and attention to repetitive tasks can help to maintain order. More than that, though, there's genuine affection between them: Tigh makes sure that Adama gets more than his fair share of rest, dubbing him "old man" and reminding us that Adama is neither young, nor infallible. Mistakes will happen, it's inevitable, and the whole episode is a waiting game to see how disastrous that first — maybe final — mistake will be.

And disastrous it is: the loss of the 1,300 souls on board the *Olympic Carrier* is devastating on a collective level — with so few humans left alive, they can ill afford to lose a single person — and on a more immediate level for Apollo and Starbuck, who carry out the destruction order. The scene is painfully stark, with lots of closeups to illustrate the very personal nature of the task before them, but the two pilots (and actors) really pull it off — it's an unimaginable task for them, but their duty to the fleet and their superior officers comes first, a fact that Adama not only counts on but continually works for.

The episode closes with a shot of Mary McDonnell's face, as President Roslin is overwhelmed with emotion at the week's events — and, specifically, overjoyed at the fleet's first birth since the Cylon attack on the Colonies. After an entire episode of destruction and fallout, the strength of that single birth has a startling quality because of the depressing state of affairs: the humans are running ragged and wild, without destination, and with survival as their sole purpose. Interestingly enough, it is Six who mentions procreation in "33," couching it as a divine order. According to the Christian Bible, in Genesis 1:28, God said, "Be fruitful and multiply, and fill the earth and subdue it. . . ." That's pretty much exactly what the Cylons are trying to do — subdue the humans.

One of the most exciting things about *BSG* is how effectively the element of surprise is handled, where things that seem small and insignificant can eventually become huge parts of the show. Faith was not intended to be a big part of *BSG* at first, but it is an integral part of Six's character and becomes a central plot element later in the season. Show creator Ronald Moore wrote in his blog, "The religious angle was something that evolved after the first draft of the miniseries. In that draft, I had mentioned, almost in passing, that Number Six believed in God and [...] the Colonials in the original [series] were always mentioning the 'Lords of Kobol' and I decided to make that literal rather than figurative and give them a polytheistic religion and the Cylons a monotheistic belief system."

"33" gives us an entry point into a world that is no longer the world the characters knew. It's a world that will make everyone question who they are and what they do (the foreshadowing of Boomer's upheaval, as she starts to understand she is herself a Cylon), a world where intellect-numbing, impossible decisions have to be made on a daily basis (the order to destroy the *Olympic Carrier*), and a world wherein survival is the *only* thing that counts. It's a thrilling start to both the characters' journey and our own, with all the show's main themes making an appearance in one way or another: faith, hope, death, rebirth, love, passion, anger, religion, loss, betrayal, identity, judgment, and responsibility.

Headcount: At the beginning of the episode, the whiteboard gives us 50,298 survivors. By the end, it's down to 47,973.

Are You There, God? It's Me, Gaius. This episode marks the beginning of Gaius's own conflicted relationship with God and religion, and just the first in a series of repentances, which seem so sincere and true at the time (and probably *are* true to the character at that point in time) but which ultimately show him to be a man who believes in one thing — his own survival. Gaius is the individual embodiment of the fleet's collective goal: to survive.

Numbers: In numerology, which is an ancient method of divination, 33 is known as a "master number" (along with 11 and 22, of which 33 is the sum): when the number 33 is associated with someone's name, that person is thought to be extraordinarily developed from a spiritual perspective.

In the Christian faith, 33 is also said to be the age of Jesus Christ at the time of his crucifixion, death, and resurrection.

The number can also be seen as a double 3, which is considered one of the most sacred numbers: the Holy Trinity in Christianity (Father, Son, Holy Spirit), the Great Triad in Taoism (Heaven/Human/Earth), the Three Jewels of Buddhism (Buddha, Dharma, Sangha). According to the Chinese, 3 is a perfect number, and to the Egyptians, it is the number of the cosmos comprising three elements.

Interesting Fact: As the pilots leave the briefing room, they each touch a picture of a man looking out over a destroyed city. Ronald Moore explains the connection between that photo and the events of 9/11, "The photo was inspired by the famous shot of the firefighters raising the flag at Ground Zero that became iconic. I thought the Colonies would have their own version of this — a snapshot taken in the moment that becomes a symbol of the day they can never forget and of all they had lost" (see page 13 for the photo).

Did You Notice? Apollo asks Boomer how it is she's coping so well when everyone else is running off the deep end with sleep deprivation and stress, and Starbuck jokingly calls her a Cylon.

The (understandable) lack of humor in this episode. A couple of deleted scenes between Starbuck and Apollo provide a bit of levity. In one, as they're out on patrol, Starbuck asks Apollo how many patrols they've done. When he says "two hundred and thirty-seven," Starbuck says, "You telling me I missed two hundred?"

LEE: That's exactly what I'm telling you. . . . What, were you planning something special?

STARBUCK: Nah. Just like to keep track of things like this. I mean, two hundred was such a nice round number, and I'm going to have to wait for three hundred.

LEE: Don't even joke about it.

Also in the episode, Six tells Gaius, "I want us to have a child, Gaius." Look out for Six's words and their accompanying scripture ("Procreation is one of God's commandments") — they will become something of a catchphrase for the Cylons, as well as a major thread in the whole Cylon/human mythology.

So Say We All: TIGH: Yes, we are tired. Yes, there is no relief. Yes, the Cylons keep coming after us time after time after time. And yes, we are still expected to do our jobs!

102   Water

Original air date: January 14, 2005
Written by: Ronald D. Moore
Directed by: Marita Grabiak

The Galactica's water supply is sabotaged, leading to a desperate survey of nearby planets for water.

The minimalist atmosphere of this episode fits in with the theme and title — water, which every human requires in order to survive. Water is a heavily symbolic element for us, and *BSG* carries this symbolism along with it, expanding and playing with its significance. While the miniseries and "33" focused on the much more clear and present danger of the Cylons, "Water" brings the story back to the basics: forget the high-tech Cylons, forget the fact that the fleet doesn't know where it's going: without water, it's not going anywhere.

"Water" packs a visceral punch, focusing on the characters and what drives them. Bare-bones sets and dark lighting frame this episode, fittingly enough, as we wander in and out of the characters' subconscious minds, confronting their fears and regrets. "Water" takes place nearly entirely inside, giving it a claustrophobic feel that's evident from the first gripping scene. Interior space is another place where *BSG* plays with themes and tackles difficult subjects. Compare Boomer's tiny exterior space with the large interior space Gaius has with Six: while Gaius's world has been irrevocably exploded, Boomer's world is inexorably closing in on her. With an episode like "Water," where so much of the drama occurs inside a character's head, it's a smart move to open that way. Even though *we* know that Boomer is a Cylon, we panic right along with her as she goes from confused to frantic at her situation, making "Water" quite literally a watershed moment for her character. Her whole arc stems from that moment when she looks around her and doesn't know how she got there.

Later in the episode, another pivotal scene featuring Boomer hinges much of its power on that locker-room moment. As she scans a planet, the inner struggle she has with herself shows the character's every conflicting instinct: to betray her human side, or override her

Cylon programming? Which one is true? Which one is *right*? Her ultimate victory over her Cylon programming is poignant because she doesn't even know she's won anything: in her mind, she's simply managed to see the monitor and its message clearly. This scene opens up a key part of the Cylon arc: can every Cylon overcome his or her programming? If so, is it by design — were they created with free will and the ability to choose the way they would evolve? The parallels with human creation myths — many of which feature humankind being endowed with free will — raise a lot of unanswered questions. If machines can look like humans, feel like humans, emote like humans, then how are they different from humans? If we can never be sure who we are, then how do we construct identity? These questions are contrasted with the events of "33," where the stimulants the pilots take ironically make them able to function without rest — like machines.

Grace hams it up for the camera

(CHRISTINA RADISH)

"Water" continues to delve into the darker side of the *Galactica*'s crew, in particular Apollo. Apollo's not all military-gung-ho like his father but not all diplomacy-ahoy like the president. He's certainly a military man, and takes his job and its responsibilities seriously (you only have to check out the difference in style between Apollo's pilot briefing and Starbuck's in the next episode, "Bastille Day"), but he's also someone who wants to look at what's going on emotionally. Apollo is haunted by his own actions in "33": he has visions of the *Olympic Carrier*, and he second-guesses himself and the decisions that were made. Lee *is* emotionally invested in what he does, and he won't just ignore what he's feeling. Roslin and Adama represent two sides to this story. On the one hand, they're at war, and any way they look at it, there was no choice but to destroy the ship. Second-guessing and doubt are luxuries the crew of the *Galactica* simply can't afford — in fact, Adama places that responsibility firmly in history's hands. On the other hand, Laura reminds Lee that he is — that *they* are — all leaders now, and that their decisions affect a whole civilization: how could he take that responsibility lightly? Rationality and emotion both have a part to play, and it seems they're going to be played out primarily within the character of Apollo.

Helo's story line continues to be presented as a separate narrative from the *Galactica*'s, leaving us to wonder why, exactly. What purpose does it serve for Helo to be isolated from the rest of the crew, stranded on Caprica, fighting for his life? While forging a sense of

Ecological Footprint

In "Water," we learn some interesting facts about how *Galactica* and the fleet operate. Adama says "*Galactica*'s water recycling system is close to one hundred percent effective." What does that mean? Living in space on a ship would definitely put a crimp on things like running to the corner store to get a bottle of water, but how do they "recycle" water? Other science fiction stories have also looked at this idea. Frank Herbert's *Dune* series of science fiction novels had "stillsuits" that caught every bit of water that the body produced, distilled it, and then made it available again to drink. While we're not told specifically how the water is recycled on *Galactica*, it seems like they need to take very little water out of other environments to function.

An "ecological footprint" or "water footprint" is a measurement that determines approximately how much water is used by an individual to produce the goods and services they require — and it's more than what is needed for a person for them to *live*, it's how much they *use* on average, because different people use different amounts, depending on factors like location and economic standing. The XO Tigh, says, "Civilians don't like hearing they can't take a bath or wash their clothes or drink more than a thimble a day." Since the *Galactica* is a military vessel, its inhabitants are used to more stringent allowances of resources like water because they were trained to be — sort of like us with recycling plastic, paper, and glass. But other ships, like the *Olympic Carrier*, are civilian ships and not used to rationing. In North America, where fresh water is abundant, we rarely even think about how much water we use, whereas in a nation with very arid land, like Australia, water is always scarce and people have grown up with severe restrictions placed on their water use.

It may seem a little odd that Gaius would be able to figure out how much water, grain, and meat are needed on *Galactica* and in the fleet, but each ship must function like a planet. Because the ships are self-contained, logs have to be kept of consumables like food and water, because if they can't meet their needs, they have to go elsewhere for their resources. And since humans can't go for more than a few days without any water (if we go by the "3-3-3" rule of thumb — 3 minutes without air, 3 days without water, 3 weeks without food), it would be pretty important to know how much you've got, and how much you use.

community (fragmented though it is) within the fleet is essential to the *Galactica*'s characters and stories, so too is the isolation that Helo's experiencing an essential part of his development. Without any information other than what he already knew when he arrived on Caprica, Helo has to forge his own way. It's a different kind of survival, and a fight that clearly becomes a whole lot easier when Sharon shows up. She just raises more questions though: it's impossible to tell whether she really believes she came back to find Helo, or whether she's knowingly lying to him and is aware of her Cylon identity. And if she *is* lying, why?

For many cultures, water symbolizes the subconscious as well as rebirth. The episode "Water" works both angles — for instance, the first scene of Boomer reborn into the locker room, wet and confused, and her subsequent "rebirth" when she overcomes her programming and recognizes the presence of water. (Also, Gaius's subconscious mind nearly always features a view of water.) "Water" takes a look at the humans' most basic needs and gives us a glimpse of their most basic fears. Boomer fears she's a Cylon agent; Apollo fears it was wrong to destroy the *Olympic Carrier*; Gaius fears he'll be found out as the traitor of the human race. And the deepest fear of them all is their very uncertainty, the murky depth of their minds, which, like water, can drown or nourish. Boomer can't know who she is until a foolproof Cylon detector is created; Gaius can only heap deception upon deception; and Apollo will never know if the *Olympic*'s 1,300 passengers were on board.

Headcount: The whiteboard on Roslin's ship has been updated to read 47,958.

All of This Has Happened Before: Water plays a central role in the creation myths of many a culture. In all cultures, water is life, and represents fertility, growth and birth. Not only does water appear in creation stories to explain the origins of humankind, but also in scientific theories: Charles Darwin's theory of evolution is the foundation of modern biology, and it holds that humankind emerged from the water in one form that slowly evolved into its current shape. Water's role as both a birthing agent and a form of subconscious communication will come back in big ways in season 2 ("Downloaded") and in season 3, where we'll find out that the Cylons have a specific use for water.

Interesting Fact: When "Water" was first written, it ran a lot longer and then had to be edited by more than ten minutes. Ronald Moore noted, "I was always uncomfortably aware of the 'cheats' involved. That is, the dropped scenes, the internal cuts made to scenes that made a hash of some of the logic I'd tried to lay out, the half-expressed thoughts, the missing emotional beats, et cetera."

What's In a Name? William Adama: the name most obviously comes from the original *BSG*, but going farther back, the name "William," an extremely common name, carries with it connotations of victory and war dating back to William the Conqueror. The king of England from 1066 to 1087 when he died, William is widely recognized to have changed the course of English history through his rule. He wasn't an ostentatious leader in terms of military strategy: he often went for the simple, direct plan (very much like Adama), and if he was at a disadvantage, he immediately withdrew (very unlike Adama). Pious, he took a great deal of interest in the welfare of the church. The fact that the commander of the fleet may be named for a historically renowned conqueror and military leader offers a sense of warship, battle-readiness, and, ultimately, hope for victory that pervades the series even when things are at their worst. William Adama is definitely a conqueror, definitely *not* pious in a strictly religious sense; he is pious, however, in the sense that he believes deeply in the survival of humankind and in the strength of the human spirit, and nothing will sway him from that belief.

Adama's surname is reminiscent of Adam — the first human being — because in many ways, Adama can be seen as the first human male in the postapocalypse, with Roslin as a type of Eve, together recreating the world.

Imagine, then reimagine: old Apollo, new Apollo (CP PHOTO/RICHARD LAM)

103   Bastille Day

Original air date: January 21, 2005
Written by: Toni Graphia
Directed by: Allan Kroeker

Apollo tries to recruit a ship of incarcerated men to help mine for water; the situation turns ugly when he finds Tom Zarek, a political prisoner, in charge of the prison.

In a clear parallel with history, the episode "Bastille Day" takes a look at a central issue in *Battlestar Galactica*, that of military versus civil order. In a situation where you're at war and are constantly fighting to evade an enemy, a question arises regarding what comes under military purview and what does not: where do you draw the line between martial law and civil law? The show's third episode examines this issue through four characters: Commander Adama, President Roslin, Apollo, and Tom Zarek. The title "Bastille Day" seems like it's speaking to the events that take place at the prison, with the military and political representatives (Apollo, Dee, Billy, and Cally) being taken hostage by the unshackled prisoners, and that's definitely one way to look at the episode. It's also possible, however, to look at "Bastille Day" in terms of each character individually: Cally fights back against her oppressor/rapist and bites his ear off; Starbuck stands up to Tigh when he criticizes her lack of professionalism in the briefing room; and Apollo finally chooses a side — and it's not the side either his father or the president expected.

Lee's ethics are often placed side by side with Adama's, and while both characters always fight for the greater good, their approaches are totally different. In "Bastille Day," Lee shows

Richard Hatch (Tom Zarek)

....

Date of birth: May 21, 1945

Did you know? Not only did Richard play Apollo in the original *BSG* series, but he's also the coauthor of seven *BSG* novels. He tried for years to get the show back on the air, without success.

On the new *BSG*: "Nothing will ever replace the original show. It had an incredible chemistry and originality, and it would be lovely to see that show either made into a movie or some kind of reunion special where you could catch up with those characters and resolve and tie up a lot of loose ends that were left by the cancellation of the original series. I think the fans, in a sense, are still unrequited because that story has never had a chance at resolution. The sad part is that fans have been asking for twenty-five years for a resolution to the original. And, you know, if someone wanted to reimagine . . . that's fine. If somebody wanted to do the *Pegasus* story, that's fine. I just think that first they should have done some kind of a four-hour miniseries, you know, bringing the original show back, bringing it up-to-date, resolving a lot of things . . . and giving closure [. . .] and there would have been a lot more acceptance."

his idealist nature when he tells Zarek that the presidential elections will be held within the year, and then saves him from being shot by Starbuck's sniper bullet. Apollo then stands up to his father's and the president's anger, telling them that all he's doing is upholding Colonial law — and if Colonial law is no longer in effect, then what are any of them fighting for, anyway? It's Apollo's revolution just as much as it is the prisoners', and you can see how firmly he believes in the society that is slowing being built back up. Lee does some real maturing in this episode, going from a character who "didn't know we were picking sides" to one who promises elections and stands his ground with both main authority figures in his life.

"Bastille Day" introduces Tom Zarek's character. He is either a freedom fighter or a terrorist, depending on who you're talking to, and, as many fans know, Zarek is played by Richard Hatch, who played Apollo in the original *Battlestar Galactica*. Zarek is presented as the underdog with charisma; he plays on the fascination he inspires, saying: "I am Tom Zarek, and this is the first day of a new era." He clearly enunciates his political goals, and the intensity of his dialogue and ideas challenge and play into the fleet's political uncertainty. Zarek appears in this first episode as the figure of the revolution, one who, having spent twenty years in prison, has nothing to lose but his life — which he doesn't seem to value all that much. But as events unfold, we realize that Zarek's apathy for life is just another political tool he uses to get what he wants.

The semantic play between terrorist and freedom fighter, which is fiercely debated by Dee and Billy (they're totally focused on each other and clearly stimulated by the discussion, but respectful of each other's views, despite their respective passions) speaks directly to the real-life political situation in Iraq. Moore explained that he was interested in applying the particulars of contemporary history to the show, so that viewers could have a current framework while pointing to the fact that these issues are ongoing and universal.

The scene between Mason and Cally is brutal: it's the first time the show has really focused on her, so we have no sense of her personality or strength. Dee assures Billy that Cally will be all right, that they've all been trained for just such situations, but there's still an awful moment of tension where they wonder if Cally will survive. The situation is all the more frightening because, after all the dangers the fleet has faced — Cylons, death by dehydration, and more — being raped and murdered by a Colonial prisoner probably didn't seem all that likely until the time when it did.

There's a subtle parallel drawn between the situation on the *Astral Queen* and the situation between Commander Adama and President Roslin. There are at least two different types of prisoner on board the *Astral Queen*: the Zarek type, all rhetoric and political ideas, and the violent type, like Mason. Despite the united front that the prisoners present, "Bastille Day" shows that there will always be a difference in agenda. In the same way, the commander and the president represent different agendas, despite their united front.

Historically, Bastille Day refers to the overthrowing of a monarchy; in a larger sense, however, it is symbolic of the overthrowing of a whole regime, including its religious and political scaffolding. That same theme is present in this episode. When, back on Caprica, Helo says "Someone must be watching out for us," our immediate thought is that he's referring to a deity of some kind. The fact that Caprica-Six is watching Helo and Sharon as they make their way around the devastated planet, however, gives the sentence deeper meaning, and draws a parallel between the Cylons and god(s). This brings up one of the show's most intricate and long-standing questions: What does it mean to be a human? A machine? A god? Humans created the Cylons — by some definitions, that makes them gods. The Cylons created human-looking Cylons — by the same definitions, that makes *them* gods. Whose god is watching out for Helo and Sharon? It all gets kind of complicated!

Whichever way you choose to look at "Bastille Day," whether as an individual revolution, a collective revolt, or an overthrowing of a larger enemy, it marks a turning point in the fleet's existence: not only are they now aiming for survival, they're also hoping to recreate a civil, law-abiding, democratic society.

Are You There, God? It's Me, Gaius. Gaius finally comes clean about the fact that he's no closer to creating a Cylon detector than he was when he first started, but he's quickly turned back to the "dark side" when Six transfigures into a sort of supernatural demon and reminds him that his life is on the line. Six's fury is emphasized through the application of makeup, light-colored contact lenses, and large fake teeth. There's nothing overtly wrong about her, but she just looks . . . well, *wrong*. Gaius stumbles along the path she sets him on, figuring out piece by piece how a nuclear warhead can help in Cylon detection, but we're never quite sure whether Six and he are making it up, or if it's scientific genius at work.

Social Contract

Broadly speaking, a social contract is a philosophical term that refers to the fact that humankind adapts itself to living in society, and without the limitations imposed on us by society, we would live in a state of nature – that is, without any form of boundary or any notion of right or wrong. To avoid living in this state of nature, which would allow everyone the same liberties and create a world of chaos that follows only the laws of nature, we implicitly involve ourselves in a social contract that gives us civic rights at the cost of obedience to the same laws we expect others to abide by.

Social contract theory was all the rage in the seventeenth and eighteenth centuries, but its three main proponents were Thomas Hobbes, John Locke, and Jean-Jacques Rousseau. In 1651, Hobbes wrote his major work, *Leviathan*, in which he defined the state of nature as a state of war, where each person took what they wanted without regard for anyone else. Hobbes believed that the only real way for the state of war to be ended was for a social contract to be enforced by the appointment of a sovereign, who was absolute and was sworn to protect the people.

Locke placed the burden of the social contract on enforcement of generally recognized criteria for right and wrong. He believed that obeying the civil government was contingent on that government's protection not only of the human being, but also of each being's private property – if that contract was violated, the people would be well within their rights to overthrow the sovereign.

Rousseau's theory varied wildly in that for him, the state of nature was unwarlike, and he defined man in that state as simply "undeveloped" in terms of social responsibility and morality. It was only through the social contract that humankind could gain civic awareness and a sense of moral obligation; the government rested on the "general will" of the people to submit themselves to it.

"Bastille Day" discusses in part a form of social contract in which a bond of trust is formed between the military and political leaders of the fleet and the civilian population embodied in the prisoners. In all societies, there's a need for authorities to be well defined, and their processes transparent; in a situation such as the one the Colonials are living in, such transparency and authority are problematic because it's a totally new way of experiencing government and civic duty. Would the military or government ask prisoners to risk their lives to perform arduous physical tasks on a hostile planet if they weren't in a postapocalyptic situation? Perhaps, but there's no doubt that it would be instant media fodder, and probably a really unpopular move. Roslin and Adama each have to establish and implement their own social contract within the fleet – and Apollo takes the first step for both of them in this episode by explicitly extending an offer of democracy in order to "buy" the prisoners' help.

Adama and Roslin appear in the roles of sovereigns (military and government, respectively), and they're gaining awareness of the fact that they're there by default – not because anyone chose them to be, but because they were in the wrong (or right) place at the wrong (or right) time. The onus is on them to prove that they can maintain the social contract and that it will allow the fleet to enjoy civic liberties such as they enjoyed on the Colonies. (Look for the first of those liberties to be threatened in season 2's "The Captain's Hand.")

Numbers: Tom Zarek's prisoner number 893893 is a multiple of 47, which is a long-standing in-joke number in television. It apparently has its origins in *Star Trek: The Next Generation* and was featured in all of its spin offs and appears prominently on *Alias*. In *BSG* it's been used quite a few times: it's the number of the last lottery ticket drawn on Caprica to decide who got to fly out with Sharon and Helo, and Boomer has flown 47 Raptor missions.

Interesting Fact: The original draft of "Bastille Day" had Cally dying after being raped by the prisoner, but writer David Eick decided that she should fight back during the rape scene instead.

What's In a Name? In Greek mythology, Apollo was the god of the sun, truth, archery, music, and poetry. He was seen as the god who made humans aware of their own guilt and relieved them of it. He presided over the construction of cities and over religious law, and he was also known as the messenger for his father's will (his father was the king of the gods, Zeus). Lee sure has a lot to live up to, but so far, the mythological reference seems to suit the character well. Lee is a moral person, one who doesn't just do what he's told but tries to figure out the rights and wrongs of a particular course of action before choosing what he believes to be the best path. In this episode, he tries to ensure that the reconstruction of Colonial life follows as lawful a path as possible by promising that elections will be held, making him in many ways the protector of Colonial civic life. Like the god Apollo, Lee is more than a messenger for his father's will. The Greek Apollo was a fierce warrior, but, unlike Lee, he was known for his use of distance in a battle — he was a great archer, while Lee's style is up close and personal, both in terms of his fighting strategy and his relationships with other.

Did You Notice? Is Colonial religion based on Greek mythology? At this point in the series, what appears to be the Colonists' prevalent religion hasn't had too much to do with the story; it's not until the end of season 1 and through most of season 2 that it becomes more integral to the plot. Until then, it's the Cylons' monotheistic religion that gets all the airtime.

In the miniseries, the *Astral Queen* was said to be a passenger ship carrying 500 passengers. But in "Bastille Day," the ship is carrying 1,500 passengers (in the "Previously on *Battlestar Galactica*" segment, Billy's line regarding the number of passengers has been re-dubbed) and is a prison ship rather than a passenger liner.

Zarek calls the survivors of the Cylon attacks "children of humanity" — exactly the term Caprica-Six uses when she talks with the Cylon Doral on postapocalyptic Caprica. What is the significance of this reference? Does it have any relevance in the larger mythology of the show?

Starbuck wishes the pilots "Good hunting" at the briefing: this is what she rebuked Apollo for not saying in "33."

Classic *Battlestar Galactica*: The character of Boxey is a callback to the original series, the son of a survivor named Serina (played by Jane Seymour) and also the adopted son of Apollo. He's played by Noah Hathaway, and from the outset of the series, he already has a much more integral role in the show than the new Boxey does. The original Boxey is devoted to his dog, who died in the Cylon attacks and was replaced by a "robotic" look-alike. The character of Boxey becomes Captain Troy in the 1980 *BSG*. Outside of the mini-series, this is the only episode in the new *BSG* in which Boxey appears.

It's possible that the plot for this episode was inspired in part by an original series episode, "The Gun on Ice Planet Zero," in which a group of criminals was conscripted to work on an icy surface.

So Say We All: APOLLO: I don't owe either of you a damned explanation for anything.

ROSLIN: He's *your* son.

ADAMA: He's *your* advisor.

104   Act of Contrition

Original air date: January 28, 2005
Written by: Bradley Thompson, David Weddle
Directed by: Rod Hardy

An accident leaves thirteen pilots dead, forcing Starbuck to train inexperienced pilots to fly Vipers, and to remember her role in Zak Adama's death.

Every time the *Galactica* crew think they're getting a break, something horrible happens to remind them of their new reality. Flat Top's accident scene is all the more tense as it's interspersed with a carefree scene between Adama, Apollo, and Starbuck, who is recounting the Commander's own 1,000th landing. "He's thinking, 'I can get away with anything today,'" she says — and the camera cuts to Flat Top looking as though he's on top of the world. Through ever-faster cuts and increasingly chaotic camerawork, the director creates a horrific scene, and the fact that we never see the carnage but instead hear only the sound of the explosion and the aftermath makes the sudden absence that much more effective.

"Water" looked at the problem of physical resources — the bare necessities for survival; "Act of Contrition" takes on an equally critical problem — in a time of war, with a population that's been all but obliterated, how can the fleet keep providing the services required for survival? Fighter pilots are the first stratum of the population to come under attack, since it's they who protect the fleet from the Cylons, and stupid accidents like the one in this episode only make matters worse. Not only does the fleet lack qualified fighter pilots, they also lack qualified instructors. So Starbuck's recruitment as fighter pilot instructor seems very real. The realism is further highlighted when we get a good look at the "nuggets," as the new Raptor pilots are called — they're just so *young*-looking. Starbuck, Apollo, Gaius, not even Boomer could be considered old, but most look like they have a few years under their belt both in terms of life lived and professional experience. That's not the case for the new recruits, who look like they've just been called straight from an academy campus. We already feel like we've come a long way since seeing the young faces of the main crew in the miniseries — and it's only been four episodes.

Each act in the episode starts with the same sequence of Starbuck in freefall from her plane. There's a tie-in between the emotional states of Flat Top and Kara through the use of the camera, suggesting that even though their feelings — elation and despair — are different, these feelings are similar. One of the most effective uses of the freefall sequence is at the end of the confrontation between Starbuck and Adama: Adama's gaze turns ice cold, the affection he'd directed at Starbuck vanishes, and he tells her, "leave this office, while you still can." As she leaves, we see that she is holding her head in despair, and the scene cuts to her plane in freefall in the moon's atmosphere. There's a clear parallel between Starbuck's emotional state after being rejected by Adama and her being forced to eject from her aircraft — she's been cut off from everything that's important to her.

Mary McDonnell, classy as ever
(ALBERT L. ORTEGA)

But how tough would it be to find out that the woman he thinks of as a daughter is partially responsible for the death of one son, and for his consequent estrangement with his other son? That's got to be hard to take, and it also more than likely brings up Adama's own feelings of guilt regarding Zak's death, since he pulled the strings to get Zak into flight school. It's just as obvious that Kara's also in real anguish: she feels like she betrayed her fiancé, and Apollo and Commander Adama. The repeated flashbacks to loving, domestic scenes between Starbuck and Zak Adama have worked to show Starbuck's emotional vulnerability in this episode — making the whole episode her own act of contrition.

Although Starbuck has a central role in "Act of Contrition," a lot of other threads get pulled into the spotlight as well. Dr. Cottle confirms that Laura Roslin's cancer, which she put down to "allergies" in the last episode, has progressed well beyond the point of operation and rebukes her for having gone five years between breast exams. "I was busy," Laura retorts. How ironic that now that she is busier than ever, and has the responsibility of 50,000 lives, she has to deal with terminal cancer. Roslin looks tired and scared but not defeated, and that's one of the things that viewers and Colonists alike have admired in her since her rise to power.

"Act of Contrition" is all about the humanity of the characters. "We know each other very well," says Adama of Starbuck, but his statement could also be an ironic comment on Gaius and Laura, both of whom are deceiving the people around them in different ways — Laura with her cancer and Gaius with his secret betrayal of the human race. The same, too, can be said for Chief Tyrol and Boomer who think they know each other, or Helo and Sharon who also think they know each other.

Ronald Moore wrote in his blog, "We're showing people doing what people really do and not all of their choices are smart ones. We smoke, we drink, we have sex with the wrong partners — we make lots of bad choices and some of them we do knowingly and in full cognizance of the risks and consequences." We forgive all these indiscretions because the characters are just so human in their various flaws. Boomer keeps doing wonderful little human things, like kissing the chips she wins at poker; Starbuck has a great maniacal laugh when she's shooting the Cylon Raider near the end of the episode; Laura talks back to her doctor. It's these moments of pure humanity that make cliffhangers like the one at the end of "Act of Contrition" so effective.

Are You There, God? It's Me, Gaius. Another entry in the humans as gods portfolio: Starbuck tells the nuggets to refer to her as "God," and later informs Apollo that her "word is scripture" and that if she says the nuggets aren't good enough for fighter pilot training, then that's all there is to it. On the one hand, others — as well as Starbuck herself — have repeatedly commented that she is the best pilot they've ever seen, so her confidence is hardly an exaggeration. Even Adama tells Lee that he believes Kara only needs one day to tell if the nuggets have the goods. On the other hand, however, Starbuck has a tendency toward extreme reactions, so Lee's caution and second-guessing isn't unwarranted. It's also worth noting that, God or not, Starbuck doesn't have much choice when it comes to the recruits — it's them or even less-experienced nuggets. Either way, it's an interesting look at the idea of divinity — even as a god, she has to follow certain rules.

Interesting Fact: The accident scene in the hangar was inspired by a similar real-life accident from 1967 on the *USS Forrestal*, when a missile accidentally went off and knocked off an on-board aircraft's fuel tank and started a fire. This set off a series of explosions and fires throughout the ship, which ultimately left 132 of the crew dead and 62 injured.

Did You Notice? When Starbuck is training the nuggets, she mentions a maneuver called the "thorch weave." This could be based on a real defensive maneuver, the thatch weave in which two aircraft cut across each other's tails to prevent fighters from closing in. The thatch weave is said to have first been used in World War II by U.S. Navy Commander John S. Thatch.

Viper pilot "Hotdog" is played by Bodie Olmos, son of Edward James Olmos. In an interview, the younger actor revealed that, "The character of Hotdog is very interesting for me because it's one that was really wide open for me to develop. He is a washed-out fighter pilot, from flight school, who was really a hotshot type of pilot, which ends up getting him thrown out of the academy. That being said, he always thinks he is a little better than he actually is."

105   You Can't Go Home Again

Original air date: February 4, 2005
Written by: Bradley Thompson, Carla Robinson
Directed by: Sergio Mimica-Gezzan

Apollo and Adama use valuable resources to try to find Starbuck.

"You Can't Go Home Again" opens with Boomer rescuing Hotdog — the poor guy is so shaken up by his close call with the Cylon Raider, he throws up in the Raptor. Crashdown comments that he's "not the first to lose it in combat" and "won't be the last" — a sure foreshadowing that things aren't going to get any easier for the *Galactica* crew.

"You Can't Go Home Again" is a fitting title for this episode, in which a number of things are put to rest. Not least among these is the unsettling tension between Commander Adama and Apollo. Their relationship has apparently been uneasy since Zak's funeral and since Apollo accepted President Roslin's request that he act as her advisor on all things military in "Water," and the rift between father and son has grown all the more evident, with snide remarks and a lingering sense of disappointment in their interactions. In "Bastille Day" for instance, Adama insists that someone *purely* military be involved in the prisoner negotiation — casting doubts on Apollo's own military expertise and loyalties.

While this episode allows Apollo and Adama to reforge a bond, to unite in their common desire to get Starbuck back alive, it also allows Commander Adama to come to terms with Starbuck's confession from "Act of Contrition." His anger at her in that episode comes full circle here: he worries about her, spends valuable and scarce resources on rescuing her, and finally comes to the realization that they're family — and you don't give up on family. His love for Starbuck eventually helps him to make that final step towards Apollo at the end of the episode, when the father — not the military man — says, "If it were you, we'd never leave."

It's hard not to see both sides of the issue: Adama and Apollo are hell-bent on rescuing Starbuck, but, while Roslin has ample empathy and patience, it becomes clear that the rescue operation is verging on futile and they're wasting resources — both human and material. Roslin finally loses patience, marches onto *Galactica*, and demands that Apollo and Adama get their heads on straight and move the fleet out of danger. We're so used to Roslin as the diplomat that her angry tone comes as quite a shock. It's the first time Roslin has had to really call Commander Adama on anything since the miniseries, when she convinced him to walk away from the fight against the Cylons so they could all survive; in the same vein, here she asks him to walk away from someone he loves so that the rest of humanity can survive. It's easy to look at Roslin and resent her for making them give up on Starbuck, but they all have heavy burdens to carry, and while Adama's assertion that "sometimes you break the rules" holds true, it's equally true that sometimes you have to uphold them.

Besides, while all this is going on, Starbuck is out saving herself. The episode leans heavily on irony, cutting from the futile rescue attempts to scenes of Starbuck binding her injured knee, climbing to higher ground, locating the Cylon Raider she shot down, and finally saving herself. No matter how bad the situation is, she won't just sit back and take it. And she does whacked-out so well: covered in a Cylon Raider's blood and gore, sucking oxygen through its innards, she pep-talks herself through the whole scene, chuckling madly and with a wild glint in her eyes. As the first human to be in such close contact with these advanced "machines," her horror and mania seem, well, appropriate.

The creative use of her call sign painted on the Raider's wings, which allows Apollo to recognize her towards the end of the episode, is loads of fun, as is the little wing-wiggle the two perform to greet each other. The chemistry between these two characters has been present since the miniseries, but it's usually couched in the little moments like this one; Apollo might be a big one for figuring out what's going on beneath the surface, but Starbuck seems to save her delving for downed Cylon Raiders — a nice inversion of the typical binary, which has women wanting to share their feelings and men resistant to the idea. It's also the flip side of the first episode of this two-parter, "Act of Contrition," which focused on Starbuck's emotional side. It's good to see that even in emotional freefall, she can pull herself together and work her way through a situation. It's good not only on a personal level, for Starbuck herself, but also on a military and professional level — if she weren't able to pick up the pieces and move on, she might not be able to go wading into battle at each sign of a Cylon attack.

One of the most unsettling scenes is when Adama coldly dismisses Tigh, showing that he's lost perspective. The Colonel draws himself to attention and salutes, but for a split second, he's absolutely disbelieving that his friend and colleague would treat him so disrespectfully. It's the first time we've seen this kind of conflict between the two, and it's a bad sign. To Tigh's credit though, he wraps himself in professionalism and leaves the deck with dignity. Aside from his drunken episode in "Bastille Day," Tigh's been the consummate military officer in every situation the fleet has encountered. He takes his responsibilities seriously, not least because he's one of the few people aboard *Galactica* who knows firsthand what war is like.

Back on Caprica, Helo and Sharon are almost in honeymoon mode, with enough food, water, and anti-radiation medicine to last them a good while, and the closed set and closeup shots of the two actors convey a sense that the characters are creating a sort of postapocalyptic Eden: "We can't be the only two people left in the world," says Sharon. This setup of Helo and Sharon as a new Adam and Eve continues throughout the series. This episode highlights Helo's growing feelings for Sharon and widens the feeling of isolation that has surrounded them until now. The interlude is exactly that, an interlude, and we know it won't be long before the calm subsides and their story explodes.

Headcount: The whiteboard reads 47,958, the same as it did in "Water" — clearly, Roslin hasn't updated it to reflect the 13 pilots who died in "Act of Contrition." Bad president, bad!

Interesting Fact: Katee Sackhoff has gone on record as saying that this episode was one of her least favorite to shoot, ever. "It was absolutely horrible. Every time I climbed inside [the Cylon Raider] I screamed. I'm such a […] girly-girl. I have nails and wear stilettos and wear dresses and the last thing I want to do is go play in gook. And not only play in it, but also put it in my mouth! It was so nasty, especially because that day, we shot all the stuff on the planet before that. It was just the hardest day I ever had on the show because I had that pack on my back and it actually had forty pounds of air in it. […] So I was getting sweaty, but the flight suits are made of rubber, so it holds the wetness in and then they were turning

Tahmoh Penikett (Karl "Helo" Agathon)
....

Date of birth: May 20, 1975

Did you know? Tahmoh and his twin sisters Sarah and Stephanie are the children of the former premier of the Yukon (Canada), Anthony David John Penikett. Tahmoh also has First Nation ancestry: his mother is from the White River First Nation.

His role as Helo: Originally, Helo was meant to die on Caprica when he let Gaius Baltar take his seat on the Raptor going back to *Galactica*. Ronald Moore decided that Tahmoh's performance as Helo and the character's popularity warranted further exploration, so he wrote an entire story line around him.

On Helo's promotion at the end of Season 2: "I didn't realize until [a couple of episodes into the third season] that I was actually the XO! I thought I was simply put in Gaeta's [Alessandro Juliani] station. I am a senior lieutenant already, but I thought because of the skeleton crew, and not that many people left up there with Adama, there was a small establishment. So, I sort of overlooked the XO thing. This season, I remember reading a second time and it said 'Helo, the XO, is coordinating a mission plan' or whatever. I thought, 'XO?' I kinda got a kick out of that then!"

On his relationship with Grace Park: "The one thing I appreciate in working with Grace is that because we share so many scenes together, we have gotten to the point where we do a lot of analyzing together. If we see a scene that is worked a certain way, we are always trying to look back on the story. We just do a lot of extra work trying to figure out where we are coming from."

on this giant ten-foot fan and it was blowing cold air on me so at one point, my lips were blue. So when I did that stuff in the Raider, I had the flu. And I was putting it in my mouth, do a take, throw up, do a take, throw up. Which was not one of my finer moments."

Did You Notice? Starbuck's wearing a thumb ring in this episode, which she wasn't wearing in the miniseries. Katee Sackhoff, who plays the fighter pilot, explained in an interview, "I've had this [thumb ring] on my finger for eight years, and I've always had to take it off for jobs, and I've always lost it for like a week, and then found it. And I didn't wear it in the miniseries, and then finally I was like, 'I'm not taking this off. It hurts to get it off, and I don't want to take it off every day, because I'm gonna lose it.'"

A very humorous (if tense) face-off between the toaster and, well, the Toaster (a.k.a., the Cylon) in the restaurant on Caprica. It's machine versus machine — who will win? The use of a chrome toaster in this scene refers back to the miniseries, in which Gaius mentioned that the original Cylons, those created by the humans, looked like chrome toasters, which in turn is a reference to the original series.

Starbuck asks the Cylon Raider, "Are you alive?" when she first approaches it on the planet. That's the third time that particular phrase has been used in the series: the first was at the very beginning of the miniseries; the second occurrence was in episode "33," again with a Number Six model, but this time the question was directed towards Helo. In both these instances, the query was followed by a kiss, thereby infusing the Cylons' concept of life with their idea of passion.

106   Litmus

Original air date: February 11, 2005
Written by: Jeff Vlaming
Directed by: Rod Hardy

A Cylon suicide bomber detonates a bomb aboard the Galactica, forcing the president to reveal the existence of humanoid Cylons.

Oh what a tangled web they weave. Before the Cylon attack, the *Galactica* was about to be decommissioned; it's a reasonable assumption that many of the rules and regulations that govern a military ship had been swept aside — like Chief and Boomer's clandestine affair. With such sudden and drastic changes, in a postapocalyptic world, the management and discipline issues that could have been tacitly ignored beforehand have become a lot more important, and the boundaries between private and public must be redefined. Moore agrees: "[*Galactica*] was far from the best of the best at the time of its retirement and the people on board weren't either. The discipline was lax and many procedures had been allowed to fall by the wayside. Now, this ship and its crew are forced to operate far above what they considered to be the norm and it's not an easy transition for any of them."

Boomer and Chief Tyrol's relationship might have been tolerated before the attacks; now, though, their relationship could affect military operations and, ultimately, the whole crew. Their relationship is all the more important in this episode because Colonel Tigh told Boomer directly to end it, so on the one hand, it's not like she hasn't been given every opportunity to put an end to the relationship; on the other hand, making a change like that involves a lot of soul-searching and the sacrifice of her personal life for professional demands, and as easy as Tigh makes it sound, it's just not that simple. "Litmus" puts the relationship to the test though, and ultimately, it's Tyrol who calls it quits when he realizes how many lives and reputations they're compromising. Socinus goes from making his own distillery with Cally and Jammer to being stripped of his rank in the space of one episode. Tyrol is professional and hardworking, and we learn that he's been serving under Commander Adama for five years, so there's a great deal of trust between them. Adama's disappointment with Tyrol, and his frustration at a lack of choice when it comes to punishing Socinus, resonates strongly with the Chief, and also points to the problem that was dealt with in "Bastille Day" and "Act of Contrition" — the crippling lack of adequate human resources in the fleet. Adama *should* have punished Chief and Boomer for lying under oath and carrying on a relationship that is forbidden by military regulations — *especially* given

A Chain of Command

Sometimes it's a little hard to figure out who's in charge — and that's one of the most interesting aspects of *BSG*. By exploring the military/civil boundaries of a society, *Battlestar Galactica* can look hard at little mistakes, big ones, liars, cheats, black markets, subordinates, and racketeers — to name a few. The endless question of "who's in charge" stays interesting precisely because the parameters of each episode can change so drastically. Some episodes, like "Scar," deal almost exclusively with military operations, and we don't wonder about the individual liberties of citizens. Others, like "Bastille Day," show both military and civil heads working together to achieve their aims. And still others, like "Colonial Day," focus on civil and civic operations and expectations. But some episodes like "You Can't Go Home Again" have a real tension derived partly because military decisions (in this case using resources to find one pilot) go against civil concerns (expenditure of resources jeopardizes the entire fleet). From a strictly military point of view, here's how the chain of command works in *BSG*'s military, according to Ron Moore, the executive producer and chief reimaginer:

Officers:
Admiral
Commander
Colonel
Major
Captain
Lieutenant
Lieutenant (junior grade)
Ensign

Enlisted:
Master Chief Petty Officer
Chief Petty Officer
Petty Officer (1st and 2nd Class)
Specialist
Deck Hand
Recruit

that they were explicitly ordered to end it. But the Chief is the best person to keep the fighter planes up and running, and Adama can't afford to lose his valuable services. It's a lose-lose situation, and he's understandably angry with the Chief for putting him in that situation.

In its everyday use, a litmus test is a test that relies on just one indicator to prompt a decision: in this episode, the title refers primarily to the independent tribunal that's been appointed to find out if there are any more humanoid Cylons hiding on board the *Galactica*. It also refers to the experiment being conducted on post-nuclear Caprica, where Helo has his own unwitting litmus test to pass: he has to decide whether to try to find Sharon and rescue her from the Cylons, or to leave her and find his way off the planet. The repeated scenes of Cylon models Numbers Five (Aaron Doral) and Six definitely work to maintain an imagery of experimentation, with frequent long shots and shots filmed from above, making Helo seem like a mouse in a maze. There's also a parallel wrought between the end of Boomer and Tyrol's relationship and the growth of Sharon and Helo's. And finally, we find out that this Sharon has known all along that she's a Cylon agent and has been manipulating Helo into falling in love with her, casting a whole new light on all their scenes up until now. That's one thing that *BSG* is known for — its ability to make you go back to the beginning and see everything differently. Helo is so undecided, but as Sharon says to her fellow collaborators: "He's a good man. He always does the right thing," and true to form, he turns back to find her. Helo's goodness will continue to be his character's defining trait, and Sharon's words are telling: she's been deceiving him, but she is also getting to know him — we just don't know if she's doing it for the right reasons yet. Can she, like Boomer, defy her programming and learn to love? When Helo kills the Cylon that's dragging her and pulls the bag off her head, it's reminiscent of a twisted traditional wedding scene, where the man lifts the woman's veil at the end of the service. But it's hard to say just what relationship is being born here: is this a new Sharon, baptized in blood, or a Cylon Frankenstein's monster created for just this purpose, to deceive Helo? In that sense, "Litmus" could also be a test for the Cylons as they try to discover exactly what it is about humans that makes them human.

Sergeant Hadrian is a thoroughly unlikable character, because although her intentions seem to come from the right place, she immediately hones in on Tyrol and Boomer and apparently ignores any other avenue of investigation. Obviously, the hangar crew *is* hiding something, but Hadrian's suspicion doesn't come from evidence gathered in this episode. Adama puts an end to what has become, in his words, a "witch hunt," indicating that whatever one's intentions, it requires constant vigilance and absolute awareness to ensure that one does not become one's own worst enemy, pointing to the fact that a fragmented, suspicious crew isn't in anyone's best interests. Hadrian lacks any real insight or foresight, and ends up thwarting her own investigation — letting her personal beliefs leak into the public arena, and putting the whole operation at risk. She, too, it seems, has failed her personal litmus test.

The public/private debate is central to this episode because everything relies on it: what do people need to know in order to survive? What do they need to know in order to make the best possible decisions? It's interesting that the debate surrounding the military versus the political approaches to life on board the fleet seems to have temporarily screeched to a halt in the face of this new issue regarding transparency: both Adama and Roslin have the same concerns about private information becoming public knowledge. This transparency debate ties into the longstanding philosophical tenet that "knowledge is power" — and in a situation like the one the fleet is in, it's just plain dangerous for power to be shared in any form.

"Litmus" opened on a romantic interlude between the Chief and Boomer; it finishes with Chief suspecting her of being a Cylon. Tyrol has really changed — in "Water," he wouldn't even entertain the notion of Sharon being a Cylon, but the events of "Litmus" force him to conduct his own independent tribunal on their relationship and on Sharon herself. And while her silence matches his own decision to invoke the "23rd Article of Colonization" that grants him the right to not respond, her silence is also damning.

Headcount: In "Litmus" three people died in the suicide bombing, and thirteen more were injured. Although there's no official whiteboard, if we combine these numbers with those from "Act of Contrition," we get 47,955 survivors.

Interesting Fact: When Six turns on Gaius and says, "Don't make me angry, Gaius. You wouldn't like me when I'm angry," it's a tribute to the character David Banner, who frequently said just that before transforming into the Incredible Hulk.

Did You Notice? When Adama is called in front of the tribunal, he picks up his glasses from where they're lying on a book on his desk. The book is a *Reader's Digest* anthology. No comment.

This is the first episode where Apollo and Starbuck aren't omnipresent: Lee is entirely absent, while Starbuck features in one scene in the medical unit where she's being visited by Gaius (who's being visited by Six).

President Roslin says to Adama, "You sound like a lawyer," recalling Adama's own comment to Apollo in "Bastille Day": "You sound like some kind of lawyer." Here, we find out that Adama's father was a civil liberties lawyer: it could be that the distaste in his voice when he rebuked Lee in "Bastille Day" is related to Adama's father's occupation in some way — or, it could be just a coincidence.

So Say We All: HADRIAN: Why did you allow the relationship to continue, knowing it was against regulations?

ADAMA: I'm a soft touch.

107   Six Degrees of Separation

Original air date: February 18, 2005
Written by: Michael Angeli
Directed by: Robert Young

A Number Six shows up on board the Galactica to accuse Gaius of treason — and she has photographic evidence.

The term "six degrees of separation" came into the common lexicon in 1990, with a play of the same name written by John Guare, but the theory was actually first posited in 1929 by a Hungarian writer, Frigyes Karinthy. In the play by Guare, one of the characters states, "I find that extremely comforting that we're so close. I also find it like Chinese water torture that we're so close. . . ." This episode functions much the same way — all the human survivors are united, a common front against the Cylons; but they're also cooped up in close quarters, unsure of who to trust and who to alienate.

"Six Degrees of Separation" points to both the growing suspicion throughout the fleet that more Cylons are hiding, but it's also a play on the name of the Number Six Cylon model. The title could refer to the fact that Six separates herself from Gaius, but also to the fact that "there are many copies" of Six, and they're all different in one way or another. The flesh-and-blood version of Six, Shelly Godfrey, is quite different from the version that lives in Gaius's mind — not least because she lacks the pure physicality of that Six (oh yeah, and the wardrobe). When Gaius encroaches on her personal space in the bathroom, she tries to push him out of the way, but it ends up looking like a feeble attempt — a far cry from the physical strength we've seen in the other two Six models.

One of the most intriguing aspects of Shelly showing up on *Galactica* is that, in "Litmus," Six intimated to Gaius that the other Cylons don't know she "lives" in his mind and that they operate independently of her. However, the Cylons' actions in this episode seem to contradict that statement: it's Six's anger over Gaius's blasphemous ways that causes the other Number Six model to show up and accuse him of treason. It's also Gaius's tenth-hour (re)conversion to the Cylon God that causes the whole sham to be revealed. Do the Cylons actually act separately from Gaius's Six, or is she more than what she says she is — and what we assume she is — that is, a figment of his subconscious? Most fans believe that Godfrey is a corporeal manifestation of Gaius's Six — that she has the ability to take physical form. This in and of itself is reminiscent of the Christian belief that God became flesh and blood in the form of Jesus Christ. The fact that Godfrey simply vanishes from one moment to the next certainly supports this view of her as a physical manifestation of Gaius's Six, but she leaves physical proof of her existence — a pair of glasses — so the question isn't answered one way or the other. Gaius himself asks Six the question at the end of the episode but she ignores him, inviting him instead to have sex — perhaps not a coincidence that she wants to engage in a physical act rather than a philosophical discussion.

When the episode opens, Gaius seems prickly and out of sorts, and totally resistant to Six's idea of God — an idea he had accepted so contritely back in "33." In a nice parallel with real-life relationships, religion becomes a stumbling block between the two, and Six walks out on him as he calls Cylons "little more than toasters." It's interesting that she puts up with his flirting with Starbuck and his vacillating loyalties, but his fair-weather conversion incenses her to the point of vanishing from his mind. Gaius's about-face with religion reminds us of the man we saw in the miniseries, a genius who appeared on a talk show to vaunt the merits of hard science and fact.

The media are becoming a greater presence, and in "Six Degrees of Separation," there's again a mixing of the public and private, as Roslin's illness nearly becomes public knowledge because of the media listening in on ship radio transmissions. When she collapses while on the phone to Gaius, it's a priceless character moment: Laura sounds dreadful, but he can't (or won't) look up from his own life long enough to see anyone else's pain. Roslin obviously won't stop working or living up to her responsibilities until she's dead — that much is clear from her collapse and her instruction to Dr. Cottle to dose her up so she can face the press. Gaius is her antithesis: self-involved where she is civic-minded, obsessive where she is rational.

Genius

In the new *BSG*, Dr. Gaius Baltar is often referred to as a "genius"; he did, after all, design the defense mainframe for the 12 Colonies. He's also called an "evil genius," as he helped bring about the downfall of that very same mainframe. What is a genius? And why does the character of Gaius continue to elude and frustrate us? Is he an example of other kinds of "intelligence," a sort of parallel to the Cylons in that he is driven, obsessive, seems bent on world domination (or at least becoming more powerful than any other human)? Is he a ray of hope for humanity, with his endless repentances to God, Adama, Six, whoever happens to be listening, and his ability to do the "right thing" just moments after we're sure he'll do the wrong thing again? His character is moody, unresponsive, selfish, and he lives, sometimes literally, in a fantasy world. His off-the-cuff responses to situations seem crazy and farfetched; we catch ourselves saying, "that would *never* happen in real life."

Sometimes Gaius's character seems a little too smart: not only did he design a defense mainframe — no small feat of engineering, among other things — he's also apparently a stellar physical scientist with intimate knowledge of the properties of plutonium ("Bastille Day"), as well as a brilliant biologist well versed in the makeup of human blood ("Epiphanies"). The series sets Gaius up as a sort of scientist *Übermensch*, a suprahuman brain filled with knowledge — with a penchant for sex. Lots of sex.

While the sexpot part of Gaius may be tailored for *BSG* specifically, the genius part does hold more water, so to speak. Studies conducted in the 1980s and 1990s show that there has always been a sense that the idea of "genius" carried with it concepts of bizarre behavior or what we today might term "psychological disorders." While we usually think of artists and writers in the category of tortured genius, anecdotal evidence about scientists like Louis Pascal, Isaac Newton, Johannes Kepler, and Copernicus reveals that it's not necessarily just artistic genius that suffers. A scientist, supposedly the most rational of us all, can have just as many irrational behaviors as a composer or a painter, and that very irrationality seems to be linked to a little thing called *creativity*.

Some theorists believe that there are certain commonalities in exceptionally creative people, like *divergent thinking* (trying to expand, rather than limit, the options to an answer); think of Gaius casting about when he speaks to Six and inadvertently saying something damning out loud. Other theorists point to the unconscious workings of the mind as a source for creative responses. And Gaius's ability to inhabit a daydreamy world often results in him coming back to the "real world" with the answer to a complex problem that neither he nor anyone else could figure out with conventional thinking.

Another factor that many scientists believe is necessary for creativity is dogged determination, even in the face of defiance or ridicule. Gaius Baltar often seems to be motivated either by an urge to revenge himself on other people, like President Roslin or Commander Adama, or by his own ambition, no matter how craven that ambition may seem to us. In fact, the ridicule of others, whether it's shipmates or enemies of Six, seems to trigger in Gaius an immediate "I'll show you!" response.

Are geniuses always creative? The jury's still out on that one. It's important to realize, though, that researchers in this area do not conflate *intelligence* (general mental ability) with *creativity* (the ability to find new and novel ways of solving problems). Instead, they see them as different conceptual forms of mental ability; they may have some overlap, but they're not the same thing. And it's in between those two places – intelligence and creativity – that Gaius Baltar has free reign.

Despite the serious themes, "Six Degrees of Separation" has gone down in sci-fi history as being the first episode of the genre to feature a scene taking place in a bathroom. It's a long-standing joke that for all its hundreds of episodes, *Star Trek* never once indicated the presence of bathrooms or the crew's "eliminatory needs."

This episode isn't *all* about Gaius, however. Tigh proves to be a great help in Starbuck's recovery, which is unexpected because there's been no love lost between the two from the start of the series. In fact, the last time we saw the two interact was when Starbuck tried to call a truce and Tigh called her on her professional flaws ("Bastille Day"). Tigh's snide comments and use of reverse psychology to get Kara back on her feet prove to be exactly what she needs. The tension between the characters relies on the fact that they both need to prove the other wrong — revenge as a driving force.

And back on Caprica, Sharon and Helo have sex in the middle of a highly symbolic downpour. For Helo, the act of making love with Sharon is the mark of a new beginning, but Sharon's motives are a lot more complicated. This scene plays on their identities as a post-nuclear Adam and Eve, but Sharon could also be the snake from the biblical story, placed there to bring down humankind. It remains to be seen if there are "six degrees of separation" between the humans the Cylons.

Are You There, God? It's Me, Gaius. This whole episode is a message from Six to Gaius about the need for Gaius to develop a personal relationship with God. A couple of additional points, however. Gaius refers to his attempts to develop a Cylon detector, calling his mission "the Church of the Mystical Cylon Detector." This ironic name calls attention to two things: firstly, that humans have a tendency to create religion out of anything as long as it holds importance for them; and secondly, that despite his waffling attitude towards faith and God, Gaius still holds science — however ironically — up as both the means and the end to his life.

Finally, in the very beginning of the episode, Six tells Gaius that he is "tempt[ing] fate" by his blasphemy. It's unclear as to whether she's warning him of the perils of taunting God, or herself — a distinction made even more unclear by her disappearing act and subsequent reappearance as Shelly. Six maintains that "God has a plan" for Gaius — but her ambiguity fuels questions about the nature of humanity, machinery, and deity.

All of This Has Happened Before: We learn that Boomer believes she's from Troy, which begs the question: is she some sort of Trojan horse in the fleet? According to the Greek story of the Trojan War, when the war had gone on for ten long years, the Greeks devised a ruse to end the fight once and for all. They built a giant wooden horse, hollow, wherein they hid arms and soldiers, and dragged it to the gates of the city of Troy. The remaining Greeks then got out of sight and the Trojans, believing themselves safe, took the horse as a sign of good-will and defeat and brought it into the city. When night had fallen, the Greeks inside the horse emerged, opened the gates for the rest of the hidden army, and the city was taken. In the current lingo, a Trojan horse is something that seems to be a gift, but is in fact destructive — say, a Cylon sleeper agent where you would never expect to find one. It adds an interesting facet to Boomer's character because we'd never blame the wooden horse itself for what it contained, so it raises the question of whether we can justifiably "blame" Boomer for her programming and actions.

Interesting Fact: When this episode aired in the United Kingdom, Sharon's back didn't glow red when she made love with Helo.

Did You Notice? The tune Lieutenant Gaeta is whistling in the bathroom is the theme to the original *Battlestar Galactica* series from 1978.

Gaius pleads with Six, "I thought we had something, something special," which is a direct quote from the miniseries where she said the same thing to him.

In the scene where Gaius is being dragged from the lab by the guards, a man holding a sound boom is clearly visible. Oops.

So Say We All: GAIUS: I don't see the hand of God in here. Could I be looking in the wrong place? Let me see, proteins, yes. Hemoglobins, yes. Divine digits, uh, no. Sorry.

108   Flesh and Bone

Original air date: February 25, 2005
Written by: Tony Graphia
Directed by: Brad Turner

A Cylon agent is discovered and he reveals he has planted a nuclear bomb somewhere in the fleet.

"Human beings can't turn off their pain. Human beings have to suffer and cry and scream and endure because they have no choice." Starbuck's pronouncement points to the main question behind "Flesh and Bone" and behind science fiction in general: what does it mean to be human? What does it mean not only to humans, but also to Cylons, who have molded themselves on humanity?

While Leoben points to the mechanics of the humanoid Cylon body as proof of the race's humanity (he sweats, he hungers, he bleeds, he feels pain), both he and Starbuck ultimately indicate that being human requires more than just the presence of "flesh and bone." Both follow religious ideologies: Leoben is the first Cylon since Six to discuss the Cylon faith in any depth, although other models have mentioned their singular "God" (Caprica-Doral, for instance). Ultimately, Starbuck proves her own humanity by reaching out to Leoben at the moment of his death: despite the differences in their ideologies and the time she's spent hating him, she sees his need for some form of connection. It's one definition of humanity: the ability to transcend differences to find common ground and simply relate and make connections. And if that is the definition of humanity, then could it be argued that Leoben is trying to connect as well? It's hard to say because Leoben's connections seem to be based on a belief system while Starbuck's last attempt at reaching out doesn't seem based on a god, but rather on a commonality of experience.

The push-pull between the two characters makes for an interesting dynamic. Starbuck would clearly rather be anywhere but where she is, but she does her job, employing a variety of physical and mental techniques to keep Leoben off balance. For his part, Leoben is enigmatic until the end, determined to get into Starbuck's head and figure out who she is. Their scenes aren't fun; in fact they're downright uncomfortable, bringing to mind some of the world's more shocking recent events (Abu Ghraib, anyone?). They do, however, make us think about the irony involved in defending one's own humanity while one inflicts torture on a sentient being. Of course, that factor is mitigated by the knowledge that the being is a machine — but therein lies the crux of the whole episode: does the Cylon's very mimicry of the human race make them human, too? They seem to have corporeal bodies, religion, free will, and emotions — where is the machine part? Have they managed to evolve beyond their mechanical origins? The episode offers no answers, but leaves us feeling not a little uncomfortable. One of the great strengths of "Flesh and Bone" is, however, that it never questions the ethical implications of torturing a Cylon prisoner: the premise of the episode has certainly been done before, on pretty much every police procedural show ever made as well as most science fiction ones, but in each of these, the ethical considerations are raised. Here, they're not, leaving us to draw our own conclusions and decide for ourselves whether Leoben is machine enough that it doesn't matter if he's tortured, whether he's human enough that the crew's actions are immoral, or whether it's some shade of gray in between.

"Flesh and Bone" focuses on Starbuck's interrogation of Leoben, but when the episode begins, it's Roslin who's having a dream about the Cylon. When Billy informs her that a copy of the Leoben model has been discovered on the *Gemenon Traveler*, Roslin appears totally disoriented by this first indication of any type of precognition on her part. This hint of prophecy sets the scene for the rest of the episode, where the cycle of time plays an important role. Past, present, and future intermingle through dreams, dialogue, and speech patterns: "All of this

The Selfish Cylon

One giant question in *Battlestar Galactica* is: Why do the Cylons have or need religion? If they're machines, wouldn't something as contested, as nebulous, as . . . *human* as religion be eradicated? How did the Cylons "get" religion, anyway? Did someone give it to them, or did they find it on their own?

In 1976 a scientist named Richard Dawkins published a book called *The Selfish Gene*, and in it he used the term "memes" to explain how cultural ideas seem to move from person to person, and generation to generation. His examples were "tunes, catch-phrases, beliefs, clothes fashions, ways of making pots, or of building arches." Dawkins, a zoologist, adapted Darwin's theory of evolution to fit cultural instead of biological circumstances.

Perhaps religion acted as a meme within the Cylons. The beginning of each episode states that the Cylons "evolved" but doesn't state in which *way* they evolved. The only thing we know for sure is that they are following Darwin's theory of evolution, which depends on variation, mutation, and competition. Perhaps part of their evolution incorporated the meme of religion, which transferred itself from generation to generation until it found a new home in the human-Cylon hybrids. Dawkins noted that memes will often propagate in matrixes of other memes – so perhaps the very idea of *humanity* is a meme to these advanced machines, and one of the elements of humanity is religion.

The theory has some problems, and seems to be waning in popularity these days. Still, Dawkins recently put out a book called *Viruses of the Mind* – where he explains his theory of how religions came to be, following much the same theory.

has happened before, and all of it will happen again," Leoben muses. A staple of apocalyptic writing, visions, dreams, and the sense that time is elastic help this episode to debate the question of what makes us human. Roslin has visions — but it seems Leoben does, too.

Until now, the characters have focused on the here and now — justifiably so: crisis after crisis has plagued the fleet, and just as Adama rebuked Lee in "Bastille Day," indicating that regret is a luxury they can't afford, so too has the future been a far-off idea, something to be thought about "later." Precognitive dreams, a mention of destiny (Leoben tells Starbuck that her destiny is to lead the fleet to Earth), the talk of death and an afterlife: finally, in "Flesh and Bone," the future becomes more tangible and the fleet can begin to look at what happens after *now*.

The episode explores this idea not only in the physical sense by mentioning the search for Earth (a largely ignored thread until now) but also in the spiritual sense through Kara and Leoben's dialogue: Leoben claims not to care about death because he believes in a form of afterlife. He believes that he'll be "downloaded" into a new body, memories complete, body whole, the entire experience of death something to look back at from the safe distance of a new existence. Starbuck, disbelieving him, plays on the fear of death she's sure he feels — it's ironic that she would try to disprove his humanity by appealing to a very human fear: what if we are, after all, nothing but "flesh and bone"? And Leoben himself seems sure of his future, raising even more questions: to be communicated with by the divine has been the sole domain of humans from ancient times, so Leoben's prophecy seem almost like trespassing on sacred *human* ground.

Two uses of foreshadowing push the boundaries of what we perceive as the "future" in this episode. Roslin's dream shows Leoben being snatched away on a strong wind, and Starbuck snarls a warning to Leoben at the beginning of their interrogation: "Maybe I push you out the airlock and tell them you never said a word." It's not until the end of the episode when Roslin orders Leoben into the airlock that we realize that hints of the future were there all along if we'd known to look for them.

"Flesh and Bone" plays on our own fear of torture and death and on our uncertainties about the characters and their respective motivations. The first scene, a blue-toned dreamscape featuring a nightie-clad Roslin, is a stark contrast to the rest of the episode, which uses lighting that seems even darker than usual. The interrogation scenes are especially gritty, with lots of nuanced toning to illustrate the shades of gray that are being played out within the episode.

Each character is looking to define themselves as human in one way or another. Boomer tells Gaius that she was born on Troy and that her parents were killed in a major mining explosion; but we know her to be a Cylon, so we know that her background is pure fabrication — it doesn't make her any less human to us. On Caprica, Sharon faces a defining moment as she has to choose between her Cylon brethren and her human lover, Helo. She chooses Helo, raising yet another question: is humanity, more than a consequence of being born to human parents, a choice that each person must make?

Headcount: The whiteboard now reads 47,954 survivors, up by 8 from "Litmus." Have there been some births throughout the fleet?

Interesting Fact: Grace Park ad-libbed the humming in her scene with the Cylon Raptor in this episode. In an interview with Julia Houston from scifi.about.com, she stated that she wants to bring more sexuality to the character: "I like bringing a deeper sexuality — that scene with the Raider, for instance. That was fun to play with. That singing I did in that scene wasn't scripted. I just started humming a Korean lullaby with the Raider."

What's In a Name? Leoben's name sounds strikingly similar to the name Leibowitz from the 1959 novel *A Canticle for Leibowitz* by Walter M. Miller Jr. Leibowitz was a Jewish electrical engineer who worked for the U.S. military prior to an apocalyptic nuclear war. He survived the war, and went on to found a monastic order that was dedicated to the preservation of knowledge and books. Eventually betrayed and executed as a martyr, Leibowitz was later beatified and made a candidate for sainthood. In the postapocalyptic novel, Leibowitz is seen as a visionary endowed with sacred knowledge. Although this seems a far cry from the character of Leoben Conoy, some similarities remain, including the visionary aspect of the character that's in full bloom in this episode. Leoben possesses information and knowledge that he chooses to share in a very prophetic tone and in language that confers an air of authority — or perhaps just madness — to him. And like Leibowitz, Leoben is martyrized — thrown out of the airlock, having created a push of sympathy in at least one person present (Starbuck). In the novel, Miller asks questions about who holds and who disseminates knowledge, and why. Leoben could be performing a similar function.

Did You Notice? Adama warns Starbuck about Leoben, saying, "He has an agenda. It's a goal you won't understand until later." This is prophetic in its own way — see season 3.

The Cylons believe in predetermination, in knowing how one's life is going to unfold. Leoben talks about Starbuck's destiny, and says, "I see the foreshadowing that precedes every moment of every day," indicating a belief in a cycle of time that's clearly defined and infinitely looped. Predetermination is a doctrine usually associated with Calvinism, expositing that everything has been foreordained by God — up to and including the final judgment and humankind's salvation.

Leoben tells Roslin that "Adama is a Cylon." Does he mean Commander Adama? Lee Adama? Since this episode really messes with the time continuum, mingling past, present, and future, it could be any number of Adamas: heck, it could be Zak Adama. If the Commander or Lee were to get married at any point, their wives might take the Adama name: would that make one of *them* eligible to be a Cylon?

So Say We All: GAIUS: You couldn't be more human if you tried.

109 Tigh Me Up, Tigh Me Down

Original air date: March 4, 2005
Written by: Jeff Vlaming
Directed by: Edward James Olmos

Roslin suspects Adama is a Cylon. Adama mysteriously vanishes but ends up bringing Tigh's wife onto Galactica.

"Is suicide really a sin?" bemoans Gaius as he stares out over 47,905 blood samples waiting to be tested for Cylon indicators. Despite the promise of a more mature, responsible Gaius, he turns first to whining about his plight, then to Six's offer of sex; the metaphysical question regarding suicide lingers throughout the scene despite the quick turn for the hilarious when Starbuck walks in on him in a compromising position with himself or Six, depending on your point of view.

The humorous tone of the episode is immediately apparent through its title. "Tigh Me Up, Tigh Me Down" is best known as the episode that introduced Ellen Tigh as a recurring character. Tigh appears quietly overjoyed at seeing his wife and eagerly follows her lead, toasting a "new start." Whether or not Ellen truly wants a new start with her husband, she's overtly sexual with Tigh, covertly sexual with Lee at the dinner table, and says pretty much whatever goes through her head. (And she's blonde, which makes the blonde roster three for the women and zero for the guys.) Placed in a throng of military men and politicians who are used to order and discretion, Ellen's certainly . . . different. She and Tigh act as enablers for each other's alcoholism and it's really hard to watch Tigh be seduced into drinking again.

Nothing stops the man from doing his job, though, and in a scene that contrasts sharply with the fire emergency from the miniseries, when the Cylon Raider first appears on-screen and Tigh realizes that Adama isn't on board, he immediately takes control of the situation and barks out orders in a firm tone, unhesitating and unwavering. The last twenty-eight days have really changed his behavior: he's gone from someone who was ready to leave the military and who hesitated before making life-and-death decisions to someone who's comfortable in his skin and his position, autonomous, and readily reliable. So Ellen's influence on him is all the more difficult for us to swallow, and we easily empathize with Adama when he asks his friend not to let anything, even Ellen, get in the way of doing his job — or in the way of their friendship.

Some of the weakest parts of "Tigh Me Up, Tigh Me Down" are Adama's own actions. As commander of the only surviving human force in the universe (that he knows of for sure, anyway), there is simply no way he would ever leave *Galactica* without letting someone know where he's going, what he's doing, and when he plans to return. To do otherwise — as he does in this episode — is sheer irresponsibility, and puts everyone at risk. It's out of character for Adama, and frankly, it makes no sense. Perhaps such caution was necessary in the beginning, when he was making sure that Ellen was who she said she was, but the trip he takes in "Tigh Me Up" is ostensibly to bring Ellen back to the ship — so he's clearly checked her out and knows he's bringing her back. Why the need for secrecy? It plays like a poorly conceived way for Roslin to justifiably nurture her suspicions about Adama being a Cylon — and this despite the fact that she *knows* that Leoben was trying to sow suspicion and distrust throughout the fleet in "Flesh and Bone."

Adama's and Roslin's suspicions are played out through both drama and comedy: the comedic aspect comes to a head in Gaius's lab, with all major players careening there for the final confrontation, but the fact remains that the underlying suspicions are far from funny. Roslin suspects Adama of being a Cylon; of betraying the fleet and leading humanity to its ultimate downfall — willingly and knowingly. That cuts to the very core of what we know of Adama and muddies the uneasy truce he and Roslin have finally been able to establish between the military and political components of postapocalyptic Colonial life.

In other news, Billy and Dee go on their first official date. The innocence of their relationship is a nice contrast to the harsh realism of Saul and Ellen's marriage, which is filled

Kate Vernon and Michael Hogan put the "fun" in dysfunctional (CAROLE SEGAL/© SCI-FI/COURTESY: EVERETT COLLECTION)

with bitterness and betrayal. Both relationships, however, retain a measure of hopefulness, which makes them wonderful and heartbreaking to watch. And Billy must be the world's worst secret agent — he's terrible at pumping Dee for information, and clearly has no clue what he's doing. It doesn't help that he's torn between his devotion to Roslin and his conviction that Adama is indeed who he says he is, or that he's totally clueless when it comes to women anyway.

Twenty-eight days postapocalypse, and Helo and Sharon are running for a different reason now — at least, Sharon is. Symbolically, the twenty-eight days she's been with Helo are an entire life cycle, as twenty-eight days is the median number for the menstrual cycle.

Humans and Cylons are moving from being tied up in revenge to being tied down in emotion. From the very beginning, Six has been the Cylon who's most intrigued by the concept of being "alive," and her yearning for love is what makes Six one of the most complex of the Cylon models. She struggles for understanding and humanity, and it's sometimes hard not to sympathize with her. All her actions, however misguided, stem from that one desire. It's also ironic that she wants to feel like Sharon feels, but the jealousy and envy she displays are human emotions, just like love is.

Headcount: Gaius says that the fleet now numbers 47,905 survivors. That's sixty-eight deaths since "33," and forty-nine deaths since the last episode, "Flesh and Bone." Something isn't adding up . . .

Interesting Fact: The operatic song playing in the episode's first scene was composed by one of *BSG*'s music gurus, Bear McCreary; "The scene originally called for Mozart to be playing. So I told him that I don't have the lyrics on me." The original lyrics to the song are in Italian but here is the translation:

Woe upon your Cylon heart
There's a toaster in your head
And it wears high heels

Number Six calls to you
The Cylon Detector beckons
Your girlfriend is a toaster

Woe upon your Cylon heart
Alas, disgrace! Alas, sadness and misery!

The toaster has a pretty red dress
Red like its glowing spine
Number Six whispers:
"By Your Command"

Woe upon your Cylon heart

If the song's directed toward Gaius, does that mean the writers are suggesting he is a Cylon, or is it another red herring?

Did You Notice? In "Flesh and Bone," Gaius told Boomer that the Cylon detection test only took minutes to perform. In "Tigh Me Up, Tigh Me Down," he claims that it takes eleven hours to test each sample.

More on the infamous song in the blood test scene: the inclusion of the phrase "By Your Command" is a wink to the original *Battlestar Galactica* series, in which it was used by the Cylons to indicate obedience to their leader. It was also the last spoken line of the miniseries.

Historically, Delphi is important because of its association with the Greek god Apollo, and, more specifically, his oracle, who was known as the Pythia and who foretold the future there.

110   The Hand of God

Original air date: March 11, 2005
Written by: David Weddle, Bradley Thompson
Directed by: Jeff Woolnough

With the ships running low on fuel, the fleet's only hope is to mine for tylium on an asteroid that's guarded by a Cylon basestar.

All the pain and mess of the last nine episodes comes to a head, and the fleet finally gets a chance to celebrate and kick some Cylon butt. It's a much needed sigh of relief.

"The Hand of God" is a lot like "Water" and "Act of Contrition" in that the fleet is lacking a vital, basic resource, and they have to figure out a way to fix the situation. Far from the prosaic concerns of fuel shortages, however, Six tells Gaius that "God doesn't always speak in words," and in the same way, "The Hand of God" emphasizes action above language, right down to the word "hand" in the title. In the end, it doesn't matter what any of the crew says, what plans they come up with, or what they're feeling: it's what they *do* that matters. Gaius can talk all he wants about God, it's not until he reaches out his hand and takes a leap of faith that he comes to a sort of epiphany regarding his relationship with God. Starbuck devises an amazing plan of attack, but it's not until the theory is put into practice and the plan actually succeeds that it *means* anything. Apollo can worry and get all the pep talks he needs, but it's not until he goes out there and makes life-or-death decisions that his faith in himself can be restored.

In "The Hand of God," Gaius's random selection for the location of the Viper strike illuminates the traits we've come to rely on in this character. Despite all his fears and hesitations, his ego outweighs any other consideration and he can't admit to Adama that he simply doesn't know what the target should be. As viewers, we're shocked, angry at the foolhardiness of the risk he's taking: he's endangering the entire human race — again. We have to remember, however, that in "You Can't Go Home Again" Apollo and Adama endangered the whole fleet on the assumption that Starbuck was still alive. It's the characters' respective motivations that make all the difference here: Gaius is acting in the interests of self-preservation, while Adama and Apollo were acting with some altruism. It's also another way to tackle the thorny problem of what makes us human: we despise what Gaius does but we have no problem recognizing the motivation — sometimes it's just all about *me*.

The scene between Lee and Starbuck in the gym provides some context for the sense of competition that seems to abound on the hangar deck — the pilots are engaged in a job that doesn't allow for any weakness so they're constantly taunting each other to make sure that they're performing as well as possible. Starbuck's been benched since "You Can't Go Home Again," and this episode shows her trying to fit her skills to the fleet in different ways, by coming up with military strategies. Tigh, a professional through and through despite his personal shortcomings (as we saw in "Tigh Me Up, Tigh Me Down"), judges Starbuck's professional performance harshly; Starbuck's every attack on Tigh is on a personal front. So far, Starbuck has steered clear of intimate embroilments, and while her relationships with Commander Adama and Apollo are deep and complicated, she's always far more comfortable in the cockpit of a Viper plane. She and Tigh are actually very similar in their absolute dedication to their jobs — they're never quite as happy as when they're working.

Much of "The Hand of God" revolves around the dichotomy between conventional and unconventional thinking. Starbuck rebukes Apollo for overthinking things while Adama recruits Starbuck to devise an attack strategy because she isn't "weighed down by conventional thinking." It's that difference in approach between Kara and Lee that makes their dynamic so interesting: they'll each look at a situation and see ten different ways out and none of them will match.

James and a very sleek-looking Tricia. They sure look happier than their characters ever do. (ALBERT L. ORTEGA)

If there's one thing that might seem like it doesn't quite strike the right note in this episode, it's Adama's attempt to rally Lee's spirits. The Commander's certainty that Lee will perform up to scratch "because you're my son" is . . . really not that reassuring. Apollo is CAG (Commander of the Air Group) for a reason: he has his own military career, his own strengths and weakness, and Adama's inability to see his son as more than an extension of himself might be restrictive to anyone other than Apollo. Still, in the context of the past strain between father and son, it's understandable that Adama would choose to reaffirm the relationship rather than the career choice.

The celebratory shots are real feel-good moments, and the human-to-human contact adds to that feeling. A much more subdued but nonetheless very true-to-character celebration occurs between Adama and Tigh, who turn to each other and shake hands somberly. They embody the reality of the situation, which is that they've had a significant victory, and it's well worth the celebration . . . but the war is far from over.

Are You There, God? It's Me, Gaius. In this episode, Gaius has a real turning point with regard to his religious beliefs. It's interesting to note that it's not until he realizes that he is "an instrument of God" that the idea of God seems to take on some real meaning for him: for Gaius, God just isn't all that interesting unless His plans revolve around him, or his genius. You have to love the fact that Gaius remains true to egocentric form, even when it comes to deities.

Numbers: Twelve is a highly significant number in the *Battlestar Galactica* universe, and it seems based on our own real-life use of the number. There are 12 Colonies of Kobol, 12 Lords of Kobol, 12 humanoid Cylon models; we have the 12 signs of the zodiac, and Christian history talks about the 12 tribes of Israel, the 12 Apostles, and even the 12 gates and foundations of New Jerusalem. In this episode, the Pythian scrolls mention 12 serpents, referring either to the 12 snakes Roslin sees in her hallucination/vision, or to the 12 Viper planes that attack the Cylon basestar. Adding to the dozens of, well, dozens, the scrolls date back 3,600 years — which is a multiple of 12.

Interesting Fact: If Apollo's flight through the Cylon basestar tunnel seems familiar, there's a reason: Ronald Moore has said that the scene pays homage to similar fight sequences from *Star Wars*. It's primarily, however, a scene that gives us some insight into Lee's character, where we see him do something reckless, intuitive, and totally improvised. Ronald Moore explained, "It's not so much the plot device of how to destroy the Cylon base — it's really a character gag. We wanted Lee to do something crazy. Like Kara would do. That was the whole point. Apollo doing really a Starbuck move to prove to himself and everyone else that he's capable of doing these kinds of things."

What's In a Name? Although the character of Gaius Baltar was taken directly from the original series, the name goes back a lot farther: in addition to its callback to the assassination of Julius Caesar (Cassius Gaius was one of the emperor's assassins) and the political ramifications for the character of Gaius Baltar in *BSG*, the name is also almost a male form of "Gaia," which is Greek for "earth." In the Greek pantheon, Gaia was the mother goddess, representing Earth; in many myths, Gaia was born of Chaos. Gaius Baltar in some ways embodies the entire human race in all its messiness. His flaws are exaggerated (he's not just a traitor, he's a traitor of the entire species), as are his positive aspects (he's not just smart, he's an all-out genius), and he vacillates from agnostic to believer, from prophet to destroyer — and it always makes sense, because he's human and flawed. It's also interesting to note that Gaius represents a link between Cylons and humans: he's the foremost expert on Cylon history, technology, and society, and he's also got a Cylon living inside his mind.

Did You Notice? Six quotes a passage from her scripture: "Though the outcome favored the few, it led to a confrontation at the home of the gods." In the earlier episode "Flesh and Bone," the Cylon model Leoben told Starbuck that she would be the one to find Kobol, "birthplace of us all." Whether the passage Six quotes refers to a confrontation on Kobol or somewhere else remains to be seen.

Both Leoben and Six quote the same passage from scripture in "Flesh and Bone" and "Hand of God" respectively: "All of this has happened before. All of this will happen again." Here, Six uses the phrase to make Gaius see that his actions are directed by God's hand, while Leoben was trying to make Starbuck realize her own role in God's plan and the Cylon/human future. The repetition of the scripture leaves us wondering if Starbuck and Gaius will share responsibility for a sequence in humanity's future and if they're somehow linked in ways we haven't yet seen.

Classic *Battlestar Galactica*: The series finale of the 1978 *Battlestar Galactica* was also entitled "Hand of God" and involved Adama attacking a Cylon basestar that was unaware of the fleet's presence. This reimagined episode takes elements from another classic *Battlestar Galactica* episode, "The Living Legend," which involved taking fuel from the Cylons.

So Say We All: GAIUS: He didn't speak to me. God didn't speak to me. So I was totally lying. I just picked that spot at random.

SIX: He doesn't always speak in words, Gaius.

GAIUS: So the fate of the entire human race depends upon my wild guess.

111   Colonial Day

Original air date: March 18, 2005
Written by: Carla Robinson
Directed by: Jonas Pate

The Quorum of Twelve meets for the first time since the Cylon attacks.

"Politics. As exciting as war. Definitely as dangerous." If "The Hand of God" was a military story with a military plot, "Colonial Day" is its polar opposite, a political story with political intrigues. "Colonial Day" is set on the luxury liner *Cloud 9*, and it couldn't look more different than the dark, gritty interiors of the *Galactica*. The ship *looks* luxurious — there's sunshine, gardens, a pool, a bar, dancing, and a conference room, where much of the episode takes place. It looks like civilization again, allowing each of the characters to play house and pretend that they're not on the run, that their world hasn't ended. The main part of "Colonial Day" is bookended by scenes of life: in the beginning, Lee and Kara act like kids together and enjoy a water fight in the sun; in the end, the main characters are all enjoying a night out, drinking, dancing, and generally having fun.

However, these scenes frame some more serious issues, and the episode starts with a panel of journalists, a device that has so far been used to indicate the presence of freedom of the press and the existence of democracy in the fleet; it's an effective entry into this particular episode which is all about democracy and gives us a glimpse of a very different fleet outside of its military operations. The fleet isn't uniform: it's made up of discreet ships, which themselves house separate factions and groupings that all hold different religious, political, and ethical beliefs. The convening of the Quorum of Twelve, the first since the holocaust, provides an opportunity for the Colonists to get involved in their way of life again. In that sense, "Colonial Day" is a follow-up to "Bastille Day," in which Apollo promised Tom Zarek that democracy was still what the Colonies were about. This is an interesting choice for *BSG* — most sci-fi postapocalyptic stories focus on the devolution of society brought about by the chaos of the apocalypse and the resulting scarcity of resources. While the resources story line has remained, the devolution has been reimagined, which may be one of the reasons why *BSG* draws mainstream drama viewers as well as genre fans.

Tom Zarek makes his second appearance in this episode, and once again seems to speak for the common person. His speech is political, but then, he's a political personage, and has always been presented as such. Hatch's performance is interesting because it really straddles the fence: on the one hand, Zarek has an air of urgency about him, which is always appealing in a crisis situation. On the other hand, Hatch portrays Zarek with a side of sleaziness that just won't dissipate.

Eddie, Aaron Douglas, and Richard Hatch at a SciFi Channel event

This episode is a revealing one for Laura Roslin. Driven by the need of the people for a government that works, for the presence of a familiar structure, she easily (although not lightly) assumed the presidency back in the miniseries. In this episode, Roslin shows that, although she hasn't always been president, she has been in politics for a long time and she can — and will — make decisions that serve her political purposes without regard for personal feelings. She absolutely distrusts Gaius, but she still asks her second-in-command to resign so that Gaius can take over because she's in it to win. She has real concerns about Zarek's motivations and she wants to serve the people in the best way she knows how — on her terms.

The two story lines of "Colonial Day" — *Cloud 9* and Caprica — have a couple of similarities. Amongst them is the idea that the characters are all playing a part in an elaborate fantasy: the Colonists continue to live and work as if their lives were the same as before, while Sharon plays house with Helo, delaying the inevitable revelation of her true identity until it can't be hidden any longer. Another similarity is the idea of community and society: while on *Cloud 9* the Colonists work to rebuild their government and Roslin recruits Gaius to form a tentative partnership, on Caprica, Helo and Sharon are like a community of two, a partnership. Both the Colonial and the couple's foundations are rocky at best, but they're giving it their best shot — at least, until a copy of Sharon shows up and is shot by Sharon. As oppositions, *Cloud 9*'s relative utopia houses discontent and strife, while the postapocalyptic Caprica houses real love.

It's day forty-seven, and Sharon and Helo have finally made it to Delphi. (For the record, it's taken them between nine and ten days, just like Sharon predicted.) It's hard to figure out exactly what Sharon is doing here: we have no idea if she's planning on leaving the planet with Helo or if she'll elect to stay on Caprica to prevent the other Cylons from going after him. And if he does leave and eventually find his way back to *Galactica* (although the odds of that are extremely slim given the amount of time that's passed, and she must know that, too), he's going to find out she is a Cylon. In the end, it's a moot point since when they get to Delphi, another copy of Sharon puts an end to Sharon's charade. The flashback sequence revisits a series of scenes with Sharon, pieces to the puzzle that finally add up to a complete picture. Helo's world was destroyed with the Cylon attack, but the realization that the woman he's been in love with since long before the attacks must feel like another apocalypse. This sequence, with its blue tinge, is reminiscent of "Water," while the monochromatic feeling also serves to mimic the feeling of learning something terrible — Helo's betrayal feels like the phrase "all the color drained out of his face" visually as well as narratively. This is definitely not a red-letter day for this Colonial.

Headcount: The whiteboard shows 47,898 survivors, seven fewer than "Tigh Me Up, Tigh Me Down."

Did You Notice? Yet another bathroom scene (that's at least two so far). Interesting things seem to happen in bathrooms in this series: in "Six Degrees of Separation" Gaius pleaded with Gaeta to let him help enhance the photo's resolution; in "Colonial Day," Roslin asks Gaius to be her candidate for the vice presidency. In an unrelated move, Gaius has sex in a bathroom stall with journalist Playa Palacios, who appears, rumpled, after Gaius's conversation with Roslin. We've seen Playa in media scenes from "Litmus," "Six Degrees of Separation," and "Flesh and Bone," but she was credited as Playa Kohn in those episodes. The name change has not been explained (and, one has to ask, why keep *Playa*?!).

If you look closely, amid the bottles behind the bar in this episode, there's a bottle of good ol' Jack Daniels.

Starbuck wears a dress in the dance scene at the end of the episode. This was actually Katee Sackhoff's idea. She reportedly wanted to remind viewers (and the character herself) that Starbuck isn't a single-faceted military pilot; she's also very feminine.

So Say We All: HELO: Now all we have to do is wait until dark, infiltrate the most heavily fortified military hub on this planet, hope the Cylons haven't completely wasted the spaceport, steal a ship, meet *Galactica*, and fly to her without getting shot to hell.

SHARON: Is that all?

112   Kobol's Last Gleaming, Part 1

Original air date: March 25, 2005
Written by: Ronald D. Moore
Directed by: Michael Rymer
Story by: David Eick

The discovery of a planet leads Roslin to believe the fleet has found the mythical planet of Kobol.

Part 1 of this finale builds tension through a montage of scenes; dialogue is scarce, and each character is shown in a vulnerable moment. The music stays the same volume, lengthening the tension and the sense that *something bad is about to happen*; Helo, Kara, Lee, Adama, and Sharon (both of them), have all reached breaking points. From here on in, it will all be different.

Until now, season 1 has been reimagining and reintroducing us to a postapocalyptic society. It's also adding something that we don't see a lot in television these days, even from its science fiction shows — responsibility. Apocalyptic science fiction is about the end of the world and the revelation of a divine plan, and season 1 has seen both. Thanks to the unveiling and exposing nature of apocalyptic writing, responsibility often figures large since the unveiling is followed inevitably by judgment. Up until now, most of the references that Six has made to God and His "plan" have been nebulous; the beginning of each episode also has its own mini apocalypse, when the screen flashes the text "they have a plan" in reference to the Cylons. At some point, it is implied, there will be judgment.

What are God's methods? Who gets to play god, and why? These are questions that *BSG* works with throughout the season. The season finale however, uproots us from our traditional idea of how things should be in television shows, nice and tidy, and it sticks us back into the framework of the unknowable. Whether the unknowable in this case is the will of the Cylon God, the Lords of Kobol, or the Cylons themselves, no one can say. What we come to expect from *BSG* (and what is delivered flawlessly in this episode) is a sense of fragility combined with an explosiveness that makes us feel like *we're* the ones sitting with the ruins of a civilization around us.

That fragility is there because before any final judgment, things get really, really bad. What's interesting about the series is that it has to expand the common notion of apocalypse to one that we are more familiar with in our secular society. This key theme of judgment is set up at the very beginning of the episode, when Adama instructs Lee to "lose control." He says paradoxically that it is because Lee is always sparring — training rather than really fighting — that he always gets beaten. Then, the scene cuts to Kara and someone having sex — we think it is Lee, but when we realize it's not him but Gaius, we're totally confounded by her choice of partner, one-night stand or not. Now that's out of control: for the whole season it's been pretty plain that Starbuck couldn't care less about Gaius Baltar.

The problem is that, unlike the kind of uncontrolled moments that Commander Adama is talking about with Lee, both Starbuck's and Gauis's situations are the result of trying too hard to hang on to control, rather than acknowledging that some things are just naturally out of our control. Gaius's manipulation of Boomer's mental state is chilling, because until now, while he hasn't exactly been a shining example of humanity, he usually gets tossed into situations rather than trying to control them from the outset. But the constant floundering and near misses have taken their toll, and the Baltar we saw in the pilot, the one who clearly considers taking an old woman's ticket to freedom, leaps to the foreground.

The Ragtag Fleet: The Ships of *Battlestar Galactica*

The exact number of ships that escaped from the Cylons in the miniseries is unknown, and has been a matter of some debate since it was first stated in the miniseries that about forty ships had FTL capability. But in the beginning of season 2, Tigh tells Adama that twenty-four ships represents more than a third of the whole fleet. Regardless, here are the names of the ships that have been named in one form or another (visually or orally):

Adriatic	Freighter 212	Picon Express
Astral Queen	Galactica	Prometheus
Atlantia	Galatia	Pyris
Aurora	Gemenon Liner 1701	Raadamanteb
Baah Pakal	Gemon Liners	Rising Star
Blackbird	Gemenon Traveler	Salpica
Boreas	Gemini	Sargon
Bretan	Gideon	Scorpia Traveler
Carillian Trader	Greenleaf	Scylla
Carina	Harrak	Solaria
Cassandra	Hexare	Space Park
Celestra	Incron Velle	Stealthstar
Chiron	Intersun	Striker
Clymene	Kara Nexal	Swordfish
Cloud 9	Kimba Huta	Tarbadeck
Colonial One	Luxury Liner	Tauranian Traveler
Columbia	Majahual	Threa Sita (the spelling
Coronis	McConnell	is debated though:
Cybele	Mercury	it's been seen as
Daru Muzu	Monarch	Theta Sita and Thera
Demetrius	Mutem Wia	Sita as well)
Diomedes	Odysseus	Tora Bashiri
Embla Brokk	Olympic Carrier	Triton
Enkidu	Pan Galactic	Valkyrie
Epheme	Pegasus	Virgon Express
Faru Sadin	Persephone	Zephyr
Flattop	Picon 36	Zeusuda

Of everyone in the fleet, it is Roslin and Adama who seem the most competent at planning, while letting go of how they want things to be. The Commander knows that each time they jump or engage with the Cylons it's a whole new ball game and they might not come out of it. When the Raptor team comes back minus two Raptors and there are ten dead crewmen from the Cylon ambush, Adama quickly moves to recoup their losses, abruptly abandoning the initial plan to survey the planet in favor of getting his people and getting the hell out of there. President Roslin attempts to lead the people with a strong but elastic arm, even planning for her own demise as the cancer she can't control continues to consume her. But the fragile sense of security that radiates from these two is not only a serious foreshadowing of what happens in the second part of this mini-arc, but also reminds us of the larger idea of the inscrutable ways of non-human entities (Cylon or otherwise).

"Kobol's Last Gleaming" shows that only by losing control, by going down avenues other than rigidly defined reason, military training, and brute force, can people (and Lee in particular) become the kind of leaders that are needed. It's hard for Lee, straitlaced officer that he is, to let go and leap into the unknown, but it's a necessary step. The same goes for Starbuck: Lee's afraid that he'll make the wrong decision as a man, while Starbuck is afraid that she'll make the wrong decision as an officer. For everyone, the rules of life are changed, the comfortable boundaries are altered with no way back. The very framework of humanity has changed, and it's the restructuring of and adapting to that framework that the crew of the *Galactica* and every other ship must deal with. Roslin's movement from minor schoolteacher with strong scientific leanings to president of the Colonies about to embark on a holy relic hunt is a good summation of everyone's personal journey. She goes way beyond thinking outside the box — there *is* no box anymore. Roslin and Adama's ability to lose control and not just spar but play for keeps is one of the reasons they and the fleet are still alive.

Headcount: Whiteboard says 47,897 survivors, accounting for Valance's death in "Colonial Day."

All of This Has Happened Before: Although the Scrolls of Pythia are not real-life artifacts, in Ancient Greek mythology, Pythia was the god Apollo's oracle, and was stationed in Delphi. She traditionally "belonged" to Gaia (the earth), but was either taken by or given to Apollo. The Pythia would enter a trance by eating laurel leaves, and in such a state would utter her prophecies. These were usually extremely ambiguous and were interpreted by priests. In much the same way in *Battlestar Galactica*, the Priestess Elosha interprets the visions Roslin has under the influence of the chamalla leaves.

Interesting Fact: In ancient Persian, the word "kobol" actually means "heaven." It's also an anagram of "Kolob," which is, according to the Church of Jesus Christ of Latter-Day Saints (Mormons), the name of the star closest to the "residence of God." It's a fitting symbol for the name of a planet that will supposedly lead the fleet to the promised land of Earth.

Did You Notice? When Adama asks Starbuck what she's doing firing up the FTL drive, she answers, "Bringing the cat home." This is a direct quote from the miniseries, where Adama instructed Kara to "grab your gun and bring in the cat" — first prior to the decommissioning ceremony, then while she was bringing Apollo's plane back in.

Roslin asks Kara if she believes in the gods, just as Leoben did in "Flesh and Bone." Starbuck rebukes the president for asking such a personal question, but does answer in the affirmative, unlike the earlier episode, where the question went unanswered.

113   Kobol's Last Gleaming, Part 2

Original air date: April 1, 2005
Written by: Ronald D. Moore
Directed by: Michael Rymer
Story by: David Eick

While the crew of Raptor One *struggles to survive on Kobol, Starbuck finds the Arrow of Apollo on Caprica, and Adama and Roslin go up against one another.*

The second half of season 1's finale takes place in three separate locations: on Kobol, the *Galactica*, and Caprica; each panel of this triptych follows a separate drama. Part 2 doesn't start with a slow montage of scenes, as Part 1 did, gradually easing us into each character's moment of truth and jeopardy. Instead, Part 2 throws us into the immediate consequences of the first half, starting with the Raptor's crash on Kobol. The scenes on the planet's surface are intense, but they add a new dimension to the show because they focus on secondary characters who until this point have only played parts in the main characters' story lines.

Separated now from the rest of the fleet, the group has to take matters into its own hands and it's quickly clear that Crashdown is unprepared for the responsibility that's been thrust on him. As the senior officer, he has to take charge until they're rescued, but it's Chief who maintains the clear head. It's a nice way to emphasize Chief's strengths as well as show us a different side of Crashdown: every scene the lieutenant has been in before has shown him as efficient, mostly calm under pressure, and good at his job. This is the first time we've seen him have to assume control of a situation, and he's obviously going to need some time to let the new role sink in. The problem is that he doesn't have the time he needs, and it's an indication of his professionalism and his respect for Chief that he acknowledges his strategic error in judgment.

Gaius's story on Kobol takes a different path. In Part 1, we saw his relationship with Six go south. He emphasizes that he's not breaking things off with her, but that he needs the time alone on the planet to breathe. So he's doubly surprised when Six appears to him and leads him through the flames on the downed Raptor. There are a lot of interesting shots of Six in this episode, as if we're seeing her in a new light. (The lighting on Kobol is bright, shot with a sharp filter, which makes the greens and blues appear cleaner.) When Gaius wakes up after collapsing onto the grass, we look straight up at Six and see her from his point of view. It's not a terribly flattering view and she looks almost like an ugly angel swooping in to rescue Gaius. In Part 1 of the finale, Six looks pained when she realizes that Gaius actually likes Starbuck, that he's a little bit in love with her; that, combined with Gaius's request for a break, splits open the mold of their relationship. They're on all-new ground now.

Back on *Galactica*, tensions don't even get the *chance* to mount: Adama goes from zero to *coup d'état* in less than two minutes. Pacifism is rarely considered in the reimagined *BSG*. Unlike many other science fiction shows, which sort of glance sideways at things like court martial, torture, rape, or the atrocities (and spoils) of war, *BSG* not only looks them straight in the face but challenges them to come forward and do their worst. Can humanity survive one catastrophe after another? Part 2 has the fleet fragmented, at its worst — and the two people we count most on, Roslin and Adama, are at odds with each other, stalwart, edging ever closer to violence. This sets up the unease that exists between an arm of society devoted to change through consensus (politics) and one that uses more stratified authority (military).

Apollo's story line plays out much as we would have expected it to: he follows his own path, treading the fine line between politics and military, torn between his duty and his beliefs, but ultimately needing to stay true to himself. In the end, though, Apollo does what he always does — he sorts through things methodically and acts decisively when he's come to his own conclusion. He has to know as he points the gun at Tigh that he's putting his relationship with Adama in jeopardy. Considering the difficulties they've had throughout the season, climbing to even ground and coming to a sort of understanding about their past, and a place where they're able to forgive each other and move on, the decision Apollo makes isn't a light one. It's hard, it's tough, and it's what *BSG* is all about: making the decisions we know to be right, standing up for what is true in our hearts — because otherwise, the Cylons have won.

"We are all playing our parts in a story that is told again, and again, and again, throughout eternity." Roslin's words from the first part of the season finale remind us that there's a larger story being told, and that the characters are all merely players in a galactic, universal tale. Both parts of the season finale work to incorporate the increasingly important prophetic aspect of the story, weaving in elements like scriptures, ancient scrolls, ancient religious artifacts, and sacred planets. Kobol is the largest part of the mythology so far, the birthplace of humans and therefore of the Cylons. It's that sacredness that's reinforced when Roslin looks at the survey images of the planet and sees not the ruins of a lost civilization but a thriving urban center. The planet could have remained a thing of the past, little more than an artifact of archaeological significance; instead, it's brought into the here and now of the fleet's journey, making the Colonies' mythology and religion less a field of study and more a clear presence with the potential for real impact on everyone's lives. As more than one character points out, we need hope to continue.

The fact that Roslin sees Kobol at its best rather than as it is in the present, ancient and uninhabited, speaks to her ability to rise above the immediacy of a situation to see beyond it to the solution, but it also paradoxically presents her as a visionary. She's the voice of reason within the fleet, totally pragmatic, and hasn't been swayed by her personal feelings — until now, which makes it all the more strange for her to suddenly become a messianic voice of prophecy. "I think it's interesting to note that she comes to that idea, not as a woman of faith, not as a woman who has a quote-end-quote personal relationship with her gods, but she comes to it logically," said Moore. "She looks at the puzzle around her; she looks at the pieces, and the clues, and what's been laid out for her, and how they add up."

Finally we come to the third panel of this triptych episode. The museum serves to tie in the themes of past and present, history and apocalypse, reminding us of the scope of things beyond the fight. However, this finale could just as well have been called "Starbuck's Terrible, Horrible, No-Good, Very Bad Day": in the last twenty-four hours, she's slept with a man she doesn't even like, called out the name of the man she's really in love with, had a knock-down fight with said man, found out that another man whom she thinks of as a father has been lying to her and the entire fleet about the location of Earth, been asked by her president to betray her commanding officer, gone back to her devastated, demolished home world, been violently attacked by the enemy, and, as the cherry on top, discovered that one of her best friends is a Cylon.

Starbuck doesn't just hit rock bottom emotionally, however — she has to go through physical hell as well, which culminates in a cringe-worthy fistfight with Six. When it finally ends, with Six's demise, Starbuck has a moment to realize that Helo's alive before the harsh realities of the last twenty-four hours hit her. Discovering that Sharon is — and always has been — a Cylon is the last straw. A terrible way to leave the character, and one that recalls Gaius's words from "Water": "Everyone has their limit."

The ending of this episode ranked #98 in *TV Guide*'s Top 100 Most Unexpected TV Moments, but it really deserved to be ranked much higher. The final two minutes of season 1 took everything we thought we understood about Boomer's personal journey and turned it on its head. We knew she had demons to exorcise, we knew she was having trouble figuring out what she was doing, but everything in her story told us that she would claim victory over her Cylon programming — from her significant victory in "Water" to her emotional struggle over the last twelve episodes. When she finally comes face to face with the numerous Cylon clones of herself, she keeps herself tightly under control, and she looks to be genuinely basking in the praise Adama heaps on her and Racetrack when they return, victorious, to *Galactica*. But we go to hiatus destroyed: blood pools under Adama, Apollo's about to be thrown into the brig, Starbuck's stranded with Helo on Caprica. It's a terrifying moment of realization: the Cylons really *do* have a plan — and we have no idea what it is.

Headcount: There were 10 people lost when one of the Raptors was destroyed in "Kobol's Last Gleaming, Part 2," bringing the total survivor count to 47,887.

Are You There, God? It's Me, Gaius. Gaius's role in this episode starts out on a really flimsy note, but his appearance on Kobol gains momentum as he gets his very own mini-apocalypse: Six shows him the "face of things to come" — his child. The light play in the episode really adds to the sense that Gaius is receiving some sort of privileged information. Unlike traditional apocalyptic prophets though, he'll be keeping his secret knowledge to himself.

All of This Has Happened Before: A little known myth could be the basis of the show's focus on the Arrow of Apollo. According to the ancient Greek poet Iamblichus, a gem engraver's son was born with a golden thigh; the son, named Pythagoras (who later became a well-known mathematician), was thought by many to be the son of Apollo, and a priest passing by believed that the man *was* Apollo, and gifted him with his most precious possession – a sacred arrow said to be the arrow that Apollo himself had used to kill Python in an earlier myth. The priest, Abaris, explained that the arrow had mystical powers: it would allow the bearer to fly over obstacles like mountains or treacherous rivers, and it could also heal the ill and purify cities. In *BSG*, the Arrow of Apollo seems set to fulfill the same purpose – helping the Colonials overcome the obstacle of vast swaths of space, and find their true direction.

The Scrolls of Pythia say that by taking the Arrow of Apollo to the Temple of Athena on Kobol, Roslin will find the way to Earth. In Greek mythology, Athena was the goddess of war, and was known as the protector of the city. She was also the goddess of reason.

There was no Temple of Athena in Ancient Greece, but there *was* a Temple of Artemis. Artemis was Apollo's twin sister, and her temple was built around 550 BCE; it was destroyed in 262 AD, and although it was never rebuilt, it is one of the Seven Wonders of the World.

Artemis, goddess of the hunt, was known for her arrow-slinging abilities, more than Apollo. There is one myth wherein both gods use poisoned arrows to kill the family

Interesting Fact: The scene with all the Sharons on the basestar might look simple, but it's actually the result of a lot of intense and expensive work. In the podcast for this episode, Moore said, "This is motion-control work, which is time consuming and complex. […] It's all Grace walking into camera with very carefully done shadows so you don't see the 'naughty parts.' And you have to shoot this over and over again. […] Just doing the motion control and […] matteing them all in and comping them in correctly and getting the perspectives right and the shadows — that's expensive."

Did You Notice? Adama asks Sharon to lead the basestar mission, but it's not clear whether he's asking her because she's a good pilot or because of her recent suicide attempt. She passes it off as an accident, but Adama is a shrewd man, and can probably see through that façade. He also makes specific mention of the high-risk quality of the mission, as if to make sure she's aware it could very well be a one-way trip.

In the miniseries, Roslin warned Adama that it would take a military coup to get her to resign; in "Kobol's Last Gleaming, Part 2," the situation quickly escalates to an all-out coup, as predicted. However, when push comes to shove, Roslin can't live with the idea of causing more bloodshed, and she hands herself over to Tigh.

"You can't fight destiny, Sharon." The words of the Cylon models on the basestar echo Six's certainty in "Colonial Day" that Boomer would carry out her mission, regardless of her fears, anxieties, and suicide attempt.

Sharon knew about the Arrow of Apollo, as did Caprica-Six, and Leoben talked competently about the Lords of Kobol ("Flesh and Bone"). So far, the Cylons seem to be fairly well informed on the humans' mythological and religious beliefs. That's a thread we'll see continued in season 2.

If you look closely, you can see a crewman standing huddled in a corner as Starbuck shatters the glass case containing the Arrow of Apollo. He looks like he's trying to be as inconspicuous as possible, but he's still clearly visible.

SEASON TWO — July 2005–March 2006

201　　Scattered

Original air date: July 15, 2005
Written by: David Weddle, Bradley Thompson
Directed by: Michael Rymer

Adama fights for his life and Tigh takes over a chaotic command.

"Scattered" picks up where "Kobol's Last Gleaming" left off: we thought things couldn't get much worse for the fleet — but they do. This first episode of season 2 continues the split between three locations — Kobol, Caprica, and *Galactica* — and the trend will continue for quite a few episodes.

"Scattered" handles a handful of personal, individual dramas, cloaked within the major problem facing *Galactica*: how to figure out where the rest of the fleet jumped to. While Tigh might have hesitated back in the miniseries, or even in the beginning of season 1, before taking command of the ship, the war against the Cylons seems to have given him back a real sense of purpose. And when Tigh has purpose, he's clear-headed and driven, showing no hesitation or insecurity; it's only when he's faced with everyday issues related to leadership that he's uncertain. Here, he's thrown into a situation that's possibly the most chaotic the fleet has seen since the Cylon attack fifty-plus days ago, but he quickly assesses and handles each crisis one at a time.

The scenes and dialogue in "Scattered" have a wonderful rhythm to them, with a lot of quick cuts from one scene to the next (from Tigh's quarters to the command deck, for instance) and an effective repetition of thoughts and phrases: "This is Bill's ship," Tigh says, which cuts to "This is his command," following the same thought in a different location. Later, Billy cautions Roslin, "*If* [Starbuck] retrieves the Arrow," only to be reprimanded with, "She'll retrieve the Arrow." The words and rhythm of the show pull us into a tense feeling of warning, while at the same time layering that warning with hope — a classic trope of apocalyptic science fiction — as each character makes their own way through the crisis. This dynamic holds true for Tigh as it does for Helo and Apollo.

Back on Caprica, Helo and Sharon have their own choices to make. Like it or not, they have been through a lot of hardship together over the last seven or so weeks, and Helo had feelings for her before the attacks — so his choice isn't all that surprising, especially considering Sharon's pregnancy. Starbuck is clearly unhappy about his decision, and she makes a face of sheer disgust and contempt, snapping, "My gods, men are so painfully stupid sometimes!" Starbuck's relationships are all so fraught with angst — she never seems peaceful — that it's interesting to see her interactions with Helo; the situation is messy and they're on opposite sides of the fence, but neither is worried about what the other one will think, they just make their case and know that the other will continue to be a friend as well as comrade.

These look like women who can have some serious fun!

It's ironic that while Helo is defending Sharon to Starbuck, Sharon quietly takes off, stealing the Cylon Raider. Talk about a slap in the face . . . Helo must just be reeling in confusion as well as relief at realizing that the human race isn't dead, that the fleet survived, and that his friends and colleagues are still around.

On *Galactica*, things aren't looking so rosy. It was Tigh's first few minutes in command, and he goes and loses the fleet. Much like Apollo does by not apologizing for his actions, and like Helo does by defending Sharon, Tigh has to stand on his own two feet: he can't rely on Adama, because Adama is slowly bleeding to death, so he has to figure out how he, Tigh, commands, and find his own identity as a leader. It's not an easy step for him, and his journey is made all the more clear through the flashbacks we see of him and Adama as young military recruits (well, youngish). Young Adama is ambitious, driven; young Tigh just seems tired and worn out. It's the first time we hear the phrase, "So what's your plan?" which is something of a leitmotif throughout the episode, and a question that can be applied to nearly all the characters. What is Boomer's plan? What is Tigh's plan? Lee's? Starbuck's? Sharon's? Crashdown's?

This also holds true for the poor medic who is responsible for performing open chest surgery on the leader of the fleet, the man most people love and admire — the man who is leading the way to Earth, the future of humanity. Like Tigh and Crashdown, the medic is not ready for the responsibility thrust upon her, but she has to do what is necessary. It's a strong scene, and it's nice to see some minor characters embracing roles they're unprepared for but willing to take on. In a scattered fleet, the crew's very determination and courage are a testament to the humans' strength and perseverance.

Boomer's story in "Scattered" has parallels to the emergence of the id, which is, according to Freud, the seat of a person's drives, which are usually repressed by the ego and super-ego, or are in some other way essentially subconscious. This seems to be how the Cylon programming works in terms of humanoid Cylons who are programmed to think they're human; the program works beneath the surface of the agent's subconscious, while the surface struggles to come up with rationales and explanations for their "dark thoughts" ("Kobol's Last Gleaming") and actions.

When Tigh starts to interrogate Boomer, it's a hard scene to watch because despite everything, she *is* different from the rest of the Cylons. Every day she fights her programming is a day she *chooses* to be human. Story editor David Weddle said, "The Sharon interrogation scenes are not in any way meant as a comment on gender roles or domestic abuse. They embody one of the main allegorical themes of the show, which is the tendency to dehumanize the enemy in times of war."

The outer space battle scene in "Scattered" is, as always, spectacular. Each time one of these scenes airs and we see the sheer enormity of what the *Galactica* is up against, it's awe-inspiring. There are just so *many* Cylon Raiders, and so few Colonial ships, it's mind-boggling to think that the humans are still alive, still fighting against the locust-like Raiders. One of the main themes of the series until now has been the horror and ugliness that hides behind beauty, and this battle scene really highlights that, with explosions — each one a death, a loss — going off like fireworks. It's the same way that Ellen appears so attractive on the outside but is so full of venom and sly temptations, and that Sharon seems so human but can pull her gun and shoot Adama point-blank in the chest.

Headcount: The whiteboard gets replaced by the credits, which now update with each death. At the beginning of the episode, the number of survivors is listed as 47,875. That's a loss of twelve people since "Kobol's Last Gleaming, Part 2."

Interesting Fact: The medic in this episode is played by Jamie Bamber's real-life wife, Kerry Norton.

Did You Notice? This episode marks the first use of a new credit sequence: it is set to the theme music previously only seen in the United Kingdom, the text has changed to include the number of survivors as well as a new line, "In search of a home . . . called Earth." The intro also drops the rapid sequence of clips from the episode, making for shorter credits. Moore explained in the podcast for this episode, "I think end of the day, basically everybody agreed that the theme that we had season one was not as evocative and interesting as the UK version so we all agreed to do that. The reason behind losing the second half was to just make the whole thing a little faster to get through the main title a little quicker, and also there were complaints. [. . .] Some people just don't like seeing scenes from the upcoming show."

So Say We All: STARBUCK: She's right, huh? Sharon the Cylon is right. It's all just, "Listen to Sharon the Cylon." "Do whatever she says." 'Cause *that's* a good idea.

202   Valley of Darkness

Original air date: July 22, 2005
Written by: David Weddle, Bradley Thompson
Directed by: Michael Rymer

The Galactica *fights the Centurions who made their way aboard in the previous episode.*

"Valley of Darkness" has a very different tone from any other episode to date. It's structured very much like a horror movie or a thriller: there's a plethora of dead bodies littering the ground, more than a few spurts of blood, a handful of races through darkened corridors with nothing visible but the cast of a flashlight, screaming, and more. The episode opens with something totally new, a different take on the fight with the Cylons. So far, the fight has been seen either from very close (the respective struggles of Boomer and Sharon for instance) or from a distance (the outer space battle scenes between Raptors and Raiders).

There is excellent use of color in this episode, with the standard blue, gray, and red being used to good effect. The gray tones used for the shipbound scenes emphasize the metaphorical shades of gray that each member of the crew must exorcise, while the bright greens and blues of the scenes on Kobol (particularly in Gaius's dreamscape) bring to mind the ideas of fertility, birth, and hope — all of which are embodied in the figure of the baby. The yellow tones of Caprica, sepia-like, raise a sense of nostalgia and homesickness, a feeling of the past being resurrected in some way, although at the same time those tones harbor the sense of post-nuclear sickness that "Kobol's Last Gleaming" showed so well. Still, the tonal qualities on Caprica are much more relaxing than any of the others, which is fitting for an episode where Starbuck and Helo revisit the former's old dwelling, put their feet up, and simply exist for a bit, which gives us some context for her character. Her apartment seems free-spirited, from the painting and poetry on the walls to the eclectic accumulation of mess, and a far cry from the Starbuck we've seen up until now. In an interview with *Cult Times*, Katee Sackhoff revealed, "My character is constantly moving. Starbuck doesn't feel comfortable sitting still or allowing her brain to pause because then she has time to think, especially about the past, and she doesn't like to do that because that's where her pain is. So she'd always rather be physically and/or mentally challenged and looking ahead."

Science fiction has long been derided for playing to gender stereotypes, and although that is waning as time goes on, it's still funny to see Dee telling Billy that if he *has* to stick that phallic gun down his pants, he should at least turn the safety on — and later reminding him to turn it *off* if he wants to get any use out of it. These two are the embodiment of young love in the fleet, and as such they represent hope — the hope of the triumph of love and life over death and destruction. They're both strong, morally unambiguous characters, thrust into a situation where they're forced to take on a lot more responsibility than they had bargained for, and they're still visibly feeling each other out (and up!). Their every move is public in one form or another, so they have additional barriers to overcome — but they're obviously very much infatuated. Their scenes have a nice, natural feel, tentative in

Revelation

The last book of the Christian Bible is called the Book of Revelation, but it's known in some historical circles as the Apocalypse of John or the Revelation to John. Its authorship is hotly debated; the only real consensus is that it's written by someone who identifies himself as John, and many scholars agree that it's probably not John the Apostle.

The interesting thing about the Book of Revelation is that it describes the end of the world from a Christian perspective. It has as many interpretations as it has readers, and it's the most widely contested and controversial book in the Bible; some believe that it's a literal description of the end time while others believe it's more allegorical or metaphorical. The text itself is often seen as being split into two distinct parts, the first using very "real-to-life" phraseology and the second a more esoteric account of events. The text begins, "The Revelation of Jesus Christ . . . unto His servant John," making the Revelation something that shines down from above – very much like a scene later in the series, "Downloaded."

When we talk about revelation today, it's often used in the sense of an unveiling of some kind. In fact, the end time as it was told by Jesus (through the prophet) in the Book of Revelation is an intricately planned and designed occurrence. In *BSG*, Leoben Conoy plays the part of the seer as he reveals God's plan for the humans, Cylons, and Starbuck in particular. As with most apocalyptic texts, warning plays a huge part in a revelation. For the warning to work, however, it has to come at an appropriate (read, crisis) time, and the prophet has to appear to be outside of mere "mortal" concerns.

In prophetic texts such as the Book of Revelation, the prophet uses vague and ambiguous language that is often weighted by metaphor and symbolism – something Leoben also does very well.

the way young love can be, and while we really hope they make it, it's hard to forget that in a postapocalyptic world, not much makes it through intact.

Although this episode doesn't end on a cliffhanger, each interwoven scene still moves towards a larger sense of danger and jeopardy, much like a thriller or a mystery story does. In this case, form and content meld, and while Centurions, the president's group, and Lee's troops move inexorably toward aft command, so too does the episode move to a climax.

The absence of Commander Adama has been keenly felt over the last two episodes, but his unseen presence looms large over the crew. Until now we have seen Adama as mostly a benevolent leader, subject to a few "my way or the highway" moments, but "Scattered" and "Valley of Darkness" cast him as a god or judge — a very old thread in Judeo-Christian apocalyptic texts. We are chilled at the thought of Adama's judgment; that is, we hope that Adama will somehow be able to make all things right *and* punish the wicked. The problem is that we don't know who the wicked are: Lee, who stood up for his beliefs? Tigh, who did his best in a chaotic situation? Roslin, who was acting on faith? We know that there will be retribution, but we don't know who we're rooting for. Heck, we don't even know *why* we're rooting for them! And that's just one reason we keep on watching, so we can figure out our own loyalties as the characters figure out theirs.

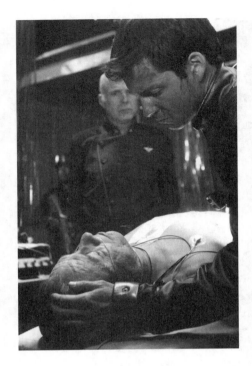

Adama's near-death experience changed everything — for fans and characters alike (CAROLE SEGAL/ © SCI-FI/COURTESY: EVERETT COLLECTION)

Headcount: The opening credits list 48,874 survivors, either to account for the death of Tarn on the surface of Kobol in "Scattered," or the death of the *Galactica* crewman just before the credits in this episode.

Are You There, God? It's Me, Gaius. Gaius displays something we've never seen in him before — compassion — as a concerned parent confused and horrified as he watches Adama drown the human/Cylon hybrid baby. Ronald Moore said, "David [Eick] and I kept fighting for [this scene to be included], and kept saying, 'Oh, this is important. This is about the threat to the child that Baltar's investing in,' and you're basically setting up a marker that Adama in some way, shape, or form, is the threat that Baltar must face to fulfill [...] his destiny *vis-à-vis* the child." The scene is also a clear callback to the miniseries, in which Six snapped the baby's neck: the question is, in some ways, whether or not Gaius can ever get to the point where he is willing to sacrifice something that's important to him.

Interesting Fact: Katee Sackhoff wrote the poems on the wall of her character's apartment on Delphi. "That, to me personally, is not art," she said in an interview with IGN TV. "It's just a bunch of scribbles on the wall. But that would make sense for her. It is a very angry type of free, crazy, erratic art, I guess. What I liked more, which is something I chose to do, was the poetry. That made sense to me; that she wrote her feelings down in poetry. [...] I just said that I wanted to go in and spend some time in the apartment and use some paint and paint the poems on the wall, so I think I did, like, three of them on the wall."

Did You Notice? This is the first episode where Sharon doesn't appear at all — in any incarnation. On *Galactica*, she's still in the brig. Sharon could be anywhere by now since she made off with the Cylon Raider.

Although Kate Vernon is listed in the opening credits, Ellen Tigh doesn't actually appear in the aired episode. She's in a couple of deleted scenes, however, that never made it to the screen.

The piano piece that Kara plays in her apartment is a solo by composer Philip Glass, called "Metamorphosis One." It's performed by *BSG* composer Bear McCreary, although Starbuck attributes the playing to her father.

Lee quotes the infamous "hard six" line from "The Hand of God" but when questioned, admits that he doesn't know what it means — it's just something his father says a lot. Nice wink to the viewers who have been asking for the meaning of the phrase since its first utterance — now they have an answer. Or a non-answer.

203   Fragged

Original air date: July 29, 2005
Written by: Nicole Yorkin, Dawn Prestwich
Directed by: Sergio Mimica-Gezzan

Things go really bad on Kobol when Crashdown decides to take out a group of Cylons. Roslin suffers from withdrawal and Tigh declares martial law.

The introductory sequence of "Fragged" strikes some false notes, in part because it seems overly ambitious. We find out soon after the false sense of jeopardy is due to the fact that it's a red herring — the Cylons aren't trying to annihilate the valley, they're aiming much higher. This false jeopardy feels all the more false given the breathtaking final combat scene on Kobol, where there's a feeling of real danger as Chief, Cally, Gaius, and Seelix go up against the Centurions. It's a great action scene, and you never stop to wonder what's going to happen because there just isn't time — you're swept along with the jeopardy and all you can do is go along for the ride.

"Fragged" is the first episode that doesn't feature the planet Caprica. Among the threads followed throughout the episode is Gaius's struggle to identify himself: it's interesting that he chooses to define himself in negatives — *not* a father, *not* a guardian, *not* a leader — and indicates that he's still searching. Gaius is forever looking for answers — he's stuck with an absolute mystery inside his own head and it must drive him crazy. As a scientist, he needs to both seek out answers and define things — so it's fitting that he would label himself as he does. Throughout season 1, Gaius actively resisted responsibility and leadership, defining himself as scientific genius *in absentia* rather than through deeds. Like Tigh, he doesn't want the responsibilities of being a leader; unlike Tigh, he does want the prestige that comes with it, as evidenced by his repeated claims of "I'm the vice president."

When we cut to Gaius's dreamscape, the house, the view, and Six are just as crystal clear and pristine as ever, but Gaius himself appears bedraggled, dirty, bloodied — exactly as he is on Kobol, in fact. It's the first time the "real" Gaius has intruded on the clarity of his dreamscape, since usually his fantasy persona is clean, shaven, and groomed. It could be that Gaius is coming closer to defining himself and so his real self is gradually emerging, even in his psyche. It could also be that Six's words, her denigration of the human race, is insidiously making itself known in Gaius's mind, and he appears as she sees him — as a representative of evil, greedy, envious humanity.

During the crises of "Scattered" and "Valley of Darkness," Tigh held his own, gracefully taking command and leading the fleet through some very dark moments. It's not until the pressure is off that he starts to come apart — and it comes as quite a shock to us that, just a few minutes into the episode, he starts surreptitiously drinking. "Fragged" is an episode that takes us to the darkest places in each character: Crashdown, Roslin, Tigh, and Gaius — showing us the worst that humanity has to offer, and Six's litany of our flaws follow us all the way there. Roslin's descent is both physical and mental: she's mostly incoherent, muttering and screeching, in a scary antithesis of the practical, sensitive leader the fleet has come to know.

While Adama has never been a big fan of politics or diplomacy, he carried the fleet through some very tense situations by virtue of knowing how to talk to people and by virtue of his personality — his confidence comes from reflection not reaction. Tigh is the polar opposite: he shouts for no reason, and makes off-the-cuff decisions that ultimately jeopardize the future of Colonial democracy. It's just who Tigh is: he's happiest when he's second in command, able to remain loyal to Adama. He hates politics and the media and he doesn't know how to exist in that world. At the end of the episode, he dissolves the Quorum of Twelve and declares martial law, a stark contrast to the centrality of the theme of democracy that has been overwhelmingly present since the miniseries. His words as he leaves the press conference allude to his descent, as he says "Get these people the hell off my ship." Until now, it's been Adama's ship, and Tigh has just been standing in. Not anymore.

There's a direct contrast between the situation on Kobol and the situation on *Galactica*. On the one hand, Chief yells, "This is not a democracy" when Gaius questions Crashdown's plan; on the other hand, Tigh, Roslin, and the Quorum of Twelve are actively engaged in a struggle to preserve or dissolve the democracy of the Colonies.

The title sounds like the famous four-letter word "frak," but it's actually a word that is first thought to have appeared during the Vietnam War, meaning to throw a fragmentation grenade at a superior officer and kill him — especially one who is considered to be overly enthusiastic with regards to combat. The word is particularly fitting for this episode, in which Gaius shoots Crashdown — who has definitely become overly zealous — to save Cally and himself. Crashdown's descent has been more gradual than either Roslin's or Tigh's, so we're a little more prepared when he starts acting even more controlling than usual. A soldier shoved into a situation he can't control, Crashdown overreacts by trying to control everything to maintain his sense of authority. He's both touching in his insecurity and frightening in his intensity; he clearly believes that he's doing the right thing by going after the Centurions.

A character's slow slide into the misguided is one of the most fascinating aspects of the

And God Abandoned Kobol

In the episode "Fragged," Six tells Gaius that, "God turned His back on Kobol. Turned His back on man and the false gods he worshiped. What happens on Kobol is not His will." Her phraseology has a scriptural tone to it, and her words are reminiscent of a passage in the Old Testament of the Bible, in which the speaker talks about God having abandoned humankind for their trespasses. The passage is part of Psalm 78 (Book of Psalms) and is said to have been written by a number of authors, including King David. The relevant portion of the psalm reads:

But they put God to the test
and rebelled against the Most High;
they did not keep his statutes.
Like their fathers they were disloyal and
   faithless,
as unreliable as a faulty bow.
They angered Him with their high places;
they aroused His jealousy with their idols.
When God heard them, He was very angry;
He rejected Israel completely.
He abandoned the tabernacle of Shiloh,
the tent He had set up among men.
He sent the ark of His might into captivity,
His splendor into the hands of the enemy.
He gave His people over to the sword;
He was very angry with his inheritance.
Fire consumed their young men,
and their maidens had no wedding songs;
their priests were put to the sword,

and their widows could not weep.
Then the Lord awoke as from sleep,
as a man wakes from the stupor of wine.
He beat back His enemies;
He put them to everlasting shame.
Then He rejected the tents of Joseph,
He did not choose the tribe of Ephraim;
but He chose the tribe of Judah,
Mount Zion, which He loved.
He built his sanctuary like the heights,
like the earth that He established forever.
He chose David His servant
and took him from the sheep pens;
from tending the sheep He brought him
to be the shepherd of his people, Jacob
of Israel his inheritance.
And David shepherded them with integrity of
   heart;
with skillful hands he led them.

The parallels between Six's words and the psalm are telling. On the one hand, she seems to be indicating that the "one true God" the Cylons believe in has abandoned the Colonists – and did so a long, long time ago – and turned His affections to the Cylons. On the other hand, if that parallel holds true, then it follows that the Cylons would believe that they are in a position where they are guiding the humans – making the Cylons into a sort of David the shepherd to humanity. It puts a whole new spin on what the Cylons believe their purpose is.

writing in *BSG*: the spark of righteousness, the lingering question of motivations, right and wrong, moral and ethical, faith and hope, life and death. Six warns Gaius, "One of you will turn against the others"; it seems obvious that she means Crashdown, when he pulls his gun on Cally. But Cally refused to do her job; Seelix didn't stand up either way; Chief turned his gun on Crashdown; and Gaius not only shot Crashdown, he's actually more or less responsible for the whole situation because he lied about watching the Centurions continuously. Crashdown might very well have chosen a different plan of attack had Gaius told the truth. So who's really the traitor in this situation?

Headcount: There are 47,862 survivors at the start of this episode, which means that thirteen people died in the Centurion invasion from "Valley of Darkness."

Are You There, God? It's Me, Gaius. Gaius appears to have accepted the Cylon God as his own and is applying a scientific mind to his religious questions. He asks rational questions about God's motives and actions, and tries to incorporate them into his worldview. His journey and Roslin's are very similar, they're taking the same path to different destinations. While Roslin applies a logical mind to the Scrolls of Pythia, Gaius applies reason and investigative qualities to the "One True God" worshiped by the Cylons.

All of This Has Happened Before: "God turned His back on Kobol. Turned His back on man and the false gods he worshiped. What happens on Kobol is not His will." Abandonment by deities is one of the cornerstones of a number of mythological and religious stories. In the Torah for example, God sent a flood to wipe out the world after humankind had turned to false idolatry, murder, and sin. The fact that the gods abandoned Kobol and the Colonists only serves to emphasize the fact that the humans are alone in this fight, and have been for quite some time.

Did You Notice? The climactic scene of Chief shooting furiously at the Cylons with his handgun until it explodes, wondering how he did so much damage, and then realizing the plane above is responsible for the explosion, is very similar to a scene from the war movie *Saving Private Ryan*. In fact, episode director Sergio Mimica-Gezzan was first assistant director in that movie.

Six tells Gaius that humans "invented murder. Invented killing for sport, greed, envy. It's man's one true art form." This is an echo of her sentiments from "Valley of Darkness" when she said, "Then your true nature asserted itself. Your brutality, your depravity, your barbarism."

204   Resistance

Original air date: August 5, 2005
Written by: Toni Graphia
Directed by: Allan Kroeker

Roslin organizes her own escape from prison. Starbuck and Helo join forces with a large group of survivors on Caprica.

"Resistance" works with both the resistance to martial law throughout the fleet (as well as resistance against the Cylons on Caprica) and the human tendency to take the path of least resistance. The episode opens

Michael Trucco credits *BSG* for his rise in popularity (ALBERT L. ORTEGA)

and closes on blood, framing the story with a sense of foreboding and foreshadowing the rage and helplessness that follow the characters, ending in Boomer's death.

From Tigh's frustrated lashing out at Chief, Gaius, and anyone in his path, to Chief's anger with Boomer; from Ellen and Tigh screaming at each other and segueing directly into sex, to Cally beating on Jammer, rage is one of the defining features of this episode. Tigh's story line over the last four episodes has been intense and explosive, and while it's surprising to watch him make bad decision after bad decision, it's also understandable. He has a pattern of making the wrong choices — his marriage being a prime example of that — although, as he pointed out to Starbuck in "Bastille Day," his flaws are personal: alcoholism and an emotionally abusive relationship with Ellen. David Eick said in an interview with *iF Magazine*, "In the second season, we went for four episodes where every single frakking thing the guy said was wrong. Every move he wanted to make: wrong. Every decision he wanted to make: wrong. Every point in the strategy he want to espouse: wrong."

The harsh emotions of this episode are framed by some fleeting moments of cleverness. One of the best is when Dee hands Tigh a bunch of papers to sign, and he flips through them, signing rapidly, and both Dee and the audience believe he's not paying attention, think that he's just signing without looking at the papers. But all of a sudden he stops and asks why Causeway B is being closed, and we realize that he's been paying attention the whole time. It's a great way to make us take another look at Tigh and realize that he's not as incompetent as some might have believed. As Eick noted in the same interview, "But after a while he can't always be wrong. The guy is the XO, he should have a point of view occasionally that doesn't spell out disaster and ruin for everybody."

"Resistance" sets up a lot of the threads for the next few episodes. When the episode ends, things are not good in the fleet, so it's heartening that when Adama limps into Tigh's quarters, there's no reprimand, no rebuke, no accusatory statements — there's just forgiveness and practicality. It's a nice contrast to the last few episodes, where Adama has been a still and silent giant, set to judge Lee and Tigh and Roslin. Instead, here he is, visibly human, visibly weakened, and all he wants is to put the fleet back together again. There'll be resistance, because in a population of more than one there will always be differences of opinion and resistance to ideas. Contrary to expectation, Adama is immediately set up as the bringer of unity, instead of the patriarchal bringer of judgment.

We've seen Cally defend Chief before ("Litmus"), but their stay on Kobol could only have deepened their bonds of trust and friendship — and, it seems, a little more on Cally's part. She blindly rushes from one extreme to the next, blackmailing Gaius, striking Jammer, before finally putting an end to the person she believes has caused all the trouble — Boomer. Actress Nicki Clyne said in an interview, "I think she was still in a state of shock, because when your reality is invaded by something you thought totally threatening to your life and to your world, it shakes you. Like the things you thought were important might change. I think Boomer represented all the things that were wrong for her at that time, including her relationship with Tyrol."

On the flip side of rage and hatred is love, which Gaius bet on earlier in the episode: it was love that led Boomer to search her subconscious and save Chief. That scene is pivotal in the presentation of love as it's perceived by the various characters. For Chief, love is something that got him seriously hurt; for Boomer, it's the definition of her humanity; and for Gaius, it's a card to be played. And yet, at the end of the episode, Gaius tells Chief that love is love, no matter where you find it: "Love is a strange and wonderful thing, Chief. You'd be happy you experienced it at all. Even if it was with a machine." Gaius's words apply to himself as well as to Chief, and they allow us to see that his time on Kobol changed him, as it did Cally. He went to Kobol needing a break from Six; he returns having realized the scope and magnitude of their relationship — recommitted to his existence with her.

While "Resistance" ends on a bitter note, it ultimately provides hope. Tigh could very well have shot Apollo and Roslin's shuttle down — he doesn't. Roslin could have quietly remained in the brig, but she takes a stand and escapes. Chief could have ignored Boomer even as she lay dying — he doesn't. Starbuck and Helo could have continued on their way alone — instead, they join forces with fifty-three other survivors of the human race. And finally, Adama wakes up. While this episode could have been an illustration of humanity's flaws, as "Fragged" was, it can actually be seen as more of a tribute to the strength and perseverance of the human spirit.

Michael Trucco (Samuel T. Anders)

Date of birth: June 22, 1970

Did you know? Michael's real name is Edward — Michael is actually his middle name, but it's the one he goes by personally as well as professionally. He's the lead guitarist for a band called Simpleworld, and although he graduated with a BA in theater arts, he actually started out in sociology and criminal justice in California.

On BSG: "This is an amazing cast and crew to work with. They've set a level of professionalism and personablility that's hard to find on just any set. There's a reason this is a critically acclaimed series, and it shows in everyone I work with. I really respect the talent of everyone involved. I mean, can you get better writing!?!? For an actor, this is the cornerstone to any good project . . . Not budget, big names, high profile network, special effects, etc. While all that stuff *is* important, it doesn't mean anything without a good script . . . And Ron Moore and David Eick and their team of writers consistently deliver."

On the cast: "Honestly, there isn't one member of the cast of *BSG* that I don't get along with fantastically. I know that sounds a bit trite, but it's true. There is no tension among the whole group with any of them and that is a rare thing when you have such a large 'ensemble' cast."

On the tattoos Anders and Starbuck sport in the season 2 finale: "They're our 'wedding bands.' Mine's on my right arm, hers on her left. They match up to form one set of wings and the circles overlap when we're facing each other. Each of us has half of the constellation of Capricorn (a reference to Caprica obviously) and a small symbol of the planet as well."

Headcount: There's one less survivor than the previous episode, due to Crashdown's demise. The headcount is now 47,861.

Interesting Fact: Ronald Moore has explained that the shooting on the *Gideon* was directly inspired by a 1770 massacre in Boston, fittingly enough called the Boston Massacre. In March 1770, five civilians were killed by British troops in an event that eventually led to a declaration of civil war. The atmosphere in Boston at the time was similar to the ambiance throughout the fleet — a heavy military presence, with brawls and riots breaking out on a regular basis.

What's In a Name? Samuel T. Anders is a mouthful of a name! The first name could refer to the biblical figure of Samuel, who has two books named after him in the Old Testament. He was presented as a seer or prophet. But there are countless other instances of the name Samuel throughout history. Anders, however, is a variant of the Scandinavian for "man," which is itself a variant of the Greek for "valiant" — certainly a fitting name considering that we meet *BSG* Anders in a scene of physical prowess. In more recent history, Wladyslaw Anders was a prominent army officer who commanded the Polish forces in the Middle East and Italy during World War II and went on to become a leader in the fight against communist forces. Samuel Anders is definitely a leader, and much like the historical figure, he's fighting not only an army that has invaded his homeland, but also the ideology embodied in the Cylons — that of humankind's unworthiness of life. Side by side, the two names "Samuel" and "Anders" give the character a double edge: he's both the figure of the virile man and the figure of the irrepressible, undaunted leader.

Did You Notice? "Let [Adama] decide what to do with you," Tigh spits at Chief. This is an echo of Lee's words at the end of "Valley of Darkness" when he said that when Adama woke up he would decide what to do with both his son and his XO.

The gun that Sue-Shaun holds to Starbuck's back on Caprica is an SA80 rifle, used by the British Army. It's not commonly used in television or movies, but it was chosen for this scene for its futuristic look — which would make sense, considering Anders' group apparently just raided a couple of armories.

Chief's first name, Galen, is mentioned in this episode. In "The Hand of God," Gaius mentions a philosopher named Galen. In real life, Galen was an ancient Greek physician who died around the year 200 AD and was renowned for his theories on anatomy. He performed operations that were far beyond his time (including brain and eye surgery). In this episode we learn that Chief Galen Tyrol's father was a priest, and his mother an oracle.

Boomer's death in this episode mirrors the death of Lee Harvey Oswald, who was accused of assassinating John F. Kennedy in 1963. Oswald was shot at point-blank range while being transferred from a jail cell to an interrogation office. According to an interview with Aaron Douglas, who plays Chief, the scene was specifically set up to resemble the real-life occurrence; the producers went so far as to show footage of Oswald's shooting to all the cast members in the scene so that they could better mimic the real-time reactions.

"You're human. You have a soul. You swim in the stream. We heard it before." Anders' words to Starbuck are a reference to the Cylon belief system we first saw in depth in season 1's "Flesh and Bone."

Classic *Battlestar Galactica*: The original series presented a game similar to pyramid, called triad. Its rules were laid out in the script for the episode of "War of the Gods," but Moore mixed up the card game from the original series with the ball game, and so the two are reversed in the reimagined series.

So Say We All: ROSLIN: I need your help. But it's illegal, dangerous, and in violation of your oath as an officer.

COTTLE: You're a lousy salesman.

205   The Farm

Original air date: August 12, 2005
Written by: Toni Graphia
Directed by: Allan Kroeker

Starbuck wakes up injured in a strange hospital on Caprica.

Talking about "The Farm" immediately gives way to a whole lot of thorny issues about procreation, feminism, responsibility, and survival of the species. It's an extremely contentious episode, and Ronald Moore has admitted as much. "Here is a female character, heroine, who we put the screws to all through the episode. It deals with a lot of fertility issues, reproductive issues, some of which may be potentially uncomfortable or distasteful. And the question is, does that drive female audiences away, or does it bring them to the party?"

In part because of that controversy, "The Farm" makes for compelling viewing, paving the way for two important story lines: Starbuck's medical rape, and her relationship with Anders. While both tropes — tough-skinned rebel falls in love, and woman gets her insides probed for the purposes of childbearing (*Dune* or *The X-Files*, anyone?) — are unsurprising in the sci-fi genre, what *is* surprising are the motivations behind the events. Starbuck isn't just any tough-skinned rebel — she's a flawed human with a past that we're just beginning to see. With the eyes of a new lover (very much like Anders), we learn that she was physically abused as a child. In season 1, Leoben told Starbuck, "You were born to a woman who believed that suffering was good for the soul, so you suffered" ("Flesh and Bone"), but until now, that suffering has remained nameless and faceless. "The Farm" shows that even if the suffering is faceless, it's there, beneath the surface, in the form of fractured fingers and broken bones.

The Cylons' motivation for their biological tampering is what makes the trope so interesting in "The Farm": despite all their machinations and evolutions, the Cylons can't reproduce. It's the one reason Sharon was given the mission to seduce Helo and get him to fall in love with her. According to Cylon faith, they have a duty to God to reproduce, and the fact that they've so far been unsuccessful to do so can't help but feel like an overwhelming failure to respect God's wishes. They go about rectifying the situation in two completely different ways: they experiment with love, to see if love is the missing link (and what a fascinating idea, that biology could be somehow fundamentally changed by emotional factors), and they set up "baby farms" throughout the Colonies, stealing women's ovaries and forcing them to breed.

The scene where Starbuck discovers Sue-Shaun is horrific, and Sue-Shaun's plea for Starbuck to kill her alludes to the apocalyptic nature of this episode. There's probably nothing women like Sue-Shaun and Starbuck want less than to become breeding machines — for humans, let alone the Cylons — and they would rather die than face a fate that is, for them, the end of the world. Starbuck destroys the breeding room, filled with anger and despair, and it's a terrific, awful scene — and wonderfully ironic of her to use a pair of forceps to shut the machine down. The episode might seem on the surface to be lacking in feminism, but taken from a different perspective, it's actually one of the most feminist episodes the series has done: despite emotional, mental, and physical torture, Starbuck fights back, literally rages against the machine, and, having fulfilled her duty to the president by finding the Arrow of Apollo, leaves Caprica a changed woman. And Sue-Shaun chooses to die rather than serve the purposes of the Cylons. These are women with agency;

they might not be choosing what's happened to them, but they'll be damned if they're not going to fight to make sure that what ultimately happens is *their* choice.

Ultimately, "The Farm" revolves around one of the series' central themes — that of love and what it makes us do. All forms of love show up — love between lovers (Anders and Starbuck, Chief and Sharon), love between friends (Helo and Starbuck, Anders and Sue-Shaun), familial love (Adama and Sharon, Apollo and Adama). "The Farm" isn't *all* about Starbuck, but it does focus on her pretty decisively. Back on *Galactica*, Adama makes a much-anticipated return to the CIC. In an emotional scene, he's greeted by warm smiles and a standing ovation. It's obvious his near-death experience has altered him because he opens up to the crew, saying that they don't say they love each other often enough. It's a heartwarming moment — the crew has missed Adama as much as we have — and it feels like things are finally going to start getting fixed on the fleet. The feeling doesn't last, however, and the end of the episode brings us back to where we were at the beginning of season 2: a fractured fleet, divided families, and love lost. Adama takes a first step towards understanding in this episode, crying over Boomer's body in the morgue, but for Apollo, Adama, Starbuck, Helo, Anders, and Sharon, it's going to be a long row to hoe to make it back "home."

Headcount: There are 47,857 survivors this episode; this accounts for the deaths of the civilians aboard the *Gideon* in "Resistance," as well as Boomer's demise. So they're counting Boomer as a human . . .

All of This Has Happened Before: Zarek calls Adama "Zeus" again, as he did in season 1's "Bastille Day." In Greek mythology, Zeus ruled Olympus and the pantheon of gods. Originally worshiped as a weather god, he was responsible for thunder, lightning, rain, and wind. He was known as the father and protector of both gods and men. Zeus led the gods in victory against the Titans.

Numbers: Tigh says that 24 ships is the equivalent of nearly a third of the whole fleet. This would mean that the fleet includes more than 72 ships. In the miniseries, however, only 40 ships have the ability to jump with *Galactica*.

Interesting Fact: The scene in which Laura, Zarek, Lee and the rest of the group are in cold storage was originally intended to be set in a meat locker, but the production crew couldn't find a meat locker, or the ones they found were way too cold, or way too cramped.

What's In a Name? The newest in the Cylon group is Simon, whose name is both common-place and significant in the biblical canon. In Hebrew, the name is a variant of the verb "hear" or "listen," and is often translated as "he who hears." In the New Testament, Simon Magus (known today as Simon the Magician or The Sorcerer) was a magician who awed audiences to the point that they believed him to be "the great power of God." When Simon met the disciples of Jesus, he was himself awed by the power they demonstrated, and offered to buy the power of the Holy Spirit with silver — a blasphemy for which he was quickly rebuked. (The term "simony" comes from there, and means to buy or sell sacred things.) To many scholars, Simon's reaction to the rebuke indicates a singular lack of repentance — he merely asks that Peter mediate with God on his (Simon's) behalf so that he not be punished

for his misstep. The Cylon Simon similarly shows a real lack of empathy with Starbuck, and a stinging lack of remorse regarding his actions — both past and planned.

Is it just me, or does James really look like Michael Jackson here?

Did You Notice? The credits have changed yet again in this episode: the first four episodes of the season featured only the vocal theme, without the clips of the episode. "The Farm" marks a return to the old format — although the episode snippets are reduced in length; the final result is an amalgamation of the two credits: the clips return, but the "UK" theme music remains.

"Procreation, it's one of God's commandments, be fruitful." Sharon's explanation for the Cylons' "baby farm" echoes Six's words from the season 1 episode "33": "Procreation is one of God's commandments."

So Say We All: ROSLIN: I know exactly what I have to do. How does this thing work?

206   Home, Part 1

Original air date: August 19, 2005
Written by: David Eick
Directed by: Sergio Mimica-Gezzan

Roslin and her followers try to find the Tomb of Athena; Adama struggles to find a way forward.

We start "Home" in the middle of a fractured fleet, with the divide between the religious and the military ever more raw and ragged. It's hard to watch Adama shut himself off so completely — he doesn't want to hear about the *people* they lost to Roslin's crusade, just the *resources* they lost — but it makes sense in the larger arc of his near-death experience. Not only does a "near-death experience definitely change your perspective" (in the words of Edward James Olmos in an interview with *Cult Times*), but it must seem to Adama that he's being betrayed all over the place. He's angry, hurt, and he feels like he's given everything — including his life's blood — for this ragtag fleet of survivors, only to have them turn on him. In the same interview, Olmos said, "By the end of the season he was a completely different person towards Roslin and towards everyone. As a matter of fact, he couldn't make decisive decisions. It was very difficult for him because he was too emotional." Adama seems caught in a place where he has to be hard, uncaring — when underneath it all, he's filled with rage, hatred, fear, and grief.

Unfortunately, the only way for those repressed emotions to come out is through some less-than-stellar decision-making. Although no decision he makes leads to disaster, any of them easily could have: he chooses possibly the worst pilot we've ever seen on the series to replace Lee as CAG, and he conducts one of the least adept press conferences in the history of press conferences — second only to Tigh's own attempt in "Fragged." Adama's obvious turmoil makes a wonderful counterpoint to Dee, who conveys a peaceful determination that Adama sorely needs. Although Dee is a secondary character, and rarely has more than a few lines to speak in any given episode, she's one of the steadiest presences on the ship. We come to rely on her, the composed, soothing voice that relays instructions, guides pilots home, and provides the "missing link" between what's being said and what's being done. And as we rely on her, so too does Adama, quietly; he might not like what she has to say, but he knows that she's *there* — and that's more than he can say for a lot of people at this point in time. Their scene is tense and filled with emotion, and it's a turning point for both the episode and Adama himself.

While families are torn apart throughout the fleet, aboard the *Astral Queen*, families are coming back together. The reunion between Starbuck and Apollo was a highly anticipated one, considering that they had parted on bad terms after Starbuck had slept with Gaius and Lee found out about it ("Kobol's Last Gleaming, Part 1"). Their hug and kiss in this episode are perfect for the characters, and speak to their history and close bond — they easily forgive each other and put the past behind them.

The reunion is quickly cut short by Sharon's appearance. Because we've been following the Caprica story line, we've had the opportunity, alongside Helo and Starbuck, to work through how we feel about Sharon over the last few episodes. Apollo and Roslin haven't had that chance, and it's especially difficult for Apollo given his recent history with Boomer: Sharon is such a familiar presence, but her very existence is questionable and disturbing on a number of levels. It immediately becomes a point of contention between those willing to trust her, and those who can't. Sharon is just one more wedge to fracture the fleet. Now, factions are appearing even within factions, a fracturing that is further compounded by the scheming that's going on between Zarek and Meier.

"Home" focuses both on the details of the fleet's existence, like how to successfully conduct a refueling operation, and the larger arcs that drive the characters and their stories

— Roslin's religious quest, Adama's sense of betrayal, and the Cylons' need for love. "[Sharon] thinks she's in love. Even if it's software instead of an emotion, it's real to her. She wants her baby to live. She wants Agathon to live," Roslin notes. It's fascinating to watch throughout the series how love drives the Cylons more than any other emotion: in all incarnations we've seen, Six has been motivated by love — she has other drives, certainly, but it's love that gets under her skin, love that confuses her, love that moves her. Doral expresses the same confusion and curiosity about love in season 1's "Tigh Me Up, Tigh Me Down," and Leoben is entranced by the "love that bonds everything together" ("Flesh and Bone"). Sharon is the model that takes love a step further — she believes it, feels it, enacts it.

Roslin's words don't just apply to Sharon, though: it's the same for Roslin herself. In the end, it doesn't matter if the prophecies are true or not — she believes they are, and her actions and their consequences are real. The fleet *is* split, Kara *did* find the Arrow of Apollo, the group *is* going to Kobol: whatever truth does or does not lie behind her beliefs,

Sibyl

The Sibyl, a pagan oracle who came to prominence in ancient Greece, was the name given to a woman (usually an older woman), who made prophetic utterances about the future after entering a trance or ecstatic state. A sibyl is not a proper name, but rather the title which they held. Sibyls are found in many cultures, including Japanese, Persian, and European. The ancient type usually did their prophesying in one spot, such as a temple or a shrine, but sibyls of later times would wander from place to place – this type of prophet is the one contemporary audiences are most familiar with. The Sibyl of Cumae, an ancient Roman sibyl, is one such seeress, and was thought to have been prophesying under the guidance of the god Apollo. In Virgil's epic *Aeneid* there is a famous scene between Aeneas and the Cumaean Sibyl in Book VI: 10. In the *BSG* episode "Flesh and Bone," we see Roslin floating about the forest in a nightgown, dreaming about the future, and in "Fragged" the chamalla she takes for her cancer seems to induce visions of an ecstatic nature. Her aide-de-camp's name, interestingly, is Lee Adama, whose call sign is "Apollo." In a later episode we see Apollo floating in a lake. Both dreams and lakes are symbols of the unconscious – perhaps he and Roslin have a deeper and older relationship than they know. . . .

her actions and the actions of her followers have defined the reality of their existence at this point in time. This is another facet of the thread that's been slowly woven into the series from the very first episode: it is, above and beyond all, our actions that define us.

This is both true and false for Gaius, whose manifestation of Six and subconscious projection of his house on Caprica make his mindscape an essential part of who he is. This is not to say that the thought and emotions of other characters are less important than Gaius's, but it seems obvious that Gaius's mental path has been leading him to identify less and less with the humans of the fleet, and more with the Cylons. In "Home, Part 1," Gaius is still a little confused about exactly where he's heading, and hasn't made any decisions about his loyalties. "Why are you talking to me like I'm not one of them?" he asks Six, as he observes the flow of people moving through *Galactica*'s corridors. His stance is very similar to the stance adopted by Doral, Sharon, and Caprica-Six when they watched Helo in "Litmus" — the similarity probably isn't a coincidence, given Gaius's inner turmoil about his role in the larger arc of the human race's struggle for survival. For all the characters of *BSG*, whether simple or complex, likeable or despicable, home is where the heart is.

Headcount: With Helo back amongst the fleet, the survivor count increases to 47,858 souls.
Interesting Fact: In the early versions of the script, it was Billy who died on Kobol, not Priestess Elosha. The rationale was that the trip to Kobol was Roslin's crusade; it was Roslin's decision to bring them there, so she had to pay a price. Ultimately, the decision was made that Elosha's death was more interesting in terms of Roslin's character. David Eick added, "Because Laura's role is the 'prophet' or 'seer' and the story is about to reach a conclusion, and spin the character into a different direction, [...] it seemed right that metaphorically you would kill the person who represented that chapter of her life."
Did You Notice? Sharon says, "We all know about the tomb," indicating yet again that the Cylons have been studying human history and religion. This is a thread we saw quite a bit in season 1, but this episode adds a layer of foreboding with Sharon's prophetic words: "Even if you find the tomb, even if you find the map, and even if you find Earth, the price you pay will be too high." It doesn't seem likely that she's alluding to Elosha's death; it seems like something much larger.

This is the list of resources lost when the fleet fractured: 18,000 people, twelve transports, seven freighters, two construction platforms, one private cruiser, and one mining ship.
Classic *Battlestar Galactica*: The idea of finding the way to Earth from within the tomb echoes back to the original *BSG*. In an episode entitled "Lost Planet of the Gods," Adama discovers Kobol and tries to find a way to the 13th Colony from there.
So Say We All: DEE: You let us down. You let us down. You made a promise to all of us . . . and ans earth, to find us a home. Together. It doesn't matter what the president did or even what Lee did, because every day that we remain apart is a day that you've broken your promise.

Original air date: August 26, 2005
Written by: Ronald Moore, David Eick
Directed by: Jeff Woolnough

Tricia: just a down-home girl from Alberta (ALBERT L. ORTEGA)

Adama goes to Kobol to reunite the fleet.

This episode plays like an action movie, full of intrigue, scheming, mystery, high emotion, and plenty of twists and turns. It starts with Adama making good on his vow to reunite the fleet and bring the human family back together. He's in full detective mode, books cracked open and research team (a.k.a. Tigh, Gaeta, and Chief) at the ready.

It's not just traditional families that are brought together in this episode, although it is wonderful to finally see Lee and Adama hug and make up — their relationship has shifted through so many different dynamics over the last twenty episodes, and, like Lee and Starbuck, they were on such bad terms when Adama was shot and Lee imprisoned, that their reconciliation is a metaphor for the reconciliation of the whole fleet.

Other families are reunited, too — Billy and Roslin, Kara and Adama, Adama and Roslin, Sharon and Chief, Six and Gaius — and even Six, Gaius, and the unborn baby. And, through them, the religious and the military, the conservative and the rebellious, the Cylons and the humans are all united.

Some of the best moments in this episode are given to Six, who makes some astonishing changes to her personal appearance and performance, and who leads Gaius on a hysterical wild goose chase. Poor Gaius — he's ridiculously easy to manipulate, which seems strange considering the sheer brainpower the man has. His suggestibility points to the critical difference between brainpower and willpower, however, and scores another point in the "it's our actions that define us" category. From naked sex machine to woman-next-door, Six undergoes a total transformation. What's interesting in that scene is that the transformation comes directly on the heels of Gaius taunting her about his relationship with Starbuck, and it's obvious from Six's reaction that she doesn't appreciate the comparison: "You're in dangerous territory now," she tells him. And funnily enough, the next time the camera lands on her, she looks exactly like Starbuck. She's wearing clothes that Starbuck would wear, her hair is in a little ponytail — exactly like Starbuck's — and everything from her posture, her speech patterns and rhythm, to her laughter screams "Starbuck." Her linguistic choices even sound like Starbuck — "Wake up and smell the psychosis" is something that Six would never say, but it does sound exactly like something Starbuck would say. Six usually speaks slowly and distinctly, her words evenly spaced and enunciated; in this incarnation, she speaks like Starbuck — the words are more rushed, there's more of a lilting pattern to them, and her voice goes down at the end of sentences.

What's even more interesting in this sequence is the motivation behind Six's transformation. As a Cylon, Six is already a clone; "there are many copies" of her, but she's also distinctly individual in that she's the only Cylon model we've seen so far that seems to live exclusively inside someone's head. And it's fascinating that she, as a clone, would *choose* to mimic someone else. But Six has exhibited jealousy for Starbuck since Gaius first started showing interest in her in season 1. She's probably the Cylon model that's the most driven by her emotions — one could argue she's nothing *but* emotion. Of all the avenues the series has found to look at the complexity of defining humanity, Six is one of the most interesting, because she's so emotional and so human, as volatile as a five-year-old. You never know when she's going to blow up, decide to shove your head into a mirror ("Kobol's Last Gleaming, Part 1"), or rescue you from a burning spacecraft ("Kobol's Last Gleaming, Part 2").

On Kobol, Adama and Roslin have united their quests and are working together again to find the way to Earth. While the stress fractures apparent in Part 1 are still in play, they're a lot less critical, and the fact that these potential hotspots have been smoothed over is important because it indicates that each member of the group is putting their own feelings aside and working for the greater good — the survival of the fleet. It's a great way to bring back the sense of unity and pursuit of a common cause, both of which have been lacking since the end of season 1.

Sharon's presence makes it uncomfortable for everyone, because they look at the Cylon identity — such as it stands — and question their preconceptions. In "Resistance," Six pointed out that the term "toaster" is considered a racial epithet to Cylons; in this episode, the slew of suspicious glances and obvious distrust points to the fact that the group can't dehumanize Sharon in the same way that they've been able to dehumanize other Cylon models in the past. She's real, familiar, and each person there has a history with her, and so they have to come up with a whole new way of identifying themselves — and her — and of relating with her.

This two-parter was intended to close the *BSG* era that started in the miniseries. With the fleet back together, families reunited, betrayals forgiven, and a quest partially fulfilled, "Home, Part 2" does feel like the end of an era. The penultimate scene, with the *Galactica* crew gathered in the hangar deck for Adama's speech, echoes the penultimate scene of the miniseries. If Adama's speech in the miniseries served to offer the survivors hope, then his speech in this episode offers them unity, purpose, and truth. The people gathered before him are no longer the same people: they've lived and died a hundred times since the Cylons first attacked, they've learned a thousand lessons they never knew they needed, and they've come farther than they ever wanted to come — but they're still there, together. And now they, too, have a plan.

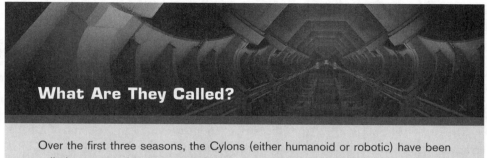

What Are They Called?

Over the first three seasons, the Cylons (either humanoid or robotic) have been called pretty much every name you can think of — and a few you might not have caught. Following is a list of as many epithets as I could find.

Toasters

Frakkers or motherfrakkers

Chrome toasters (miniseries)

Chrome dome ("Torn")

Chrome job (*The Resistance*)

Clankers ("Rapture")

Bullet head ("Downloaded")

Skin job ("Downloaded")

Carburetor ("Torn")

Sparrow ("Maelstrom" — designates a
   Cylon Raider)

Turkey ("Maelstrom" — designates a
   Cylon Heavy Raider)

Tincan ("Torn")

Lightbulb ("Torn")

Humanity's children (miniseries)

Final Five ("Torn")

Transistor ("Torn")

Microchip ("Torn")

Headcount: There are 47,855 survivors in this episode. Although we only saw two people die in "Home, Part 1" (Elosha and one other), it's plausible that another of Roslin's group died off-screen.

Are You There, God? It's Me, Gaius. The interesting thing about Gaius's conversion is that it isn't necessarily about a religious conversion. In this episode, he's determined to figure out what Six is, exactly, and he started by having Dr. Cottle check him for an implanted chip in his brain. Allegorically speaking, it's hilarious to have him looking for "god" — or perhaps an "angel of God" (in Six's own words) — in the form of an electronic chip, but it's also really fitting for Gaius, whose one true love was science, at least until season 1's "The Hand of God." He's asking the same questions most people ask of religion and God, whatever they conceive God to be: What are you? Where are you? Why do you exist? And what are you doing in my life? Except that Gaius, being Gaius, is starting with the most scientific, rational explanation.

Interesting Fact: Chief Tyrol says sardonically, "Topography's for pansies." The original line was actually, "Topography's for pussies" and, later in the episode, Adama was to say, "Adar was a prick." In the podcast for this episode, Moore explained the change of wording: "[The network] wouldn't let us say 'pricks' or 'pussies.' [...] I actually called broadcast standards and made some whole eloquent pitch about, 'Well, it's context and he's not calling someone a pussy. It's not used as an epithet. It's really just a general statement of life and that '"Adar's a prick" is a joke.' […] And they just [said], 'Oh, that's really interesting. No, you can't say it.'"

Did You Notice? This is the first episode where Roslin and Adama call each other by their first names, Laura and Bill. They're usually much more formal, addressing each other as "Commander Adama" and "President Roslin."

The Lagoon Nebula is, like all the other stellar landmarks visible in the Tomb of Athena, an actual constellation. In astronomical terms, it's known by catalogue numbers NGC 6523 and M8, and is an ionized-hydrogen region located in the constellation Sagittarius (and not Scorpio, as indicated in "Home, Part 2").

"And Zeus warned the leaders of the twelve tribes that any return to Kobol would exact a price in blood." This is the third time Adama has been called "Zeus": first in "Bastille Day" and then in "The Farm."

Just after Sharon hands her gun over to Adama, there's a series of shots where you can see the rest of the group behind Adama. There's a shot where Katee and Mary have some strange facial contortions going on as well. According to Paul Campbell, who plays Billy, the cast was having a hilarious discussion regarding horse names you might choose at random at the racetrack, and they couldn't stop laughing.

So Say We All: COTTLE: Will you stop going crazy in there?!

GAIUS: I'm not crazy!

208   Final Cut

Original air date: September 9, 2005
Written by: Toni Graphia
Directed by: Allan Kroeker

A journalist gains full access to the Galactica *to write a story on the truth about the "guardians of the fleet."*

"Final Cut" is a shift in tone and direction after the arc-heavy story lines of the previous two episodes. It offers a glimpse of everyday life aboard *Galactica* and some small moments of insight into some of the characters we see every day, but don't get to know as well as the main players. Dee, Helo, Kat, and Gaeta all reveal things that help us understand their lives better. Their revelations aren't particularly surprising; rather, the information seems to blend in with what we already know of the characters to make them more textured and layered. Dee, for example, has always carried an aura of sorrow around her, a quiet melancholy, and even though we didn't know the particulars until "Final Cut," her interview still makes perfect sense in light of what we *did* know of her. It seems that, nearly halfway through season 2, we should know the crew of *Galactica*, and it's shocking to realize that, like the rest of the fleet, we don't really know a lot about the minor characters' inner lives, their individual sufferings.

D'Anna Biers attempts to find the real story on *Galactica*. What she finds is that it's not as simple as asking whether or not the decisions made were the right ones, or whether or not everyone is performing up to scratch; the situation demands that she — and the rest of the fleet — abandon the idea of black and white, right and wrong, and instead look to the innumerable shades of gray in between.

D'Anna is another layered character, and "Final Cut" is really all about her personal journey from suspicion and bias to understanding. The title of this episode is an obvious reference to the final cut of D'Anna's report on *Galactica*, but it also points to the fact that it's the final cut that kills you — a phrase that rings especially true of this episode, where we realize that her entire journey has been a lie and she's actually a Cylon. While it's clear that D'Anna is no angel — she hides the tape of Sharon, she entices Tigh to drink — we're still invested in her emotional and intellectual journey, so it's a slap in the face when that voice rings out in the last scene — minus the New Zealand accent — and the camera pans oh-so-slowly over to D'Anna's face. She hasn't just betrayed the human race; she's betrayed us, and it stings. Adama, Roslin, Tigh — even *we* think that she's changed, that she embodies one of the most thrilling virtues of the human race, the ability to open one's mind and accept new possibilities, that she has come to know the "truth" — but her empathy and compassion are just a façade to hide her own truth.

The style of the episode also contributes to the unsettling feeling of being outside *Galactica*'s inner circle. This is very different to that of other episodes, especially with regard to the camera work. A lot of handheld shots give an up-close and personal look at the crew, and the different photographic techniques immediately convey that we're on the outside looking in. The documentary perspective provides a lot of interesting insight (Gaeta has a tattoo!) but it also imbues the episode with a sense of loss — it feels like we've lost *Galactica*'s trust because we're thrust into a different point of view.

Budgetary restrictions usually force television shows to have a "clip episode" every season: this episode takes moments from a lot of prior episodes and assembles them into a clip show, with short, intermittent moments set in the present time to frame the flashbacks. While not a clip show, "Final Cut" serves to slow down time on board *Galactica*: there are no chases, no major character developments, no health crises. This episode is about stopping the momentum so that a record can be made of the present moment.

Lucy Lawless (HOWARD WISE/SHOOTING STAR)

There are some wonderful scenes that also play into the series' philosophical inquiries, in particular the question of humanity, and how it's defined. Helo says, "They try to turn off the human part of you because that's what'll get you killed." The poignancy and irony of that statement is awe-inspiring, because it's so true on a purely factual level. The fleet can watch out for the mechanical Cylons — the toasters, the Raiders — because they show up on DRADIS, or they have red glowy eyes; but the human Cylons are just there, amongst the humans, and people have no idea who they are or when they'll strike — or even what they want. It's the human Cylons that are going to kill them, because they can't fight what they can't see. Helo says all this, and it's a terrible, poignant moment; and it's not until the end of the episode that the real terribleness appears, because he said all of this *to a Cylon*.

The premise of this episode is one that's been done to death: many shows have done an episode wherein a documentary crew comes in to film the characters and give the "real story" behind their lives. But while many such episodes merely gloss the surface of what's going on in a given universe, "Final Cut" provides some real perspective shifts that add dimension and texture to the *BSG* world. During the course of the documentary, the Cylons attack, and for the first time, we don't witness the battle from the pilots' point of view; instead, we're stuck in CIC and we have to wait alongside Adama, Tigh, Gaeta, Dee, and the documentary team as the future of the human race is played out in space, beyond their vision or control. As viewers, we take it for granted that we'll be privy to all the important moments and battles. "Final Cut" plays with our preconceived ideas — and in the end, what's important isn't always what we see, rather, it's sometimes what we don't see that matters. That holds true for D'Anna as well — we think she is what she is, a ruthless seeker of scandal, but it's what we don't see — her Cylon identity — that's actually important.

Headcount: The whiteboard is back! It's such a small prop, but it's such an essential part of the fleet's existence — and Roslin's position as president. There are 47,853 survivors. That's a loss of 2 from "Home, Part 2" — Meier and the unnamed man Apollo shot in the head.

Interesting Fact: Executive producer David Eick originally wanted Lucy Lawless to audition for the role of Ellen Tigh, back in season 1, but Lucy couldn't see herself in the part. David and Lucy go back a long way, and Lucy explained in a September 2005 interview with *Cult Times* that, "A few months ago, though, David phoned me about the D'Anna Biers role. My youngest had just turned three and I'd been working more, so it was the right time for me. [The] character of D'Anna is such a good one that I'd have been a fool to turn it down."

Did You Notice? The acronyms following the crew's names and ranks have specific meaning: CF is Colonial Fleet, CFR is Colonial Fleet Reserve, CMC is Colonial Marine Corps, and CMCR is Colonial Marine Corps Reserve.

"What a strange little man," D'Anna says of Gaius Baltar. That's close to what Roslin said about him in the season 1 episode "33": "He's a strange one, isn't he?"

The poet whose verses are written on Tigh's mirror is Kataris; it's likely a play on the real-life Roman poet Catullus, who lived in the first century BCE. He was a very influential poet who shocked readers with his explicit verses.

Classic *Battlestar Galactica*: The music playing in D'Anna's documentary is the music from the original *Battlestar Galactica*. The only other time we heard that particular music was in the miniseries.

So Say We All: STARBUCK: "From the darkness, you must fall, failed and weak, to darkness all." Kataris. Not one of his best. Can I be a suspect again? Please?

209   Flight of the Phoenix

Original air date: September 16, 2005
Written by: David Weddle, Bradley Thompson
Directed by: Michael Nankin

A Cylon virus is spreading through Galactica. *Chief starts to build a new fighter plane from scrap material.*

"Final Cut" gave an oddly impersonal look at the personal lives of the *Galactica* crew through the lens of a documentary camera; "Flight of the Phoenix" offers a much more

intimate view of a few key characters. The main thrust of the episode is in the construction
— rather, the creation — of the stealth ship that starts out as Chief's pet hobby and turns
into a ship-wide arts-and-crafts project. The entire episode reads like a metaphor for the
hope that lies in working together.

So many loose ends are waved around in this episode: Adama takes another chance on
Sharon, and she does what's asked of her but is ultimately sent back to her cell without winning any ground with the commander; Starbuck and Apollo demonstrate some awesome
teamwork when the virus locks them in the shooting range without oxygen; Roslin finds
out she has a month to live. Big, life-changing events that blend seamlessly into the background of the episode and provide additional texture for the need for something new to
come out of their lives. If humanity can't create, then what are they living for? For the
chance to fight another day? What happens when that's no longer enough?

The *Blackbird* story line is set against the backdrop of a more technical problem, that of
the "ghost in the machine." With *Galactica*'s systems going haywire, it's only a matter of
time before the ship becomes totally redundant, leaving the fleet wide open to a Cylon
attack. The idea of the ghost in the machine, or computers becoming almost sentient, is a
classic sci-fi trope, and one that is put to effective use in this episode. The twist here is that
while it's the Cylons that planted the "logic bomb" in the first place, it's also a Cylon who
manages to turn the virus back on its originators. The scene of the Cylon Raiders teeming
in for the kill and then suddenly stopping, dead in space, is awesome and a sorely needed
victory in the wake of the last eight episodes of emotional and physical trauma. Like the
pilots, we shout gleefully as the Cylon Raiders go down *en masse*.

We never really got to see how Chief and Boomer got together, but we do find out in
this episode that they had talked about marriage and kids, which puts Chief's decision to
break it off with her back in season 1's "Litmus" into its proper perspective. For someone
who seems to have such anger management issues, Chief's done a good job of masking his
feelings about Boomer since the break-up. He's had to subsume all those feelings into his
work, and that was going fine until Helo and Sharon came along.

The physical confrontation does seem fitting for the two characters (although somewhat more in character for Chief than for Helo, who's only shown violence once, immediately after he realized Sharon was a Cylon) but when Chief reaches for the wrench to hit
Helo with it, there's a stark moment of horror. How could it have gotten this serious, this
fast? It seems surreal, which is exactly how it *should* feel because there's nothing right
about one crew member hitting another with a wrench — especially when there are so
many more important things going on. Moore noted that the two writers of this episode
were uncomfortable with Chief's actions, but it *should* be uncomfortable. The situation is
unbearable, stifling, claustrophobic and stilted aboard *Galactica*, and no doubt
throughout the fleet; it's an uncomfortable scenario that's made all the more awkward by
the fact that not only do these two men have to share physical space, they're also having
to share the same emotional space. That Sharon is not Boomer doesn't really matter; to
Chief, she *is* Boomer. She *is* the woman he loved, the woman he feels betrayed him,

Aaron Douglas (Galen Tyrol)

• •

Date of birth: August 23, 1971

Did you know? Aaron is a *huge* ice hockey fan, and he roots for the Vancouver Canucks. He originally auditioned for the role of Apollo, and got a callback for the role of Lieutenant Gaeta. It was executive producer David Eick who pushed for him to get the role of Chief.

On his character: "I really like the Chief. If somebody said, 'Which character would you like to play?' I would probably pick him. He's a blue-collar guy who just works really hard, is especially loyal to his friends and family and to his workers. He has his flaws and his foibles but they're not borne out of any sort of narcissism. He's not an egomaniac. He's just doing the best he can and he makes mistakes and pays for them and he's repentant."

On Chief's relationship with Cally: "I think we had an inkling that it was going to happen, but I was a little sort of resistant to the inkling when it was brewing a little bit. I think Nicki [Clyne] spotted it certainly before I did, and yeah, it's kind of weird because it really is the big brother/little sister relationship and even in real life it's like big brother/little sister for Nicki and I. [...] Once you get past the pedophilic nature of it all, I think it's okay."

betrayed her people, betrayed herself. Sharon *is* that person, but she betrayed Helo, not Chief; she betrayed the Cylons, not the humans; and she did betray herself. There are so many messy, loose ends here that it wouldn't make sense if Chief *could* see his way through it. One of the strongest parts of the character arcs on *BSG* is the refusal to shy away from difficult topics, or difficult emotions.

The ghost in the machine story line seems almost to take a back seat to the *Blackbird* plot, and even though more time is spent on the virus than on the stealth ship, it's still the less developed of the two narratives. And there is a shudder of fascinated disgust when Sharon slides the conduit up her arm; the interesting thing about that scene is that throughout season 1 and up until now, Sharon's pretty much focused on how she's different from other Cylons, more human than they are. This is the first time she's put her Cylon identity to any use, shown it in any way, and it makes her unutterably alien to the rest of the crew.

Like the mythical phoenix, which is consumed in its own flames only to rise again from the ashes, all these people who have such a difficult time with the seeming futility of their lives rise again in this episode, through the act of creation. There's some wonderful symbolism in the fact that the *Blackbird* is built of scrap material bought with distilled alcohol. There's nothing new about it, except that it is new. It is a new ship, a new purpose, a new hope, that something can come of the miserable existence humanity now leads. The cyclical nature of recycled material is combined with the cyclical nature of life and death — naming the new ship after a dying president — to bring about a sense of renewal that breathes air and space into the ship.

Headcount: For the first time this season, there's no change in the headcount since the last episode. There are 47,853 survivors.

Interesting Fact: The DDG-62 engines used in the *Blackbird* are a reference to the U.S. Navy Destroyer, the *USS Fitzgerald DDG-62*; writer Bradley Thompson and science advisor Dr. Kevin Grazier toured the ship, and inserted the name as a thank-you to the crew.

Did You Notice? This is the first episode to take place only on board *Galactica* without a single scene on another planet or ship.

Laura returns the book Adama loaned her way back in the season 1 episode "Water" — it's called *Dark Day*.

The name of the new stealth ship is *Blackbird*: that's the name of the first real-life stealth aircraft, the lockhead SR-71 Blackbird.

210   Pegasus

Original air date: September 23, 2005
Written by: Anne Cofell Saunders
Directed by: Michael Rymer

The miraculous discovery of the Colonial battlestar Pegasus *leads to a reorganization of the fleet's crew and operations.*

Like the winged horse of Greek mythology, the episode of the same name has become a source of endless discussion and marks a turning point for the series. The whole premise of *Battlestar Galactica* thus far has been that there are some 47,000 humans left in the world, defended by one battlestar, and that they are being pursued by countless Cylons bent on their destruction. "Pegasus" changes that, introducing a new character who, not unlike D'Anna from "Final Cut," has a lot of influence and seems set on turning the status quo on its head. The *Pegasus* appears, and all of a sudden, *Galactica* isn't the only thing standing between the survivors of the human race and total annihilation.

From the first glimpse of her proud posture, it's obvious that Cain is a force to be reckoned with. When she arrives on *Galactica*, it's one of the first times we've seen any real formality on the ship: everyone is at attention, beaming with pride and joy that they've survived to be reunited . . . And Cain steps down and immediately creates a distance between herself and the crew — and the audience — by welcoming *Galactica* back to the fleet, intimating that the fleet is wherever *she* is. The *Pegasus is* the fleet, *is* the human race as far as she's concerned, and while the *Galactica* is a great resource in the fight against the Cylons,

What Did They Say?

When Adama informs Starbuck and Apollo that they're being transferred to the *Pegasus*, the two officers burst into loud, simultaneous yelling, making it very difficult to understand what they're saying. Here's the transcript of those few seconds:

APOLLO: We can't just let her come over here and frak up our entire roster on the eve of a major Cylon operation!

STARBUCK: That's a load of crap! She's just trying to frak with the "G" [*Galactica*] because their CAG has a stick up his ass.

the ragtag ships that have been following Adama around are just appendages, inconvenient at best, a hindrance at worst.

With the introduction of new people comes the inevitable introduction of new ideas, worldviews, and philosophies — and none of these seems particularly copasetic with *Galactica*'s own worldview. One of the most enduring virtues that we've come to rely on throughout the series is that, no matter what, Adama and Roslin are always trying to do what's best — and, despite some hiccups, their ultimate goal is to make sure that the human race can survive. It's not clear what Cain's goal is in this episode, except that she seems focused on the destruction of the Cylons, no matter what the cost. It's unsettling in part because there are shades of Adama in Cain — before the attacks, he was just as ambitious (as we saw from Tigh's flashbacks in "Scattered"), and when the Cylons first attacked, he wanted nothing more than to lead an attack against them. It wasn't until Roslin pointed out that the human race's survival depended on *him*, on his acceptance of defeat, that he changed his mind. His personal journey started there, and it's one that, despite all her victories in the field, Cain has not yet begun.

One of the hardest things about this episode is that Cain is right about Adama. She takes one look at the logs, at Adama and Roslin, at *Galactica*'s crew and equipment, and sees the whole thing. She sees Adama's flaws, and she's not going to hide behind politics or diplomacy — she wants the best crew possible to go after the Cylons. In that sense, "Pegasus" and "Final Cut" are two sides of the same coin: both take a look at *Galactica* from a different point of view — one from a civilian, the other a military perspective. It's hard not to wince throughout "Pegasus" as we note the differences between Cain's ship and Adama's — no worn-down boxing bags for the *Pegasus* ("Final Cut"). The differences serve to make both Adama and viewers feel like the fleet is on trial and that *Galactica*'s actions must be justified. Here again the importance of context is an essential element.

Adama is probably the person most affected by Cain's arrival, but he gives up his position as commander of the fleet graciously and gracefully. He's ambiguous about giving

Humanism

In "Black Market" we saw one of the worst facets of humanity: materialism. Why did that episode make us grit our teeth and hate ourselves so much? Because *materialism* stands in stark contrast to *humanism*, and humanism is something that *BSG* works as hard to reimagine as it does the characters — it's an ideal that is central to *BSG*.

Although it seems hard to believe that a television show about the aftermath of an apocalypse could have something as uplifting and hopeful as humanism in it, when we look at what makes *BSG* such a spine-tingling, gut-wrenching, hand-twisting rollercoaster, that's what we find. What is humanism? Loosely, it's a way of looking at the world — and when you're a humanist, all things human are paramount. Although that sort of seems self-evident to us (well duh, of course it's about humans!), the term didn't actually start to get used until some time in the eighteenth century, by German scholars. They used the term to refer to a set of scholastic principals that started up about 300 years before them, in the fifteenth century. Those principles were used to define the original "Renaissance man" — the guy who could win an honor swordfight while recounting the philosophical history of mankind in grammatically correct sentences without breaking a sweat — sound like a Lee Adama we know? And the Renaissance man was actually striving to be an ideal from his past — the Greek model.

The Greek model of *humanitas* was based in virtue — physical, mental, spiritual, and political. For the Greeks, and later the Renaissance, to fulfill your "humanity" was to embrace an astonishing number of virtues; compassion, empathy, honor, eloquence, correct judgment, self-reflection. Most importantly, the person possessing true *humanitas* was not a passive observer who stood on the sidelines but an active member of the community — sound like a William Adama we know? And, while humanism begins within one person, its aim is to map this philosophy onto civilization as a whole — from one balanced individual to a society of balanced individuals — sound like a Laura Roslin we know?

up the responsibility, because on the one hand, being the only military commander in a mission to save the human race is just about the heaviest burden he could ever have shouldered, and having someone above him to rely on means that he can hand just a little of his burden over. On the other hand, he's sweated blood to see the fleet through the last six months, and he can't help but be disappointed that he's not going to be responsible for them anymore.

One of the major differences between *Galactica* and *Pegasus* is their philosophy regarding how to treat Cylons. This is the first appearance of Pegasus-Six, a very different version of Six, who's been raped and tortured since the day she was discovered as a Cylon. So while Cain's actions until this point have been more or less justified — she's a higher rank than Adama, the fleet is by all rights hers to command — by necessity and military protocol, the violence against Gina she condones is unjustifiable. Even though Gina is a Cylon and has betrayed humanity and Cain herself, it's still difficult to see her insensible on the floor. Like a lot of things about the show, this scene rings particularly true in light of the real-life issues surrounding the Iraqi prison Abu Ghraib, where serious allegations were made against U.S. military personnel regarding their treatment of prisoners. This scene is a harsh reminder of the real-life politics that inform the show as a whole, and the disgust we feel is mirrored by Cally and the rest of the female crew who get up and leave when the *Pegasus* crew starts talking about the fun they've had raping Gina. Whether or not Cally's reaction is due to her own near-rape in season 1's "Bastille Day" is left up to the viewer to decide.

The end of the episode is brutal: it was somehow easier to watch Cally kill Boomer than it is to see Thorne rape Sharon in "Pegasus." It's a horrific scene, callous and unflinchingly disturbing, and it doesn't feel like it belongs on the *Galactica*. The *Pegasus* might have brought hope, resources, and relief, but it's also brought suffering, ethical quandaries, and a lot of pain.

Headcount: With *Pegasus*'s arrival, the survivor headcount reaches 49,605; the number hasn't been that high since the very first episode of season 1, "33," which starts out with 50,298 survivors.

Are You There, God? It's Me, Gaius. Gaius is, ironically, learning to embrace his humanity by bonding with a Cylon. Granted, that's nothing new, since he's been doing that since the miniseries (Six is gradually teaching him to love — and how hilarious is it that he loves someone who only exists in his own mind?) but in "Pegasus" he reaches out in a new, physical way, gradually shifting toward the Cylon cause.

All of This Has Happened Before: In Greek mythology, the Pegasus was a winged horse that was born of the blood of Medusa when she was beheaded by the hero Perseus. With a bridle given to him by the goddess Athena, the hero Bellerophon tamed the horse and rode him into battle against the fire-breathing hybrid monster, Chimera. When Bellerophon was unseated, killed, or lamed (depending on which version of the myth you read), Pegasus became a constellation and servant to the king of the gods, Zeus. Over the years, Pegasus has been viewed as a metaphor for the immortality of the soul, as well as a symbol of poetic inspiration.

Interesting Fact: Although the Number Six model being held prisoner on *Pegasus* isn't named in this episode, she's officially known as Gina, in a play on the acronym GINO — "*Galactica* In Name Only," which is used by fans of the original series who were opposed to the reimagined one.

Michelle Forbes as Admiral Helena
Cain (CAROLE SEGAL/© SCI-FI/
COURTESY: EVERETT COLLECTION)

Grace Park had this to say in an interview, "I think one of the funniest things that I can remember, after the rape scene, even though it sounds pretty morbid, but we'd done it so many times . . . Lt. Thorne always had to pull down my pants. I was wearing something underneath, but still, when we were done, I said, 'Now that we're done here, turn around and drop your pants.' And I was joking, but he said, 'Sure,' and he turned around, and dropped his pants. So I saw his butt, too. I thought that was pretty funny. Then we shook hands, and we said, 'thanks.'"

Did You Notice? Admiral Cain dismisses the president, saying to Adama, "The secretary of education?" This is a direct echo of Adama's own words to Apollo in the miniseries: "You're talking about the secretary of education! We're in the middle of a war, and you're taking orders from a schoolteacher?" When Adama says in *Pegasus* that Roslin has come a long way, it's clear he realizes that his own journey has been just as long and life-changing.

Starbuck says that Taylor's mission plan "sucks." She called Colonel Tigh on the exact same thing when he also devised a mission plan that counted on the Cylons ignoring an obvious blind spot. That was in season 1's "Hand of God."

When Starbuck gets grounded from the reconnaissance mission during the *Pegasus* pilots' briefing, she mouths "son of a bitch" towards Captain Taylor.

Classic *Battlestar Galactica*: This episode is based on an original *Battlestar Galactica* two-parter, "The Living Legend," in which the *Pegasus* was also recovered. In the original version, Commander Cain was a male character played by Lloyd Bridges.

Original air date: January 6, 2006
Written by: Michael Rymer
Directed by: Michael Rymer

With Chief and Helo sentenced to death, tensions mount between Pegasus *and* Galactica.

"What the frak is going on?" Starbuck's message to Apollo sums up the beginning of "Resurrection Ship, Part 1," which opens *in media res*. This first part starts with a battle sequence, but it's not the usual Cylons versus humans battle we've come to expect — rather, it's a highly tense cold war between *Pegasus* and *Galactica*. The fact that not a single shot is fired just makes the tension all the more tightly coiled; when Kat yells to be allowed to fire on *Pegasus's* Vipers, she sounds like she's being physically restrained and is struggling to break free. It's total chaos out there — there are dozens of crafts weaving in and out with breathless speed, with no one sure exactly what's going on — and they (and we) are left wondering how it came so quickly to this.

"Resurrection Ship, Part 1" starts out with wide, almost panoramic shots of the vast battle scene, but it ends on a series of close-ups on Adama, Cain, and Starbuck. The very different quality of shots demonstrates the episode's move from generalized hostility to a more focused, pointed tension that's concentrated between the two battlestar leaders. Cain continues to be an invasive presence in the fleet, and the revelation that she went so far as to shoot civilians who refused to join her ship doesn't cause surprise so much as sorrow.

The thing is, it's hard to really dislike Cain. That's not to say that her actions were justified — but they make a certain sense when placed in the context of a character who's ambitious, proud, enraged at the destruction of her home and her species, and just trying to fight back. Without Roslin's influence, would Adama have made the same choices as Cain did? In a 2006 interview, Michelle Forbes (Cain) said, "She's lost perspective. People ask, 'Is she insane? Is she psychotic?' I hope that's not how she came across because that was never the intention. I think some individuals can appear to be that way, but this is a woman who did what she had to do in order to survive during some very brutal conflicts. Along the way, Cain lost her sense of judgment as well as her sense of reason and rationale." Cain's interactions with Starbuck are a direct representation of how we feel toward the admiral. Kara is all set to dislike her, to do her standard rebellion act, but Cain gets to her: Cain provides Starbuck with something she's been lacking — a sense of purpose. It's quite possible that Cain has looked over Starbuck's file, found out some of what happened back on Caprica, learned that she has been trying to get Adama and Roslin to go back to Caprica to rescue Anders and his group — and it's quite possible that Cain has taken that information and is using it to manipulate Starbuck. Whether or not she's sincere, Cain offers a tangible goal and a hope that one day the fleet *can* win back their homes.

The scenes between Kara and Cain are electric. They're both such strong characters, and they seem to have a real meeting of the minds. Physically, they're nothing alike, but their

Nice tattoo, Katee

posture speaks to a tightly bound sense of frustrated anger that seeps through their every word. And gradually, scene by scene, the two women start to *respect* and *like* each other.

At the opposite end of the spectrum is the interaction between Cain and Gina. There is neither respect nor fondness between these two. Cain is downright cruel, taking every opportunity to humiliate Gina both verbally and physically; it's not hard to see where Thorne got his orders from regarding the treatment of Cylon prisoners.

The existence of the resurrection ship changes the landscape of the fight against the Cylons. Without it, they're no more powerful than humans, leaving them prey to the same fears and vulnerabilities that any mortal has. The resurrection ship is also a very postmodern update of the idea of resurrection: just like the Cylons are "updates" (or ancestors, depending on who you ask) of humanity, so too is the resurrection ship their adaptation of resurrection, moving the resurrection out of the spiritual and into the physical. And it's just like the Cylons, too, to take something so emotionally (and spiritually) charged, and turn it into a mechanical, automated learning experience — just like they did with reproduction in "The Farm."

Stuck in a prison cell, Helo and Chief don't have much choice but to air their concerns. Their scene is the first chance we've had to find out how Helo feels about what's going on his life: "You think I don't wonder if I'm losing my frakking mind? I'm in love a woman I know isn't a woman. I'm having a baby that's, what, half machine?" It seems like Chief has moved on, however, and gone through the five stages of grief regarding his relationship with Sharon: denial (refusing to believe she was a Cylon); anger (leading to his breakup with her and later his terrible anger at her when they are in the same brig cell); bargaining (heartbroken but still trying to get Adama to go lightly on Cally); depression (in the cell with nothing to do but think about everything that's gone wrong); and finally this final stage, acceptance.

Roslin is another character who's come a long way since the miniseries. Gone is the woman who trembled as she vowed to lead the people of the Colonies; in her stead is the woman who will now turn to assassination as the only way for the human race to survive. "Has the whole world gone mad?" Adama wonders when Roslin first tells him what has to be done. Roslin would be only human to feel that the appearance of the resurrection ship is cruelly ironic when she is so close to dying; but the very nearness of her death pushes her to consider more extreme solutions to the fleet's problems. She needs to guarantee them every chance of successfully finding Earth; and she can't do that if Cain is still around.

The end of this episode is particularly interesting because no one in the scene is innocent: Adama is both victim of Cain's plot and mastermind of his own plot (and vice versa); and Starbuck is being ordered to kill Cain — but if she complies, she'll be an assassin (and the same for Fisk). The intercutting shots allow us to see the whole situation from each person's perspective — victims and assassins both — building to a moment of anticipation that doesn't let go until the end of Part 2.

Headcount: There are 49,604 survivors, one down from last week to account for Thorne's murder in "Pegasus."

Interesting Fact: If you've noticed that there haven't been many scenes shot at Gaius's house on Caprica, there's a good reason for that. Ronald Moore explains that, "[Baltar's house] is on a narrow, windy road that you have to get all the equipment in and out of, so that was kind of a pain in the ass. And then the neighbors were getting tired of it."

Did You Notice? Admiral Cain tells Fisk that he is to execute Adama if she says the words, "Case Orange." That's not the first time we've heard those code words: back in the miniseries, an official Colonial broadcast instructed all government members to go to Case Orange.

In the same vein, the code word chosen by Adama, "downfall," is a reference to a 2004 movie by the same name that focuses on Hitler's final days. It was also a code word used by U.S. Navy to indicate a plan for the occupation of Japanese islands.

So Say We All: ADAMA: What can I get you?

ROSLIN: A new body. Perhaps one of those young Cylon models from the resurrection ship.

ADAMA: I can't see you as a blonde.

ROSLIN: You'd be surprised.

212   Resurrection Ship, Part 2

Original air date: January 13, 2006
Written by: Michael Rymer, Ronald Moore
Directed by: Michael Rymer

Gaius bonds with the Number Six model on Pegasus; *Helo and Chief wait to be executed; Adama and Cain plot to assassinate each other.*

Forty-eight hours ago, chaos broke out; unlike most battles, we're not in any doubt as to how the fight against the Cylon resurrection ship is going to end, because Lee, adrift in space, both opens this second half of the two-parter and serves as leitmotif to the episode. When Lee first appears, floating in a lake in an undisclosed location, the feeling that surrounds him is one of peacefulness and quiet; when reality opens up before him once again, it's not a gentle fade but an abrupt shift, sudden in a way that a near-death experience must be. Throughout the series, water is used in various symbolic ways; here, its symbolism combines with Lee's cruciform position to create an air of sacrifice and death, and a sense of foreboding that pervades the entire episode.

Usually, in television fare that has battles of any kind — much less big space battles of good versus evil — the focus is on the battle, but that's not the case in "Resurrection Ship, Part 2." The actual physical battle is over a little more than halfway through the episode, and frames rather than drives the narrative. The Cylon versus human framing narrative is also seen in microcosm in the relationship between Cain and the Cylon captive Gina. In a sense, this episode is a great way to resurrect one of our oldest stories — the first murder committed according to the Bible — from a new perspective. Cain *is* Gina's keeper — not only because the Cylon is her prisoner, but also because Gina has made connections to the crew, to humanity, by living among them. The connection Gina has forged — a *human* connection — also raises the question of responsibility. Until she was discovered, Gina was "human" — and now what, she gets her humanity taken away? Can we do that in good conscience? Cain clearly thinks that we can; Gaius is not so sure.

Back in season 1, Gaius surreptitiously urged Boomer to go ahead with her plan to kill herself. In a direct counterpoint to that scene, Gaius is here confronted by someone who openly wishes her life to end — and he can't take that step. He just can't kill her — partly because she looks like the Six he was in love with on Caprica, and partly because Gaius isn't that kind of man. He shot Crashdown in "Valley of Darkness" but that was an action taken in extreme circumstances; outside the heat of the moment, he freezes — has a change of heart, perhaps, recognizing the value of life above all else? More than any other character, Gaius is *the* destroyer of humanity, but he's also been given the role of judge and executioner over the Cylons in the fleet, too — Boomer, Shelley, Gina, Sharon. Watching him in this scene, we can almost believe that he's changed, that he actually believes in Gina and wants her to live, wants to love her. It's the most genuine feeling he's ever had for another life-form, and it's fascinating to see him struggle with the emotions of selflessness, pity, and love, and for once, *for once*, not take the easy way out. How easy would it have been for him to shoot Gina? Not a single person on the fleet would have batted an eyelid at her death. Instead, Gaius chooses the hard route: life and love.

On the other hand, he *hasn't* really changed, because the connection he makes with Gina is based on a lie. After all, recycling stories is something that humanity is good at. Gaius takes the heartfelt story Six told him in Part 1 — a story told in an intimate setting, with Six lying naked on the bed she shared with Gaius on Caprica, and a story that places her in an emotionally vulnerable position — and resurrects it, bringing it to life to manipulate Gina into trusting him.

Floating in space, with a godlike view, Lee in some ways stands in for the viewer, watching the paradoxically beautiful scene of destruction that's being wrought in front of him. For the last couple of episodes, Lee's been at something of a loose end: he was demoted to Raptor pilot, transferred to an unknown ship with colleagues he doesn't know

Resurrection

The belief that the soul or some other part of ourselves continues beyond this life has been with us a long long time. Ancient Greeks were sure that there was a resurrection of what they termed the soul, but it wasn't until the Christians came along that the idea of the body along with the soul started to become part of the idea of resurrection (although both Islam and Zoroastrianism have doctrines of resurrection as well). For Christians, from the Book of Revelation onwards, there has been some sense that, once we die, we will be reborn in one form or another, and we will continue on. Almost all doctrines of resurrection involve the body dying, then being resurrected after some form of judgment by a deity.

The idea was cemented with the resurrection of Christ, whose bodily resurrection after three days is celebrated during Easter, which suggested that the corporeal body as well as the spirit could overcome the things Christians feared and fought the most — sin, death, and the Devil himself. A typical Easter celebration usually includes feasting of some kind, perhaps to symbolically celebrate the body itself by feeding it. In "Resurrection Ship" we see resurrection in the form of the Cylons in their nutrient bath, a sort of machine feast that combines nutrients for the body as well as nutrients for the mind — the downloaded thoughts of the previous life. Unlike any of the other doctrines of resurrection however, the Cylons do not go through a period of judgment. Although the human Cylon models do refer to God often, they do not ascribe their ability to move from one body to another after death as part of their religion — it's just a cool thing they can do that makes them superior.

and doesn't trust, and he's been asked to help assassinate the legitimate leader of the fleet. There's no way that would go down well with him, as he is a military man. And for the last six months, he's witnessed countless deaths, endless battles; they have all been living a surreal existence — and he's tired. He's tired of struggling with the world, with the Cylons, with his father, with Kara — he just wants it to end. The peacefulness of the lake he imagines himself floating in pulls us into the same mind frame. If Admiral Cain is evil and to be destroyed, and Gina is sympathetic and to be rescued, then the whole world really *has* gone mad, as Adama said in the previous episode.

Headcount: No losses since the first part of the two-parter — there are still 49,604 people in the fleet.

All of This Has Happened Before: In the Bible, Cain killed his brother, Abel, and was punished by God to wander the Earth until Judgment Day. "Resurrection Ship, Part 2" turns that anecdote on its head not only by having the main players in this scene be female, but more importantly by killing Cain — and having Gina, a prisoner that Cain allowed to be raped and tortured, kill her. In all the ways that count, "Resurrection Ship, Part 2" is Admiral Cain's Judgment Day.

Interesting Fact: Apollo watching the battle while drifting in outer space is based on a real-life event from World War II. On June 4, 1942, during the Battle of Midway, Ensign George Gay of the U.S. Navy was shot down during an attack on a Japanese carrier force. He survived the crash, and, while swimming in the ocean, witnessed the dive bombing that destroyed three of the four carriers. He was the only survivor from his squadron.

What's In a Name? The name "Starbuck" comes from the classic Herman Melville novel, *Moby Dick*, which was first published in 1851. In the book, Starbuck is the first mate on the ship *Pequod*, and the only character who opposes the captain's ardor to capture the great white whale he's been obsessively hunting. Starbuck believes that the ship's mission should be to gather whale oil and return safely home — very much like *BSG*'s Starbuck, who has wanted only to return to Caprica, her home, to rescue the resistance group she met earlier in the season. Another similarity lies in the fact that, at one point in the novel, Melville's Starbuck considers shooting the captain to ensure the crew's safety: in this episode, Starbuck has been ordered to shoot Admiral Adama to ensure the safety of the fleet and the survival of the human race. Both in the novel and in the series, the character of Starbuck is reluctant to obey the orders handed down by superior officers, but in the end, they both comply.

Did You Notice? This episode features one of the few sequences where we see the pilots and marines actually prepare for a mission — get dressed, put their casual clothes away, psych themselves up. The scene is used to great effect to increase the tension and point to the fact that these are military officers who are being asked to put their lives on the line — and then come back and shoot a commanding officer.

"Suicide is a sin." Gina's words to Gaius aboard the *Pegasus* echo Gaius's own question to Six in season 1's "Tigh Me Up, Tigh Me Down" where he forlornly wonders if suicide is really a sin, which he says while looking over the multitude of blood samples he has to test.

The look of surprise on Mary McDonnell's face when Adama kisses Roslin at the end of the episode is genuine: the kiss was improvised by Edward James Olmos.

213   Epiphanies

Original air date: January 20, 2006
Written by: Joel Anderson Thompson
Directed by: Rod Hardy

A faction that wants to make peace with the Cylons makes its voice heard.

Battlestar Galactica is often concerned with presenting "real" moments, those which seem to be incommunicable. By its very nature, an epiphany is not communicable, since it is the revelation of knowledge that is suprahuman; for a visual medium like TV, demonstrating the existence of not one but several epiphanies poses a real challenge. This episode deals with the issue by setting up a series of mute scenes, without dialogue, and relying on the force of the idea to indicate the epiphany. One such moment is Roslin's horrified gesture towards Gaius when she awakens, filled with the knowledge of his betrayal, her epiphany pointed out to us by her extended finger.

"Epiphanies" is a blend of harsh realism and dreamlike sequences, with color and camera movements adapting to the feel of each. Hazy scenes of Caprica, which appears like an oasis in the desert, replete with water, beauty, and light, intersect with gritty scenes of real life in the postapocalyptic world: political factions setting off bombs, and the decision to abort Sharon's baby before it comes to term. The outright violence of those more realistic scenes is tempered by the gentleness of the Caprica scenes, and the difference is unsettling, as if to say, look at what the world has come to. One scene in particular stands out in terms of its brutality: when Helo tells Sharon that their baby is to be aborted, Sharon displays almost animal-like behavior, throwing herself against the plexiglass wall and howling with rage and fear. Her grief rends the heart as it rends her skin, and she literally sheds her blood in despair over her child's fate. Her reaction is partly individual: this is *her baby* and she wants it to live (in fact, the scene is a physical reminder of Roslin's analytical statement "she wants her baby to live" in "Home, Part 1"). It is also partly collective: the Cylons have tried for so long to reproduce naturally, and her and Helo's child is the first sign that perhaps the Cylons are capable of following God's command to reproduce, are capable of having love and family. The baby stands in for hope of reconciliation between the two

Sharon and Helo share one of many traumatic moments in their relationship (CAROLE SEGAL/© SCI-FI/ COURTESY: EVERETT COLLECTION)

races, too, and while Roslin's reasoning is sound, it's still an emotional issue.

"Epiphanies" is a slow return to normalcy after the political, emotional, and physical upheaval of "Pegasus" and the "Resurrection Ship" two-parter. In classic sci-fi style, Roslin is miraculously cured, and the Cylon/human baby is given a reprieve, similar to the one granted to Helo and Chief in the previous episode, and Roslin's own reprieve. When Roslin recovers, she's full of vim and vigor, prompting Adama to grin, "That's my girl," as she immediately takes on the leader of Demand Peace. Her renewed lease on life will be important in the next episode, too, and will lead Fisk to ask Gaius if the president is "always so 'right in your face.'" Her epiphany serves to remind her that she's not there to take the easy route or make friends — she's president of the Colonies to make a difference and to make sure things run as smoothly as they can.

It's interesting that virtually all the epiphanies in this episode can be seen as negative, as if the events depicted were drawing back curtains and revealing dark truths to each of the characters. One of the most climactic moments of the episode (which is filled with climactic moments) belongs to Gaius, who, surrounded by an air of victory, having saved Sharon's baby *and* the president — garnering certain goodwill for the foreseeable future — sees his reality turned upside down by Roslin's letter of succession. The letter is nice, but it does reveal one of Gaius's deepest flaws: his lack of compassion for others. Unlike Roslin's, or Gina's, Gaius's moment of epiphany is cut short, and we are right alongside him, waiting in suspenseful hope that he will take the tools Roslin has presented to him and use them to become the person we want him to be — to connect to the world around him. And we really, really want him to. We want him to back away from all the darkness of paranoia and suffering that he seems to have fallen into; to make sense of his genius in moral terms that we can applaud. It never happens, though, because Gaius's personality, his ego, his pride, and his intellect, won't allow him to make that leap. What he experiences is *not* an epiphany: he doesn't even react like Roslin or Gina, who can only gesture toward their respective revelations. In true Gaius style, Baltar immediately voices his every bitter, angry, disappointed, and deceived thought. His universe, focused as it has been on self-preservation, built on the foundations of his accomplishments, his genius, and his desires, is stripped bare; his immediate reaction is vengeful, and it is clear by the end of his scene that Gaius just can't allow himself an epiphany. He is stuck within himself, his own frame of reference and reality. But it's that moment just before he chooses not to reach toward the unknowable (or is manipulated by Six into not doing it) that is the reason he remains an empathetic character. It's the "so close" moment that, ironically, also reveals his deepest sympathy as a human being.

Headcount: The whiteboard shows 49,598 survivors, down by 6 from "Resurrection Ship." Cain and the marine killed by Gina account for two of the dead; we can only assume that the rest were lost in the battle against the Cylon resurrection ship.

Did You Notice? "The interesting thing about being president is that you don't have to explain yourself to anyone." Roslin repeats President Adar's words from earlier in the episode — and also her own words from earlier in the series. In the season 1 episode "Flesh and Bone," Roslin quoted Adar, saying, "President Adar once said that the interesting thing about being a president is that you don't have to explain yourself to anyone." It's also a near-direct quote from Bob Woodward's book *Bush at War*, wherein real-life U.S. President George W. Bush is quoted as saying, "I do not need to explain why I say things. That's the interesting thing about being the president."

The manifestos found in Asha Janik's quarters feature a picture of a human either pleading or flying, inside a circle. Tigh quotes one of the propaganda pieces: "Do not be afraid, we are not terrorists, but we will not sit back while Adama's war machine continues to press us into cruel and futile conflict." Other content from the pamphlet includes: "Demand peace: a manifesto to negotiate an end to the slaughter. Demand peace [. . .] the war. The answer to our suffering lies in negotiating a peace. This is our cause. This is your cause. Commander Adama would have you believe that he will save us. But can one man claim to save the future of all mankind? Clearly the task is too great for a warrior. It demands the perspective of a statesman and a historian. In short a democratic council. Is this what we have? Despite lip service to the processes of democracy the truth is [. . .] We believe:

Only open dialogue will save mankind.

The military is the servant, not the master, of the fleet.

The Cylons will respond to reasonable dialogue.

Democracy is the key to responsible decision-making for the future of mankind.

Man and Cylon can co-exist together in peace.

We are at the dawn of a new beginning for mankind.

The enemies of peace are the enemies of mankind.

. . . Demand peace."

If you wondered how no one could have noticed Gina's resemblance to the Cylon model Six, whose picture has been shown all over the fleet, you're not alone. Moore said, "This is a push that nobody recognizes her with the glasses, it's sort of the Clark Kent disguise of the Cylons. [...] Somehow I talked myself into believing that no one would recognize Gina if we did her hair differently and put glasses on her. But you'd have to be a moron not to realize that that's the Cylon."

214   Black Market

Original air date: January 27, 2006
Written by: Mark Verheiden
Directed by: Michael Rymer, James Head

Apollo investigates a black market in the fleet.

"Did you really expect some utopian society to rise from the ashes?" Zarek asks Lee incredulously. He's referring here to the phoenix, the mythological bird from ancient Egypt, which was said to live no less than 500 years and which, at the end of its life, built a nest and set itself and the nest on fire, a myth already alluded to in "Flight of the Phoenix." From the fiery ashes rose a new phoenix — ugly but alive, vital. The phoenix was associated with the idea of immortality. Life on the Colonies has been seen through glimpses only, and although there's been evidence of conflict (the teachers' strike seen in "Epiphanies," for instance) pre-apocalypse Colonial life seems pretty incredible compared to the survivors' current lifestyle.

"Black Market" seems to point to the idea that Lee is a wandering utopian, continuing the aimless drifting that he began in "Resurrection Ship, Part 2" and remembering all his own unrealized potential. While "Epiphanies" showed Roslin before the attack — a political figure but also a woman with failing health and a failing relationship — "Black Market" gives us an idea of what lies behind Lee's façade as a pilot and as a son. Specifically, the episode introduces Lee's previous love interest — a fiancée we assume by the ring on her finger. The attacks are assumed to have occurred soon after the confrontation we see in the flashback, killing her. The physical and symbolic images of love, hope, and a potential future haunt Lee throughout "Black Market," and are also echoed in the next episode, "Scar," in which Lee admits to Kara that he did, eventually, want to have a wife and family.

What has actually risen from the ashes of the Colonies is a dysfunctional, dystopian society that reflects the hard realities of humanity's existence. The government operates from a spaceship, the entire human race is stuck in tin cans working their long, strange way to what is considered by many a planet that doesn't exist, and from the detritus of their old lives, each person has to recreate meaning. Lee is the epitome of that change, having gone from a loving, committed relationship to an apparently long-standing relationship with a prostitute.

In Islamic mythology, the phoenix was identified with the "anqa," a huge bird that was created perfect by God only to be infected with a plague and die. The parallels between that symbolism and pre-apocalyptic Colonial society are remarkable, and the analogy ties directly into what Six told Gaius in "Fragged": "[God] turned His back on man and the false gods he worshiped." It also echoes the idea that has been thrown around amongst the crew that perhaps humanity was destroyed simply because it didn't deserve to

Jamie, rough and rugged
(ALBERT L. ORTEGA)

survive. "One has to be worthy of surviving," Adama told Starbuck in "Resurrection Ship." "Black Market" plays directly into the idea that, as a species, humans are destined to "stand in the mud," because it showcases the worst of what humanity has to offer: withholding food and antibiotics for profit, child prostitution, and murder. *BSG* generally does a great job of pointing to real societal issues and looking at them in very different ways, but the child prostitution seems like a cheap way to make the situation seem *bad*.

This episode adds texture to Lee's feeling of displacement and non-belonging, and a great many characters don't appear at all. Starbuck, Sharon, Helo, Chief, Cally, Gaeta, who are all people with whom Lee interacts on a more or less regular basis, are all conspicuously absent, adding to the isolation that's enveloped the character since his space walk two episodes back.

"Black Market" is the first reappearance of the Lee/Dee thread since "Resistance." Dee once again says what needs to be said — so often, potential is thwarted by simple lack of communication, and if there are two people on the ship who firmly enact the principle of communication, it's Lee and Dee. In that sense, it seems fitting that they should be drawn to each other — no one else demonstrates the same honesty or forthrightness. That compatibility isn't enough to mask the fact that we just haven't seen enough of them to believe in their relationship yet.

The *Prometheus* is discovered to be the hub of the black market trade. In Greek mythology, Prometheus was a renowned trickster and the god of fire. His name was said to mean "forethinker." There are two main myths related to Prometheus: the first is that Zeus, having been tricked by Prometheus into accepting an unworthy sacrifice, hid fire from man. Prometheus stole it and gave it back to humankind, which prompted Zeus to create Pandora — who eventually opened a box, setting evil, toil, and disease loose upon the

Earth. Hope alone remained inside the box. In the second myth, Zeus punished Prometheus by binding him to the top of a mountain. There, an eagle was sent to eat his liver, which regenerated every day. Just as the mythological figure is said to have brought civilization (through the gift of fire) to the world, so too does the black market, which is operated by Phelan — at least until Apollo kills him — claim to provide an essential service to the fleet. And the truth of the matter is that every society has a black market, because in every society, there is need, and someone who wants to profit from that need. There *is* no utopia outside of literature — and even literary utopias are generally satirical rather than realistic in nature. The very etymology (utopia means both "no place" and "good place") makes it a myth, a projection of unrealized potential.

Headcount: There are 49,597 survivors in this episode, a net loss of one. That's a little odd considering the suicide bombing on the *Daru Mozu* in "Epiphanies" — where you can actually see at least two bodies being blasted into space and where Adama says straight out, "People are dead." However, we can assume that there are some births occurring throughout the fleet, making up the difference.

Interesting Fact: When Jamie Bamber was first introduced to the idea of the reimagined *BSG*, he was less than enthusiastic. He said, **"When I first read the script, my heart sank when I saw the title. [...] If it was done well the first time, why do it again? But then there was a manifesto that Ron [Moore] and David [Eick] had come up with at the beginning that was a mission statement about what we are and what we are not. And it was all about reinventing sci-fi on TV and bringing the drama out and losing the space opera aspect. Having real people and real situations. Making it look as much like our world as we possibly can, not as different as we possibly can."**

Did You Notice? This is the third episode of the series to use the "flash forward" technique, coming on the heels of "Resurrection Ship, Part 2," and season 1's "Act of Contrition."

Dee asks Apollo for permission to "speak frankly"; she asked Adama the exact same thing earlier in the season, in "Home, Part 1." Neither Lee nor Adama liked what she had to say.

Classic *Battlestar Galactica*: The idea of Lee being involved with a prostitute has its origins in the original series, which featured a character named Cassiopeia (played by Laurette Spang) who was a prostitute — or a socialator, as prostitutes were known in the original series. She eventually became Starbuck's girlfriend on *Galactica*.

So Say We All: PHELAN: It's hard to find the moral high ground when we're all standing in the mud.

215   Scar

Original air date: February 3, 2006
Written by: David Weddle, Bradley Thompson
Directed by: Michael Nankin

The competition between Kat and Starbuck comes to a head as the exhausted pilots try to take down a Raider they've named Scar.

Scars come in many shapes and sizes, and they're not all physical — some of the deepest scars are emotional. This episode's title provides an easy entry into its various narratives, and the episode itself is beautiful in a really sad, ragged way. "Scar" allows Starbuck to have her own epiphany, in the same way as Roslin and Lee were allowed theirs in "Epiphanies" and "Black Market," respectively, but her epiphany unfolds in some seriously messed up ways. In 2006, Katee Sackhoff explained, "I kept saying to our producers, 'Starbuck would never do this,' and they'd say, 'Yes, she would. At some point if she can't solve her problems on her own, she's going to turn to drink, drugs, something to numb the pain.'"

"Scar" is painful to watch at times because Kat is so frakking obnoxious throughout the episode; she's in Starbuck's face the entire time, and the most annoying part is that she's right about Starbuck's behavior. Kara *is* falling down on the job, she's in freefall, and she can't figure out where her life is going — or if, like Lee, she even wants it to go anywhere. If the beginning of season 2 was hard going for Adama and Tigh, then the second half of the season is equally hard for Apollo and Starbuck, when the pressure of the last six months seems to collapse in on them all at once.

The first scene in the pilots' lounge immediately sets up the uncomfortable sense that something isn't quite right with Starbuck. She's always been an extroverted, social person, obviously popular amongst the pilots, but here she stumbles around drunk, and there's no mistaking the pity and mockery in the onlookers' eyes. As a hero, Kara is meant to perform courageous deeds, stand proud and dignified, and embody a certain professionalism that the other pilots look for in her and that they emulate; her behavior in the lounge shows none of this, and that's partly the reason that Kat is so bitter about her. Paradoxically, by giving up on the status of hero and allowing Kat to take the "glory," Starbuck is able to regain her hero status.

When Kat first came to *Galactica*, she was a nugget who had barely set foot inside a cockpit; Starbuck is infamous throughout the fleet for her combined recklessness and skill as a Viper pilot. Over the last season, Kat's flown fast and hard, seen her friends and colleagues die, and become a better pilot for her mistakes.

Kat is the human equivalent to Scar: just as Scar has learned from its many deaths and resurrections, so too has Kat learned from the pilots whose deaths have paved the way for her. It's a terrible but also terribly effective analogy. Starbuck was her teacher, but Kat has reached a point where she doesn't feel she needs any further training — certainly not from Starbuck, who's lost everything but her bravura.

Another thing "Scar" and "Black Market" establish is a contrast between the different ways to deal with loss, pain, anger, and memory. How does the memory of Gianne haunt Lee as compared to how the memory of Anders haunts Starbuck? Both characters turn to sex to dull the pain, but while Lee can't help but form an attachment, even to someone he's paying to spend time with, Starbuck angrily rejects any form of relationship, even with someone she does love. When she leans forward to kiss Lee, it's immediately messy and uncomfortable,

What's In a Call Sign?

Nicknames, or call signs, for the pilots that we see on *Battlestar Galactica* have a diverse history, but there are some commonalities. A popular Web site on the F-16 fighter jet notes that the most common way to get a call sign is to "do something stupid or have it fit with your last name," but that's not the only way. Call signs (a famous movie example is Tom Cruise's character in *Top Gun*, whose call sign was Maverick) can also be derived from a pilot's actions, or their demeanor. A call sign is almost always "gifted" to the pilot by members of their squadron or sometimes an instructor or leader. Call signs can also change over time. A new pilot might be designated "Probie" (short for "probation") for instance, but later on graduate to a more heroic call sign (although sometimes they get worse, depending on the pilot's actions).

In *BSG*, call signs are also used to designate a pilot's ethics or morality. In the original series, Apollo and Starbuck were the actual names of the characters, but in the reimagined series, they have been changed to call signs. Lee Adama's character is very much like his call sign, Apollo, especially in the first season as the show was shaping out his character. Lee was noble, virtuous, courageous, loyal, and wanted to bring people together — a sort of heal-all-wounds approach. These are all aspects of the god Apollo. And Kara Thrace's call sign Starbuck is a great fit for her practical, pragmatic, in-your-face way of life, not to mention her gambling penchant . . . (Buck, a dollar . . . get it?)

Sharon Valerii's call sign Boomer is actually a holdover from the original *Battlestar Galactica*, where the character's actual name — not his call sign — was Boomer. It was a way to keep some consistency between the old series and the new, but it was also a great way to introduce some new twists to the reimagined *BSG*. Sharon Valerii does not immediately strike one as a "Boomer," but her actions prove she's courageous, more than able to hold her own, and surprisingly strong.

In the second season episode "Scar," Starbuck lists some of the pilots who have fallen in the line of duty, giving only their call sign: BB, JoJo, Reilly, Beano, Dipper, Flat Top, Chuckles, Jolly, Crashdown, Sheppard, Dash, Flyboy, Stepchild, Puppet, Fireball. Other pilots include Bulldog, Shark, Buster, Stinger, Red Devil, Catbird, Narcho, Snitch, Chopper, Raygun, Fuzzy, Two Times, Showboat, and Sever.

Here's a partial list of the main call signs that appear on *Battlestar Galactica*:

William "Husker" Adama	Karl "Helo" Agathon
Lee "Apollo" Adama	Brendan "Hotdog" Costanza
Kara "Starbuck" Thrace	Louanne "Kat" Katraine
Sharon "Boomer" Valerii	Margaret "Racetrack" Edmonson
Sharon "Athena" Agathon	

there's no naturalness to it, and the sense of wrongness pervades the whole scene. Kara is incoherent with pain and desperation, while Lee only wants to savor the moment and allow them each the chance to properly appreciate how much it's taken them to get to this point. The result is two people who are coming together for all the wrong reasons. After all Lee and Kara have been through, it comes down to an angry, aggressive grope behind a locked door, with Starbuck spinning wildly out of control as Lee stands by, helpless to do anything but watch her implode. The scars from their encounter aren't physical, but they're still there.

It's fitting that just when the past starts to make a comeback in terms of its importance for many *BSG* characters, the memorial wall also makes a return appearance in this episode. Even though the Colonists' entire history has been erased, there are very few scenes of mourning in the series — in fact, they're basically limited to the miniseries when the chaos first starts to fade and people begin to realize everything they've lost. Since then, the present has been placed first and foremost — and in fact, looking back on past actions has been actively discouraged ("Water") — because without a strong present, the past hardly matters, and the future can't exist. That denial of past makes it often seem like the characters exist in a void: a spatial, temporal, and emotional void. A lot of the events in "Scar," despite the flashforward technique, are impulsive and rapid-fire: Starbuck and Apollo's sexual encounter, BB's death, Starbuck's drinking, her conversation with Sharon. They're all moments that happen quickly and suddenly, and would seem without context, except that the characters themselves *are* the context.

One of the throughlines of this episode and the series itself is the fact that the life expectancy of a *Galactica* pilot — and, now, a *Pegasus* pilot — is not high. "You know, the president says that we're saving humanity for a bright, shiny future. On Earth. That you and I are never gonna see. We're not. Because we go out over and over again until someday, some metal motherfrakker is gonna catch us on a bad day and just blow us away," Starbuck says to Lee. His reply ("Bright, shiny futures are overrated anyway") cements a fact that should be obvious but never really is — these pilots don't expect to live through *any* battle. Lee and Starbuck are exceptions to the rule, and they've survived through a combination of awesome skill and luck until now, but some day, they fully expect their luck to run out. What sort of mindset is that to have every time you climb into a cockpit? For the Cylon Raider, Scar, his past encounters weave across the surface of his body, tattoos of bad judgment that he learns from. Each encounter shaves some metal off his body, making him leaner, meaner, faster. But for the humans, all the scars are under the skin. They only have each other to learn from. And, thanks to their inability to resurrect themselves or their comrades, they have to carry the burden of each death with them, too, as a lesson that the dead pilot never learned but they have to. Sometimes it's amazing they can even climb the short ladder to the cockpit with the weight of all that scar tissue.

Headcount: The headcount is 49,593 — four less than in "Black Market" where Fisk, his murderer, Phelan, and one other person died.
Interesting Fact: Kara's move — blocking the sun's glare with her thumb — is a reference

to a real-life maneuver devised by Colonel Gregory "Pappy" Boyington in World War II. He came up with the idea when the enemy's planes were always in the sun. Boyington had no idea that it wasn't a recognized technique or that he was actually the first person to come up with it until after the fact.

Did You Notice? There are many pilots that weren't included in the list — in "Act of Contrition" and the miniseries, at least thirty-one other pilots were killed. In addition, Ripper was killed in the miniseries, and Karma was shot in "Kobol's Last Gleaming, Part 1."

The fight diagram in the background when Starbuck's doing the pilots' briefing is a schema that writer Bradley Thompson drew to show the production crew how the battle scene was to be choreographed. The tactics come from a book called *Fighter Combat: Tactics and Maneuvering*, which is written by a U.S. Navy pilot.

If you think those Viper scenes are fun, think again. Katee admitted in an interview that, "It is very uncomfortable in that tight space. All of a sudden, you're claustrophobic, you're hot and sweaty, and then you're cold, you have to pee, you need water, but you can't drink it because you'll have to pee again . . . You have these rubber space suits and you get stuck to the seat. Gross! Then there's wind in your face and you are falling asleep because it is so hot. You are trying to memorize all this dialogue — fifty pages — all this technical mumbo jumbo. You're like, 'Break my knee again, please.' That was the best thing that happened to me in season 1. 'Scar' was really tough. It was all those scenes of technical mumbo jumbo so Luciana [Carro] and I decided to add it all together and do it as one big, long scene. We were in and out of the Vipers all day long. It is exhausting."

Classic *Battlestar Galactica*: Lieutenant "Jolly" Anders is one of the pilots mentioned by Starbuck when she proposes the toast to the deceased. The call sign "Jolly" was the name of a recurring character from the original *Battlestar Galactica*.

So Say We All: STARBUCK: To BB. Jo-Jo. Riley. Beano. Dipper. Flat Top. Chuckles. Jolly. Crashdown. Shepherd. Dash. Flyboy. Stepchild. Puppet. Fireball.

APOLLO: To all of them.

ADAMA: So say we all.

216   Sacrifice

Original air date: February 10, 2006
Written by: Anne Cofell Saunders
Directed by: Reynaldo Villalobos

A grieving woman takes a restaurant full of people hostage — including Lee, Dee, Billy, and Ellen.

Suffering is a burden we each bear alone. While "Black Market" and "Scar" showed us that no matter what we go through, the heart always remembers, "Sacrifice" looks at unresolved grief and anger when the victim is not in a position of power. Until now, the stories have focused on *Galactica*'s crew — the pilots, the people in command, who have some form of outlet for their frustration and rage: they're actively involved in the search for Earth and the fight against the Cylons. Here, Dana Delany plays a widow, Sesha, struggling to make sense of her life in the aftermath of her husband's death in a Cylon attack some ten weeks earlier. This particular Cylon attack is unseen, except in Sesha's flashbacks, and highlights the idea that grief is always in the heart of the sufferer.

Sesha has none of the outlets available to Adama, Roslin, Starbuck, or Apollo. She doesn't even have the political intrigues that occupy Tom Zarek or the sexual intrigues of Ellen Tigh. In the void left by her husband's death, she has nothing to cling to but the elusive but utterly seductive idea of revenge. The premise of "Sacrifice" is a callback to the episode "Valley of Darkness," which features the first mention of human sacrifice in the show's history. From the beginning montage of Sesha's obsession, it's obvious that the story isn't going to end well, and that something is going to have to be sacrificed on the altar of her rage.

Of all the characters on the show, Billy is the one who seems the least changed by the events of the last nine or so months. From the start, he's been straightforward and honest, carefully negotiating his way around difficulties and taking whatever path seems right to him rather than switching his opinions or ethics for whichever fair wind is blowing. He helped Roslin escape *Galactica*'s brig in the beginning of the season, but he also didn't allow himself to blindly follow her to Kobol ("Resistance"). Billy, although he is decidedly Roslin's ally, also

Even though it's Apollo on the ground, it's Billy we mourn at the end of this episode (CAROLE SEGAL / © SCI-FI / COURTESY: EVERETT COLLECTION)

has his own path and his own mind. He seems innocent in a way that Laura, Adama, Lee, Kara, Dee — even Sesha — don't.

Despite the dark subject matter, "Sacrifice" takes place nearly entirely in a vibrant bar, which only serves to emphasize the sheer wrongness of the sacrifices being made. It feels *wrong* for Billy to die, it feels *wrong* that Starbuck should be the one to shoot Apollo, it feels *wrong* for Adama and Tigh to be at logger-heads. Whether or not the tension turns to hostility, Tigh's concern about Adama's gradual but evident thawing towards Sharon is a difficult subject — for the two men and the rest of the crew. However much Sharon looks the part of the pregnant young woman in love, she's a Cylon, and it's entirely possible that she's playing the fleet for their lives. Tigh is a voice of reason in this episode as he tries to make Adama let go of the illusion of the Sharon he knew and face the reality of the new Sharon — to adapt to the changes that have occurred.

Like "Resurrection Ship," what seems to be the climax of the episode actually isn't: the slow-motion shots of Lee getting shot indicate that Apollo's jeopardy is the main thrust of "Sacrifice," and the emotional resonance of that event supports that. Dee is terrified, but fiercely determined to make him live; and Starbuck is shattered in the same way that Apollo's skin is torn apart. Despite her pain, in some ways, it's the best thing that could have happened to Starbuck, because she's been in something of an emotional freefall for the last several episodes, and shooting Apollo is a reality check of the worst kind.

Apollo isn't the focal point of this episode, though — Billy is. Billy, who embodies innocence and "down-to-Picon" ambitions — work, love, marriage — dies, suddenly and with no last words or final glances. He gets shot, he goes down, and he's gone. It's just that hard. Of the sacrifices that are made in this episode, it's only the sacrifice of innocence that finally allows the ordeal to come to an end.

"They're all good men," Billy told Vinson viciously. And indeed everyone sacrifices something in this episode. Starbuck sacrifices Lee, Dee sacrifices her sure love with Billy for the unknown relationship with Lee, Tigh sacrifices Ellen, Roslin sacrifices the closest person she has to family, and Adama sacrifices his moral certainties to save Sharon. The end of "Sacrifice" is reminiscent of several other episodes, bringing a sense of symmetry and destiny to the events: Adama throws himself on Apollo's body just as Apollo threw himself on his father's body in "Kobol's Last Gleaming," and, later, Starbuck watches Apollo and Dee bonding, just as Dee watched Starbuck and Apollo in "Resurrection Ship." Situations, people, and relationships have changed, unutterably and irrevocably, but the parallels we see here all point to the fact that "all of this has happened before, and all of it will happen again."

The final scene of "Sacrifice" brings it all back to Sharon: everything that's happened in this episode revolves around her. The last shot of her raises so many questions. She's laid out on her bed like it's a sacrificial altar — but Lee was shot *for her*; Billy died *for her*. She's a sleeper agent in the worst possible way, a complete unknown. Her motives — political, emotional, and psychological — remain an absolute mystery, but she's arguably the most important person aboard the ship.

Headcount: There are 49,590 survivors in "Sacrifice" to account for the three pilots lost in "Scar."

Interesting Fact: Fans wept at Billy's demise, but we were lucky we got to see as much of him as we did, because he had been in danger of being killed off since the beginning of season 2. In an interview with *Media Blvd*, Paul Campbell said, "They kind of gave me the ultimatum and said, 'Sign a contract for five years, or we kind of need to go our separate ways.' And I kind of put it off and put it off, then eventually they just said, 'Look, we can tell you're not really committed to the show, and we can't write story lines. So we've decided to kill the character.' It wasn't really a surprise, but I wasn't expecting it to happen when it did. But I certainly wasn't surprised that they had to do that."

Did You Notice? "How many times have I saved you?" Sharon asks Adama. Not counting the times she saved Helo or Starbuck, she's saved Adama and the fleet a number of times — in fact, she's played a central part in saving one person or the whole fleet at least five times. The first was when she stopped Meier from shooting Adama in "Home, Part 2"; the second was in "Flight of the Phoenix" when she linked herself to the mainframe computer and turned the Cylon virus on itself; the third was in "Resurrection Ship, Part 2" when she saves the fleet from all-out war with Admiral Cain by telling Adama that perhaps humanity doesn't deserve to survive; the fourth was when the blood from her fetus was used to cure Roslin's cancer; and the fifth was when she told Starbuck everything she could about the Cylon Raider Scar, allowing Starbuck and Kat to destroy it. She'll save the fleet a couple

Human Sacrifice

A pretty self-explanatory term, don't you think? A sacrifice of the life of a human. Historically, human sacrifices were performed for different reasons, but all can be placed in two basic categories. The first category is when a human sacrifices his or her life to a god. In the ancient Aztec culture, for instance, they believed that the sun needed human sacrifices to continue to shine, and they sacrificed thousands of people annually.

The second type of human sacrifice is the one that involves the entombment of slaves with their master after the master's death. One reason for the practice was because the deceased person needed a retinue in the afterlife as much they needed one in this life. This was a much more prevalent type of sacrifice than the first type mentioned (uh, perhaps because they were slaves?), but the way in which servants and slaves were sacrificed varied depending on the culture, time, and place. Some slaves were killed and then offered as a sacrifice, while some cultures actually buried the slaves alive with the dead body. Gruesome!

Little is known about human sacrifice through the ages, but one thing's for sure – it wasn't exactly something people jumped up and down to do, and it wasn't practiced nearly as much as popular superstition says it was. Accusations of human sacrifice were sometimes used to vilify a person or culture, from witches to Satanists to Jews. These false allegations are referred to as "blood libel."

BSG, as usual, takes something already fairly complicated and then complicates it even more. At the end of the episode "Sacrifice," we see the body of Sharon enshrouded and lying on a hospital bed like slab, but she could be seen as the god to whom everyone else has been sacrificed. Adama, Billy, Dee, Apollo, Starbuck, Tigh, and Ellen have all sacrificed some part of their humanity to this Cylon sleeper agent.

more times before the season ends, too.

If you wondered what Adama's order, "Cut the wire," meant, you're not alone: Moore laughs, "It's not even scripted. It was something Eddie said. He was in one of his takes — it's just a line that he threw out there as he put it down."

Sesha has categorized the Cylon *modus operandi* in the following way:

Sleep deprivation

Assault on natural resources

Emotional manipulation
Suicide bombing
Cylon impregnation and reproduction
Multiple models
Sleeper agents within the fleet
Takeover by brute force

So Say We All: VINSON: He wasn't just her husband. He was my brother.

BILLY: My brother died on Picon. He was a good man, too. They're *all* good men.

217 The Captain's Hand

Original air date: February 17, 2006
Written by: Jeff Vlaming
Directed by: Sergio Mimica-Gezzan

The new commander of the Pegasus *disobeys Adama's orders.*

One of the overarching ideas addressed in this episode is that survival demands adaptation. Despite his long career, Barry Garner proves incapable of adapting to his new environment and responsibilities. As an engineer, Garner has a distinct point of view, as did Sesha Abinell in the previous episode, "Sacrifice." It's unfortunate that Garner's character is such a caricature, and that his story is cut short. Garner is the most annoying kind of narrative cliché — he grandstands and soapboxes, and he's really incompetent; you just know he's going to bite the big one. Apollo would be a better commander than he is — and the fact that Garner has to die in order for Apollo to be promoted to a rank that would allow him to take command just seems trite. Garner spends the whole episode pigheadedly refusing to listen to Starbuck or Apollo, both of whom have a lot more military experience than he does.

Throughout the series, the characters have had to adapt to some really rotten situations. When Starbuck was stranded on the planet with the Cylon Raider, she adapted by slitting the Raider open and figuring out how to get back to the fleet; Adama didn't necessarily want Ellen back in Tigh's life, but he adapted, and brought her back to *Galactica*; Helo had no idea Sharon was a Cylon when he fell in love with her, but when he found out, he adapted, and now wants to raise a family with her. The fleet has had to adapt to living in spaceships for a good part of a year; and they've coped with water shortages, fuel shortages, an uncertain political outcomes, murky futures — they've survived, because they've adapted. They adapted from the very first time Adama decided Roslin was right and fled from the Cylon attacks in the miniseries.

At the end of "The Captain's Hand," Apollo tells his father that Garner's main flaw was his inability to deal with humans: "He was used to working with machines. Command is about people." When Lee doesn't support Garner's decision to go after the missing Raptors, Garner dismisses his second-in-command; he does the same when Lee starts to tell him that he and Starbuck believe they're being led into a trap. He just doesn't learn — and it almost seems like he doesn't want to. The minute he realizes that he was wrong and that things are rapidly going downhill, he goes back to the engineering deck and leaves the command to Apollo. Granted, it's probably the smartest decision he makes in the whole episode, but it still shows his unwillingness to adapt.

It's no coincidence that, in this series, it's the Cylons who are known for their ability to adapt. "Adapt. That's what you're good at, right?" Adama's words to Sharon in "Sacrifice" point to one of the most fascinating aspects of the Cylons: the humanoid Cylons are the very *proof* of their adaptability, because they've become so completely human that they've been able to infiltrate the fleet and make everyone believe in their humanity. Sharon, Doral, and Gina have all been part of the fleet's everyday lives and have changed to suit their environment. Here, it's the machines that are able to change, and the humans who have difficulty adapting. And in Garner's case, the unwillingness to learn leads to his death. And yeah, we get that. Which is why it's even more annoying that Lee's statement about Garner and machines seals the whole cliché deal with a giant GET THE IRONY hammer.

Another big issue raised in this episode is that of abortion (one that was first raised in "Epiphanies"). In a nice piece of symmetry, Adama and Roslin switch positions as he reminds her that if the human race is to survive, it might not be possible for them to maintain the same civil rights. The whole series so far has been about survival, but this is the first time that the Colonists' rights have been curtailed to serve what their leaders ultimately deem to be a greater purpose. Roslin has, until now, done everything in her power to ensure that the political and social system from before the attacks remains intact — providing a sense of the familiar in the absolute unknown. Roslin makes a huge decision in "The Captain's Hand," one that will irrevocably change her life and the lives of the entire fleet. Ronald Moore particularly liked the fact that Rya went through with the abortion: "This was the key moment, the moment that we talked about quite a bit. That Laura would take this step. Laura would ban abortion in the Fleet. Laura would ultimately decide that the survival of the race, that their security, would outweigh their need for freedom. That [...] she would curtail a freedom. She would start cutting back on the ways that they had lived their lives before the attack and deal with the realities of the situation that they're in now. And she would do it because she thought it was the thing she had to do, not because she thought it was a good thing to do. [...] I like the way that Mary [McDonnell] struggles with this. I think Mary had trouble grappling with this notion as well. This is a big thing, and [...] I had a lot of conversations with Mary about this story line, and about why she was doing what she was doing and her motivations for banning abortion and the reasons why she would be forced to this position." Roslin sacrifices a hugely personal issue (and one that can only be more personal now that she's fought her battle with cancer — her body taken over and ravaged, control of her own body removed) because she wants the bigger picture: she wants the human race to survive, and sometimes that means surrendering what's important. Adama and Roslin act very much like parents in this episode, making an unpopular decision that they hand down to the population in much the same way they would to children. This is the second time procreation rights have been dealt with directly ("Epiphanies") but this time *BSG* leaves itself open to debate. While the issue of abortion is generally treated in discreet specifics, like its medical rationale or its political ramifications or its religious import, "The Captain's Hand" brings everything together to see what happens. How does Roslin — how do we — make a decision when so many factors are weighing in?

Headcount: The whiteboard shows 49,584 survivors, down 6 from "Sacrifice." There were both marine and hostage-taker casualties in that episode, but they numbered 7 (Billy, Sesha, Vinson, Chu, Page, and 2 marines), so there must have been a birth since then to account for the discrepancy.

Interesting Fact: The last scene between Lee and Kara features an ad-lib from Jamie Bamber. In reply to Starbuck's "You should see the way my brain works sometimes," Apollo teases, "You have a brain?" Ronald Moore explains, "This is actually [...] an ad-lib that Jamie came up with in the table read. And the table read, of course, is when the entire cast gets together before the show and they read the script out loud and you hear it and tweak dialogue and hear what the actors play."

Did You Notice? There are a number of hand shots in this episode that illustrate the title: Starbuck's, Lee's, Adama's, Garner's, even Dr. Cottle's. Each person's hands hold the power of life and death, and are the conduits through which the characters enact their responsibility, or not.

"I'm going to get our men." Garner's words are a direct echo of Adama's own words when he himself went against a direct command in season 2's "Pegasus." In that episode, Adama swore that he would rescue Chief and Helo from Admiral Cain's execution order, saying, "I'm getting my men."

The nicknames given to the two battleships are never used again in the series, and Moore admits that it was a whimsical desire to give them nicknames that prompted him to come up with "the Beast" and "the Bucket."

This is one of few series that has a pregnant woman actually go through with an abortion, something Moore is particularly proud of: "She didn't have a last-minute change of heart and say, [...] 'Well, I know that I believe in a woman's right to choose but I've decided not to.' Which I just think is a total cop-out. I think that's trying to have it both ways: that's trying to have your liberal point of view, and not actually bite the bullet and have the character actually go through with the procedure. Which is a difficult procedure, and carries a lot of heavy weight, and I think you have to give it its weight and you have to play the reality of that."

So Say We All: GAIUS: Every time you take away one of our freedoms, every time you restrict or curtail one of our rights, we become one step closer to being like them.

218   Downloaded

Original air date: February 24, 2006

Tabula Rasa

The theory of "tabula rasa" ("scraped tablet" or, less literally, "blank slate") defines the mind as a blank writing surface of sorts, only "written on" once the human being starts to accumulate experiences. The phrase is known thanks to the philosopher John Locke, but the idea had been around for a while in another philosopher's works. In *De Anima*, Aristotle wrote, "What the mind thinks must be in it in the same sense as letters are on a tablet (*grammateion*) which bears no actual writing (*grammenon*); this is just what happens in the case of the mind." The idea came up again and again throughout literary, scientific, and philosophical history, but it wasn't until 1690 that Locke's *Essay Concerning Human Understanding* made the theory a more or less household idea. Locke combined the idea of empirical and sensory experience as the basis for all knowledge with the idea of an immutable human nature, thus nicely sidestepping the whole "nature versus nurture" debate.

The Cylons appear to be definite proponents of the "tabula rasa" theory of being, but, like Locke, they also seem to combine it with a firm understanding of the fact that they are above and beyond all Cylons. If they truly believed in "tabula rasa" in its extreme form — that is, the ability of a being to write, freely, their own story — the Cylons wouldn't have any problem allowing Sharon to construct herself as Sharon. Instead, as we see in "Downloaded," the Cylons have real issues with her refusing her identity as a Number Eight, and are going so far as to threaten to "box" her memories if she doesn't come to terms with her immutable identity as a Cylon. Sharon is perhaps the best example of the idea of "tabula rasa" at work, because it is her experiences that define her: she can't accept herself as a Cylon because she has the memories, the sensory and emotional input, of a human.

Written by: David Weddle, Bradley Thompson
Directed by: Jeff Woolnough

The physical and emotional rebirth of a Number Six and Number Eight model wreaks havoc on Cylon society.

Everything changes with "Downloaded," from the location (the story is told from Caprica, not outer space) to the central characters (Cylons, not humans), from the beginning sequence (a flashback to nine months before) to the point of view (again, Cylon, not human). This is the first time we've seen events from a Cylon perspective, and it opens up a whole new dimension to the show.

Fittingly enough, this episode begins where the miniseries began, with the annihilation of the Colonies, moving swiftly into the rebirth of the original Caprica-Six. It's said that when you die, your whole life flashes before your eyes: in this case, it's when Six and Sharon are *reborn* that they see their whole lives. The last two seasons have focused on the idea of love as a central theme in the Six and Sharon models, so it's not surprising that their memories all revolve around relationships and identity — who they were and who they loved. They are resurrected in a maelstrom of love and passion that immediately conveys a sense of abandon and abandonment: without those connections that Sharon and Six forged in their other lives, who are they? "Downloaded" looks at the definition of life and living, following the two through to their point of self-realization: they're resurrected in the first scenes of the episode, but it's not until the very end that they can say, "We're alive."

What's interesting is that, if Six died in the explosion on Caprica, it's likely that Gaius would have died too, or at least have had a near-death experience as Lee, Adama, and Roslin have each had. And for Gaius to appear in Six's head adds layers to the mystery that has been Six's presence in Gaius's mind: what are they each doing there? Ronald Moore has posited that the hallucinations show the perception of each character, show how they view each other. In some ways, that makes sense because love is commonly said to be blind — you see what you want to see when you look at the beloved. It would also make sense if death were a bonding experience — which, by all indications, it is: when Six and Sharon wake up, they are surrounded by women who express comfort, sympathy, and love. Sharon's identical counterpart tries to reassure her by saying, "We love you," but there's a basic philosophical barrier between Cylons and humans, which is that humans can't download after death, so death is the end, it's final — it's not a "learning experience" ("Scar"), it's not love, it's not bonding. And Sharon has lived her whole life believing she's human, so she can't quite make that leap.

"Downloaded" is nearly entirely set on Caprica, which is bathed in a sepia light, as it was at the end of season 1 and the beginning of season 2 when Helo and Starbuck were there. The lighting is representative of the physical and emotional rebirths taking place on the planet — rebirths of the Cylons, and of the planet itself, which is being rebuilt and replanted around its new inhabitants. Everything about the cinematography is light, airy, and spacious. In awful contrast, the explosion in the parking lot reflects the claustrophobic walls closing in on Sharon and Six, as their lives and beliefs are turned upside down. The climax of that scene is reflected by the light that pours down on the two Cylon women when the other Cylons remove the debris from above them. As they clutch hands and joyfully proclaim they're alive, the light shines down in a mimicry of a revelation: it's as if, having overcome their obstacles and discovered the true meaning of their new lives, they're being illuminated by a divine being. This sort of revelation-from-above is in direct contrast to the type of revelation we'll see in "Lay Down Your Burdens," where Roslin talks about knowing something "in her gut" — a more postmodern inner revelation.

An important moment of the episode is when Anders asks Sharon and Six, "What kind of people are you?" He doesn't call them "skin jobs," Cylons, or machines — just "people." Until now, Hera has been hailed as the "shape of things to come," a new form of life, a hybrid of human and Cylons. "Downloaded" poses the question of identity though: Sharon and Six are different, they aren't just Cylons, but they're also not humans. Could themselves not be the hybrid form, the "shape of things to come"?

Headcount: A full nine months after the Cylon attacks, there are 49,579 people in the fleet.
Numbers: Numbers are an essential factor in the *BSG* universe, so much so that the Cylons are all numbered, from 1 to 12. The Number 3 models are known as "Doral." The Number 8 models are known as "Sharon." We don't know what model numbers they are, but one model is known as "Simon," another as "Leoben." The Number 6 model is known as . . . Six. The *Pegasus* version of Six is Gina, and the imaginary version of her from "Six Degrees of Separation" (Season 1) was Shelly; but she is *known* as Six. Why is she different? What is it about her that requires anonymity? Did Gaius sleep with her for two years on Caprica without calling her by anything other than "Six"? In mathematics, six is known as the first "perfect number" because it is the sum of its divisors (that is, if you add the divisors of the number six — 1, 2, and 3 — you get 6). The number six also plays an essential part in religious history. In the Bible, God created the heavens and the earth, light and dark, animals and plants, and, finally, on the sixth day, he created humankind, his most perfect creation. Number Six might be called just "Six" because she is the "one true God's" most perfect creation — the perfect number, the perfect Cylon, the perfect hybrid between human and Cylon. She told Gaius that she was an "angel of God" ("Home, Part 2"). Perhaps she's even more than that: the perfect embodiment of the Cylon God.
Interesting Fact: Think you're confused about why Gaius and Six have a version of each other living inside their heads? You're not alone: Tricia Helfer admits she has no idea what's going on, either. "You know, I gave up trying to figure out what it was ages ago. Because

A Number Eight is reborn, tended by a Six and a Three (CAROLE SEGAL/© SCI-FI/ COURTESY: EVERETT COLLECTION)

there are so many things with the series, when it's kind of open-ended. I just really don't know! And then, you know, when 'Downloaded' happened, and we realized that there was a Baltar that was in *her* head, in Caprica's [Six's] head, I thought okay, well something had to have happened in the nuclear explosion, when Six saved him [see miniseries]. Something happened there where he started seeing her, and then after she got downloaded, she started seeing him. But that's just me as an actor trying to put some spin on it, because I don't know the answers."

Did You Notice? Anders refers to the humanoid Cylons as "skin jobs." This is a reference to the 1982 sci-fi movie *Blade Runner* by Ridley Scott that featured genetically altered beings identical to humans, called "replicants." Edward James Olmos was in that movie, too.

The beginning of the episode is a flashback to nine months before; nine months is the time needed for a human or human/Cylon hybrid baby to come to term and be fully ready to be born.

"We're alive!" Sharon and Six's exclamation of joy is an echo of the question Cylons have been asking since the miniseries. The first words of the series were Six's — "Are you alive?"

The licence plate behind Anders when the bomb has exploded reads SEXYMOM and has a sticker on it promoting the Caprica Buccaneers pyramid team — that is, Anders' team. The sticker says "C-Bucks rule."

Kara's dog tags show her military ID: 462753.

Instead of Six's usual theme music, that plays when she appears in Gaius's head on

Galactica, the same music plays whenever Gaius appears in Reborn-Six's head, but the xylophone notes are in reverse. (The violin music stays the same, though.)

So Say We All: D'ANNA: God loves me!

SIX: See you again soon.

219   Lay Down Your Burdens, Part 1

Original air date: March 3, 2006
Written by: Ronald D. Moore
Directed by: Michael Rymer

Starbuck organizes a mission to rescue the group on Caprica. A habitable planet changes the presidential race.

Unfamiliar and haunting, the opening music takes on a foreboding aspect as the camera pans over pamphlets, leaflets, brochures, campaign posters, all of which frame Gaius, who looks as tired as he ever has, red-eyed and already defeated. The music continues to wash over the slow camera movements, framing our experience of Gaius and Roslin, as the camera frames Gaius and Roslin themselves.

The episode opens with everyone uncomfortable and in a situation they don't want to be in: Gaius, Roslin, Sharon, Starbuck, Chief, and Adama are all on edge, tense, on the verge of *something* but not yet sure what. One of the first things we notice is that Gaius is all PR while Roslin is all about the issues. Even their postures tell their story. Gaius's desk is covered with promotional material; he's slouched, unshaven, and looks like he hasn't showered or slept in days. In contrast, Roslin looks jittery but she's energetic, well-dressed, and studying her notes.

This second season finale is unlike the first year finale in that there is no big military operation, no huge space battle; instead, the battle lines are drawn on the moral and political field, with Roslin's and Gaius's prose as the bullets. Nearly all the action takes place indoors, revealing an insular, interior drama, both psychological and implicit. It is nine months since the attacks and a new age is about to be born. Apollo tells the pilots, "You'll be making history just by making the attempt; [...] you'll be making part of the future"; that statement holds true for the entire fleet — by rising above their difficulties, they're weaving the threads of their past to create their future.

Sharon appears as a prophetess of doom in this episode, telling Helo that "Something dark is coming." Sharon's feeling of foreboding echoes our own as the tension slowly builds, but despite her huge misgivings, Sharon herself looks small and frail in a way she never has before. It's obvious that losing her baby has utterly destroyed her and she hasn't made her way back from her own dark place. She doesn't even walk into the pilots' briefing room on her own steam — she's led in by her prison guards, shackled to her own fate and sadness. Sharon maintains that same distanced outlook throughout the whole episode, and doesn't

A turbulent moment for Specialist Cally Henderson. (CAROLE SEGAL/© SCI-FI/ COURTESY: EVERETT COLLECTION)

show a flicker of emotion when the Caprican group and the fleet's pilots are reunited. It's a huge moment for Starbuck and Anders, and it's also of significance to Helo, but Sharon's face is like stone. She doesn't share in the joy around her, she's just completely uninvolved in their lives and her own.

"Lay Down Your Burdens" builds slowly, framed by the presidential debate between Gaius and Roslin, but the discovery of a habitable planet drastically shifts the tone and direction of the series. After nine months of nomadic wandering, the hope of a home world, somewhere where humanity can "lay down their burdens" and build a new life, shines like a beacon. The fact that it was so fortuitously discovered by Racetrack's lost Raptor can only strengthen the planet's appeal in some circles, as it appears to be ordained by the gods. Dee talks of "rivers of milk and honey," a reference to the Bible, in which Moses declares that he has been sent to rescue the Hebrews from the Egyptians. The literary and religious allusion here is to an easy, carefree life, free of worries about Cylon attacks, military operations, or constant shortages.

The political battlefield in the episode is particularly vicious and is pretty much the only thing worth talking about in the fleet. Far from the political lethargy of real-life North America, these human survivors all gather around the radio to listen to the debate and actively involve themselves in creating their own future. The scene in the pilots' briefing room on *Pegasus* is reminiscent of World War II, when the radio was the main form of communication between people and factions, bringing news to all corners of the world. In a situation where their society has been almost annihilated, blasted into near-extinction, humanity simply can't afford to be lazy about their future; they've also had their past, homes, and lives forcibly taken from them, so they have a stronger-than-usual desire to be a part of rebuilding their society, to participate and have a choice.

The political debate is thrilling in a way that really emphasizes the candidates' characters. It is, as usual, difficult to figure out where Gaius's true motivations lie, and Roslin exudes confidence and political acumen that speaks to her decades in the public arena. She's blindly confident, however, and demonstrates the same kind of ego that Gaius is typically known for. She seems to teeter on that fine line between leadership and zealous disregard for the people's wishes; her personal feelings for Gaius (though they might be rooted in her suspicion that he's involved with the Cylons) are interfering with her ability to compromise and listen.

Gaius and Roslin are not the only ones who struggle to come to terms with one another in this episode. Starbuck and Apollo have an awkward scene together, their difficulty in looking at one another illustrated by the skewed angle of the camera. Something is clearly not right between them, and it hasn't been since "Scar." Even though they started to make amends at the end of "The Captain's Hand," they're still distant and awkward with one another. Individually, however, it is a different matter. Starbuck seems to have matured by leaps and bounds since her conversation with Lee two episodes ago. When she presents the mission outline to the pilots, she's calm, in charge. Gone is the drunken, lost pilot from "Scar"; in her place is a more responsible, more able woman who knows what she wants.

Part 1 ends with jeopardy on every plane: political, military, and personal. On *Galactica*, Chief is facing up to his ultimate fear of being a Cylon, and his deepest, hidden, desire to kill himself. Until now, the issue of suicide has been seen from the Cylon perspective: both Six and Gina have said time and again that suicide is a sin, and Boomer was driven to attempt suicide because of the same sense of wrongness that Chief is feeling. Finally, while Gaius and Roslin are each facing the possible deaths of their political futures, Starbuck, Helo, and Sharon are facing a literal death at the hands of the Cylons.

Headcount: The headcount — 49,579 — is the same as in "Downloaded," which means that Hera was probably counted, but her addition was discounted by the dead baby with whom she was replaced.

Are You There, God? It's Me, Gaius. "I'm just going to sit right back and wait for the hand of God to reach down and change my political fortunes." This is a direct reference to the season 1 episode "The Hand of God," wherein Gaius came to realize that he was an instrument of God. The fact that it's Six who prompts Gaius to say, "Can you imagine if we actually had to live [on the newly discovered planet]," and that she has told Gaius that she is "an angel of God sent here to protect him" ("Home, Part 2"), creates a sense of hidden meaning behind the discovery of the planet, and its usefulness as a political maneuver.

Interesting Fact: The actress who plays Racetrack, Leah Cairns, developed a backstory for her character that involved having a crush on Helo. The backstory is inspired by a piece of

Dean Stockwell (Brother Cavil)

....

Date of birth: March 5, 1936

Did you know? Dean's father, Harry, was best known for his role as the voice of Prince Charming in Disney's *Snow White and the Seven Dwarves*. Dean was nominated for an Oscar for his role in the 1988 movie *Married To the Mob*, and he has been nominated for many, and received several, other awards over his long career. Dean's best known today for his long-standing role as the AI in the hit series *Quantum Leap*.

On getting the role of Brother Cavil: "It was one of those rare occurrences where my agent put it together. He's got Katee Sackhoff [Kara Thrace] as a client, and he just saw this opening and it worked out."

On his role on *BSG*: "They tried to tell me a little bit about what the show was about, but it's very difficult to explain it to somebody without showing it to them. So when I had done the episodes, I came back home and they got me the first season. I put it on and watched it, and I was very, very impressed. […] And then I saw that my hunches worked out very well!"

On his life as an artist: "I feel very lucky to have gotten [the *BSG* gig], because I've taken myself off the board for any series. I've been living up in New Mexico, 7,000 feet, on a tall mountain, and I'm making art. I make collages. I had a show here in Dallas, and another one in Santa Monica in October, and it's becoming more important in my life. For me, it's on a higher level of [creativity] than acting. But this just fits in."

On his approach to acting: "I approach every acting job in the same way, and that's strictly through intuition and instinct. I don't research stuff, I don't go into depth of character or anything like that, I just get ideas, and I execute them."

fan fiction that pairs Helo and Racetrack up. According to Leah, Tamhoh Penikett (a.k.a. Helo) is aware of the backstory she created, and they both play their scenes as if Racetrack is in love with Helo, and Helo recognizes but does not reciprocate it. For "Lay Down Your Burdens, Part 1," Leah asked if additional scenes could be shot that incorporated her character's reaction to Sharon being brought into the pilots' briefing room. These scenes showed Racetrack looking jealously at Sharon when Helo walks up to her, Helo notices, and Sharon does not. The scenes were filmed, but they didn't make it to the final cut.

Did You Notice? The campaign flyers on Gaius's counter read: "We deserve peace and serenity. We deserve a homeland. We deserve Gaius Baltar." Another one reads, "Peace is ours to make. On Election Day, make the choice that can save our Future. Elect Gaius Baltar as President." Yet another states simply, "Baltar for President," and one starts, "Your book . . ."

Roslin says to Gaius, "Why don't you go frak yourself?"; this is an allusion to the 2004 spat between Vice President Dick Cheney and Senator Pat Leahy, both of the United States.

In another allusion to U.S. politics, one of Roslin's responses at the debate is, "Well, my initial response is 'There he goes again.'" In 1980, a presidential debate was held between President Ronald Reagan and Jimmy Carter. Reagan said to Carter, "There you go again."

Brother Cavil "reassures" Chief that he's not a Cylon agent by telling him, "Maybe because I'm a Cylon and I've never seen you at any of the meetings!" His words are a reminder of what Six told Gaius about Doral, back in the miniseries — "I don't remember seeing him at the Cylon parties." Of course, since Doral *did* turn out to be a Cylon, Cavil's reassurance raises questions of its own.

Dee has a photo of Lee stuck to the inside of her locker. The picture is from the one of Starbuck, Zak, and Lee, that Starbuck has had in her locker since the miniseries.

Lee tells the pilots jumping back to Caprica that if the fleet finds Earth before their return, he'll personally build the pilots a bar. According to Jamie Bamber, Lee never wanted to make the military his career, and at the time of the Cylon attack, his character was looking to leave the military to open up a bar somewhere: "My little idea was that after the decommissioning ceremony, [Lee] was going to hand in his resignation and open a small bar or something on Caprica."

Lee is now wearing a wristwatch, something that hasn't been a part of his usual uniform until now. It's likely that it's Garner's wristwatch from "The Captain's Hand."

The Raptor that rematerializes inside the mountain on Caprica is number 612. The number 12 (which is also a multiple of 6) is of central importance in *Battlestar Galactica*. See season 1's "The Hand of God" for more on the numerology of 12.

220   Lay Down Your Burdens, Part 2

Original air date: March 10, 2006
Written by: Mark Verheiden, Anne Cofell
Directed by: Michael Rymer

Roslin tries to steal the election. President Baltar orders the fleet to settle permanently on New Caprica.

It seemed impossible for anything to top the two-parter "Resurrection Ship" from earlier in the season, but the season finale is astonishing in its scope. The final third of this second part skips forward more than a year, leaving viewers and characters alike with no hope for a "reset" button, or for a last-minute reveal of a dreaming Gaius or Roslin. This is reality, cold, dark, and damp as it is, and the only way for the Colonials to change it is to do as Kara says: ". . . fight 'em until we can't."

A somber episode, "Lay Down Your Burdens" shows that no matter what, you can never predict everything. Tory can take all the polls she wants, but she couldn't have predicted the discovery of a new, habitable planet; Starbuck can plan for all the contingencies, but she couldn't have predicted the Cylons would simply up and leave; Tigh and Tory can plot stealing the election to the utmost detail, but they couldn't have predicted that a spelling error on the ballots would ruin everything; Gaius can hand out nuclear weapons on a whim, but he could never have predicted that it would lead to the downfall of the human race. Prophecies, predictions, gut feelings aside — the future is unpredictable, and all people can do is make the best of the path they've chosen.

The episode draws some interesting parallels and ties up some of the loose ends left over from the first part of the finale. Cally, who has been dancing around her feelings for Chief since the miniseries, finally admits that she loves him — ironically, she does so with a mouth full of wire and a face swollen and scarred. Chief, who's battling his own demons, is taken aback, and the next time we see the pair, they're married and expecting a baby. This points to the idea that sometimes relationships have to develop away from the public eye, just as Cally's own feelings have had to remain hidden in Sharon's shadow and her own shyness until this point. Chief apologizes to Cally in a scene that's very reminiscent of Cally's apology to Chief in "The Farm." He beat Cally to a bloody pulp, she killed the woman he loved; both are seemingly unforgivable acts, but just as love has managed to overcome obstacles between Starbuck and Anders and Sharon and Helo, so too does it obliterate the challenges between Cally and Chief.

The debate between Roslin and Gaius escalates, becoming less political and more personal as they fight for what they believe in, and for their own egos. Gaius is certainly using the new planet as a political pawn, but he maintains a clear head throughout — something that Roslin does not. Gaius sees the situation and the people around him clearly, telling

Starbuck and Dr. Cottle (Donnelly Rhodes) fight for survival on New Caprica (CAROLE SEGAL/© SCI-FI/ COURTESY: EVERETT COLLECTION)

Zarek that "Laura Roslin is many things, but she is not corrupt, and she is not dishonest." Roslin, however, is so afraid that Gaius will win and lead humanity to a darker state than its current one that she betrays her own ethics and morality by agreeing to some shady — and downright illegal — political maneuverings. Roslin's deeply upset at what she's done and so disbelieving that she could ever have stooped to it, despite the fact that she knows in her gut that Gaius is a Cylon collaborator. It's interesting to take note of Roslin's journey from prophet and visionary — someone who had revelations bestowed upon her by the gods — to the woman who attributes her knowledge of Gaius's true nature to her "gut." Revelation from above has become revelation from within; this is exactly opposite to what happened at the end of "Downloaded," where Six and Sharon were illuminated from above as they realized and embraced their destiny within the dark cave-in.

It's hard for Roslin to admit that she's much like Gaius — a flawed, rash person who can be blinded by her own visions — and affected by an itchy airlock finger! How many airlock threats does that make? Four? Five? Mary McDonnell has said that this is her favorite scene with Edward James Olmos: "In terms of scenes with Ed, I do have a favorite scene, and that was the last scene we had together at the end of last season [in which Roslin confesses to rigging the presidential election]. We sat there, the two of us, with everything that had happened up until that point, in the room. I could feel the whole two years leading to that moment, sitting there in the room. I just felt the reality of the series in that scene."

While Roslin and Adama resume their role as the flawed parents of the fleet, Gaius resumes his as destroyer of humanity. Not once but three times he's led humanity to its downfall. Gaius's story line bears faint echoes of the biblical story of Peter, one of the twelve disciples of Jesus. When Jesus was taken prisoner by Pontius Pilate, He predicted that Peter would deny Him three times before the next dawn; sure enough, Peter denied his association with Jesus three times before the cock crowed. In a similar way, Gaius has betrayed humanity three times to the Cylons, turned his back on humans to ensure his own survival.

It's interesting to note that Gaius surrenders with a tear but no hesitation, but it's not the first time the Cylons have won out over the Colonials. In the miniseries, Roslin pushed Adama to recognize their defeat, and Adama did finally turn his back on the Colonies and retreat. A strategic retreat, but a retreat nonetheless. Although it's pretty much impossible to blame him for what was undoubtedly the only decision he could make under the circumstances, it's interesting that Gaius's version of surrender is so harshly viewed by his people and the fans, especially since the situation he's facing is the same: the possible extinction of the human race.

His decision comes on the heels of a series of short scenes showing the new president's own brand of leadership: his office is conspicuously empty of everyone except his "aides" — even the ever-present Six — the whiteboard that represented hope has been replaced by a portrait of Gaius, and Gaius himself seems to be perpetually drunk or on drugs. His office is the picture of decadence, an ugly contrast to the businesslike atmosphere that surrounded Roslin when she was in office. Hers was an office bustling with activity, effort, and hardship; Gaius's is empty of feeling, work, and humanity.

Political issues aside, "Lay Down Your Burdens" is a harsh but honest testament to how relationships can change over time. Lee and Starbuck are one example of this, but Starbuck and Tigh are another. When Kara sees Tigh and Ellen on New Caprica, she runs to them and she and Tigh share a friendly, intimate hug, as if the past has no bearing on who they are in the present moment. In the twelve months we missed, Starbuck and Anders have gotten married, and Starbuck seems more Kara than ever before — not only because of the telltale long hair of wifehood, but also in the way she moves and speaks: she's more openly affectionate and more able to put aside her ego to ask for what she needs. Lee, too, has changed: now married to Dee, he's pudgy and complacent. It's hard to believe he's the same person who raged so angrily against Phelan in "Black Market." Now he's the one withholding antibiotics, hoarding them for his pilots, and exerting his own form of meritocracy. Ironically enough, Apollo was the Greek god of medicine . . .

The scene between Lee, Kara, and Anders, when Anders' group had just joined the fleet, reeks with tension and unresolved issues. Kara is positively raucous and her drinking doesn't stem from despair, or a need to forget; instead, it's joyful and excited, happy and lighter, as if she's laying down her burdens. She presents a very different picture to Lee, who's extremely uncomfortable (and who wouldn't be?) as he watches the woman he loves share her enthusiasm and joy with someone else. Even though he's trying to develop a relationship with Dee, Starbuck's always going to have a place in his heart, and it must hurt like hell to watch her with Anders. Anders keeps up with Kara — both in terms of drinking and more figuratively; whereas Lee has always tried to rein Kara in, keep her in line, help her back to a more stable place, Anders lets her loose and grins exuberantly at her as she freefalls in a good way this time: he actually seems to like her drunken lewdness.

Another of the most central relationships in the series is the one that exists between Adama and Tigh. Colonel Tigh was an overarching presence in the last few episodes, but this is the first episode in a while where he's had more than a couple of lines to speak or looks to shoot. His scene with Adama is quiet and intimate, a reminder of what deep love persists between the two veterans of life; prominent between them is Tigh's wedding ring, a metaphorical and literal symbol of the men's boundaries. Ellen has always been between them, and because she wants to go and live on the planet, Adama sets Tigh free — releases him from his bond of protection and guardianship of the fleet to pursue his individual desires. It's a deeply moving scene that lovingly highlights the abiding emotions of two longtime friends.

One of the major reveals of this episode should be that Brother Cavil is a Cylon, but with everything else that happens, the revelation is nearly dwarfed. Still, it's worth noting that the scene between the two Brothers, where they realize they can't talk their way out of the situation, is one of the funniest of the whole season. The fact that Cavil is a Cylon is surprising, but it also makes a certain amount of sense given the foreshadowing in Part 1 of the finale. The discovery of his identity is difficult in the sense that it raises the question once more of what a Cylon is, and what a human is. Each time we find out someone is a Cylon, we're gutted, destroyed, because we've formed a connection with them. Sharon, D'Anna, Cavil — they all force us to relate to them, understand them in some way, and there's no way to take back the connection that's been forged once their real identity is known. It's up to us to either adapt to the new situation, or stagnate — much like the Colonials, who must decide to give in to their fate or change with it, and fight back.

Headcount: The ambush on the Caprican mission and the Raptor losses have left twenty-nine people dead, bringing the survivor count to 49,550. There's more than just that head-count in this episode, though. When the action moves to New Caprica, we're told that 39,192 people have settled on the planet. We also learn that there are at least 46,531 survivors of voting age in the fleet: 24,365 voted for Roslin, compared to 22,266 for Gaius.

Are You There, God? It's Me, Gaius. Over the last two seasons, Gaius has gone from atheist scientist to instrument of God, passing through the phases of skeptic, fair-weather convert, and true convert. While season 1 focused on his religious conversion, season 2 has focused more on Gaius's gradual but certain shift away from humanity and towards the Cylons. By giving Gina the nuclear weapon ("Epiphanies"), Gaius passed a point of no return: the first destruction of humanity was a mistake; the second is deliberate and vindictive. In "Lay Down Your Burdens, Part 2," Gaius is clearly devastated by Gina's death, but it's impossible as always to divine his motivations. Is he so upset because he lost someone he wanted to care about and nurture? Or is he upset because Gina slept with him the night before, and he's seeing a long, sexless future ahead of him? It would be nice to think that guilt about his part in the destruction of *Cloud 9* has caught up to him, but the scenes of him one year later — exactly the same man, unchanged and unmoved — speak to his immutability. It's ironic that the instrument of God has been, and becomes, the instrument of humanity's annihilation, and seems to point to a wrathful, vengeful God.

Interesting Fact: Chief Tyrol's union speech is nearly a direct lift of Mario Savio's 1964 speech at the Berkeley Free Speech Movement. Ronald Moore and David Eick got permission from Savio's widow to use the speech, and it's listed in the credits as, "Mario Savio speech excerpted courtesy of: Lynne Hollander Savio." Actor Aaron Douglas studied videos of the speech so that he could genuinely imitate the man's intensity. Mario Savio was a political activist in the U.S., and he informally led a student protest at the University of California in 1964–65. The protest was aimed at lifting the ban on on-campus political activity, and recognizing the students' right to freedom of speech. David Eick has said that this is his favorite moment in the episode: "I've had this speech taped up on my wall at home, in my home office, for the last five years. I found it when I saw the documentary *Berkeley in the Sixties* and this guy Mario Savio was just this kid in college who stirred up this hornet's nest about civil rights on the campus of Berkeley. [...] And I love that Aaron really studied Savio, too. All those little hand gesticulations he's doing are right out of the way he used to deliver speeches."

Did You Notice? The number 12 makes a comeback at the end of this episode on *Colonial One*. When the Cylons walk into Gaius's office, there are 9 humans versus 3 Cylons, bringing the total to 12 people. See season 1's "The Hand of God" for more on the significance of 12 in the series.

At the end of the episode, Adama is sitting alone in his quarters, and he brings out a lighter. It's his father's lighter, which we first saw in season 1, in "The Hand of God," when he loaned it to Apollo to wish him luck on the mission.

The shot of Gina and Gaius's linked hands echoes the scene from "Kobol's Last Gleaming, Part 2," where Six reaches into the downed Raptor to lead Gaius through the flames. In that scene there was a similar shot of Six and Gaius with joined hands.

Ah Billy, you are sorely missed. There is a framed photo of him and Roslin sitting on Roslin's desk during the election.

The crib out of which Maya takes Hera/Isis in the classroom is the same crib featured in the season 1 finale two-parter "Kobol's Last Gleaming." In those episodes, the crib was part of Gaius's vision with Six.

Although Gaeta lied for Dee when Tigh questioned him about off-log phone calls in "Resistance," his straitlaced nature comes back with a vengeance in these episodes.

Six appears as a prophet of doom twice in this episode: first, in the beginning, when she warns Gaius that Roslin knows of his connection to the Cylons, and second, at the end when she snarkily announces the arrival of Judgment Day. In Part 1 of this two-parter, it was another Cylon, Sharon, who was the prophesier of a dark time — a prophecy that's fulfilled by Gaius's actions here.

Brother Cavil says that the Cylons have thought themselves the "children of humanity." Six used the same phrase in season 1's "Bastille Day."

If you think Gaius looks bad in the scene where the Cylons jump into orbit around New Caprica, it's because James Callis actually stayed up all night drinking so that he would look as authentically awful as possible. "He really damaged himself to do this. He really wanted to look horrible and there's only so much makeup and photography can do," says David Eick.

So Say We All: STARBUCK: Oh, I'm so glad you guys are here!

ELLEN: Me, too. It's pretty . . . pretty exciting.

STARBUCK: Yeah. That wears off.

The Resistance: Webisodes

In between seasons 2 and 3, the SciFi channel made an "intermediary" season available on its Web site. The series of ten episodes — called "Webisodes" because they were only broadcast over the Internet — followed a group of seven characters through the first birthing difficulties of the New Caprica Resistance movement. Each Webisode ran between two and five minutes, so the stories are extremely compressed. Because of the limited availability of the Webisodes (they were only available to U.S. visitors to the SciFi Web site), their content only tangentially affects the events of season 3. It's easy to pick up with season 3 even if you haven't seen the Webisodes, but seeing them does make a few things a little clearer, and it adds to the layers and continuity of some secondary and minor characters.

The Resistance started airing on September 5, 2006, and aired at a rate of two Webisodes per week until the season 3 premiere. The original impulse for the Webisodes was promotional — they were used as a sort of teaser for season 3, but because of their promotional nature they didn't generate any residuals for the writers — a very bad thing in the eyes of the Writers Guild of America. The other main issue surrounding the Webisodes was the fact that they were only made available to U.S. residents, inciting the rage of many an international fan — after all, if they were available for free on the site, then why not make them available everywhere? In an attempt to "even the playing field," so to speak, the Webisodes are to be included in the season 3 DVD set, put together along with cut scenes to create an "episode zero."

Whether or not you've seen *The Resistance*, the idea in both form and content is really well suited to the *BSG* universe. The cutting-edge digital format and very brief run-time give an interesting and unique glimpse into the birth of a movement, giving us just enough that we're interested in the characters' motivations and where those motivations will take them in season 3, but not so much that we're bored by the story line. The episodes were written in record time, and the production value obviously isn't as good as the average net-worked episode — simply because there wasn't the budget for it. Writer David Weddle commented, "When they initially came to us, we could have done just vignettes, and in fact the staff thought of that approach to the Webisodes. But when Brad [Bradley Thompson, writer] and I got the assignment we thought, 'Let's just tell one story.' Network wanted it to play into the third season, so that gave us the inspiration to chronicle events that would pay off in the third season. [...] In a day or two Brad and I came up with the concept, and a day after that we pitched them to SciFi. We wrote them in four days or something like that, and shot them the next week . . . The massacre in the temple has temp tracks [temporary music used during editing] we were going to loop and fix and make a lot better, but because we were forbidden to work on them anymore they went out as is. Of course people complained when they watched them and it just made us cringe because we very much wanted to correct that."

What *The Resistance* deals with is, obviously, the birth of the Resistance on New Caprica. The episodes start sixty-seven days into the Cylon occupation that began at the end of season 2, and follow Tigh, Chief, Cally (who's now given birth to a son, Nicolas), Jammer, Duck, his partner Nora, and Jean Barolay. The main thrust of *The Resistance* is to show how humankind can not only survive under harsh conditions but also fight back — take an active part in their own survival and pursue a better life. Not everyone resists in the same way, though — Nora and Cally survive because they have faith. They believe in the Lords of Kobol; they believe that they are where they're meant to be, and the situation might not be ideal, but they're happy in their own way. Chief, Tigh, and Barolay resist by concealing weapons and pursuing the idea of the "good fight" — in the words of Starbuck at the end of season 2, "Fight 'em until we can't." Religion and war interweave in the Webisodes, and some of the characters don't end up on the side they expected. Jammer's character in particular has to make some tough choices, and what we see opens up his character in a way that the more main-character-focused episodes in season 3 just don't allow.

Some of the characters and their motivations in season 3 are a lot more fleshed out if you've seen *The Resistance*. For instance Duck becomes a major part of the plot in the beginning of the new season. So a short summary of the Webisode events is included in this section.

Ronald Moore included the following dedication to the credits of the Webisodes: "All of the above people worked above and beyond the call of duty to deliver these Webisodes to you and they did it while also working to deliver the regular episodes of the third season. They did it without any template of how these things were to be done and they did it in defiance of a limited budget and an extraordinarily truncated shooting schedule. I'm proud of them and proud of their work. I hope you'll agree."

Webisode 1: Sixty-seventh day of the occupation on New Caprica. Tigh and Chief talk about the Resistance movement, commenting on how hard it is to get new recruits. We learn that the Cylons are establishing a human police force to instill order on the planet.

Webisode 2: Chief tries to recruit Tucker "Duck" Clellan into the Resistance, but he refuses because of his growing relationship with Nora. Later, in the temple, Jammer, Tigh, and Barolay discuss moving the weapons stash into the temple. Jammer objects, believing it to be a blasphemy.

Webisode 3: Nora prays for Aphrodite to grant her and Duck a child. Tigh, Chief, Jammer, and Barolay move the weapons into the temple.

Webisode 4: Cally and Nora visit the temple and discuss the importance of religion to themselves and their respective partners. Cally tells Nora that Chief is having a crisis of faith. Having been tipped off that the weapons are hidden in the temple, the Cylons ambush it, and Nora dies.

Webisode 5: Duck has a crisis of faith — both in terms of religion because he blames the gods for Nora's death, and in terms of the Resistance, which hid the weapons in the temple.

Webisode 6: The deaths of the ten people in the temple have prompted a public outcry: the Resistance movement is gaining hundreds of new recruits. Jammer bemoans the Resistance's part in the temple massacre.

Webisode 7: Jammer is taken to the detention center by the Cylons. He's visited by a Number Five model — Doral — who frees him of his restraints and asks about the temple massacre.

Webisode 8: Jammer is interrogated by Doral in the detention center. Although initially resistant, he wavers when Doral says that bringing weapons into a place of worship is an act of blasphemy. He gives Jammer a keycard that will allow him to enter the detention center if he wants to provide information on the Resistance's movements, to avoid further bloodshed.

Webisode 9: Jammer leaves the center and is greeted by Chief, who asks if he told them anything. Jammer denies that he gave the Cylons any information. Duck starts to clean up his home, which he destroyed after Nora's death; as he holds a picture, he starts to grieve.

Webisode 10: Duck joins the New Caprica Police to act as a spy for the Resistance. Cally and Chief's son undergoes his dedication ceremony. The Resistance starts to plan a major operation, which they will set up in a granary opposite the hospital. Wanting to prevent an accident involving the hospital, Jammer walks up toward the detention center to talk to Doral.

SEASON THREE — October 2006–March 2007

301   Occupation

Original air date: October 6, 2006
Written by: Ronald D. Moore
Directed by: Sergio Mimica-Gezzan

The Resistance movement on New Caprica tries to make the situation as tough as possible for the Cylon occupation.

Season 2 ended with a bang; season 3 opens with a slow montage of various sets of hands carefully etching out their personal form of resistance. While Tigh presses his nails into the concrete wall of his detention cell, his wife clenches her fists as she rides a Cylon's body; Chief and Anders patiently create a homemade bomb; Roslin follows the lines of the scriptures, praying to the Lords of Kobol; and Starbuck sets a table in a pretty little apartment, picking up a fork and gazing at it. Far from answering the questions that the season 2 finale raised, the season skips ahead four months.

The opening credits tell the same story as the opening montage: "The human race . . . far from home . . . fighting for survival." The rest of the text fades out, but the word "survival" remains — stark and solitary on the screen as the characters remain, alone and lonely, each in their respective hells. The fight that Starbuck declared in "Lay Down Your Burdens, Part 2" doesn't appear to have happened at all, and everyone seems determined, but already defeated.

It's hard to believe that we will see anything close to what Edward James Olmos promised: "Third season is the best season we've ever put forth. It's devastating what happens this year. It reads like today's news." And yet, "Occupation" absolutely delivers.

The first two episodes of season 3 were aired together, making for a two-hour premiere that resets once again all of our preconceptions of the characters. We *think* a lot of things when "Occupation" begins, but as the story unfolds we discover that we were wrong and that what we thought was the truth is far away from any truth we could have considered. We think that Tigh has been defeated by the Cylons, his spirit and body broken; that Starbuck's mellowed, become a placid, housebound wife willing to submit to Leoben and play the game; that Ellen is voluntarily screwing around on Tigh; that Roslin has given up the fight and turned to religion as a source of comfort. And in a sense, all of this is true, but it's only with context that the reality of their situation becomes clear. And so as the episode unravels, the hands that seemed to be submissive suddenly become sharpened, turn into weapons of resistance: Tigh holds on to the small indentations that separate him from insanity, hoping eventually he'll walk out of the cell — he may no longer be physically whole, but he is, and remains, a free man, despite the walls enclosing him. By the same token, Starbuck is locked into a nightmarish day-to-

Conventions are a great place to hear what the actors have to say. This was Kate Vernon's first such event, seen here with Jamie, Katee, and Michael Trucco.

dayness that she resists giving in to by sizing up the lethal potential of the everyday objects that surround her. Ellen is caught in the web of the Cylon occupation, and the only way she can regain her touchstone, Saul, is to use her body, in a horrible, twisted mimicry of her unfaithful ways. All are trapped, unable to escape, but work to turn what they have at their disposal into weapons.

Aboard *Galactica*, the empty ship echoes, reflecting Admiral Adama, who is hollow, frustrated and guilty. Things are different on board *Galactica*, the most obvious change being Adama's relationship with Sharon. They share tea and sympathy in Sharon's "cell" — only it's now decorated, comforting — home. Instead of actively resisting, the remaining fleet has had to adapt differently, to playing the waiting game.

But things change even while we're waiting: Lee has piled on the pounds, he's married, he's in charge of the *Pegasus*; Helo is second-in-command of the *Galactica*, he's regained his status in Adama's eyes; Adama has turned his paternal love from Starbuck to Sharon. In a nice reversal from last season, he's now visiting her at her home, rather than having her brought to wherever he is — just one more sign of how things have changed. Adama has been alone on that ship for longer than the four months the Cylons have occupied New

Caprica: it's been much longer, since the Colonials all started to settle on the planet, trusting their lives to the ground and no longer to the *Galactica*.

Until our first view of Kara, the scenes from this opening episode have been claustrophobic in atmosphere. From Tigh's cell to Roslin's small tent to Ellen's "affair" (she's filmed from below, which makes the ceiling seem as if it's closing in on her), every space is tiny, closed. The space Kara shares with Leoben is wide open with light and space, but she's a prisoner there — just like Tigh and Ellen. Leoben hasn't lost any of his creepiness. Like Six and Sharon in their own ways, he's obsessed with the idea of love and when he says, "To see the face of God is to know madness," he looks insane. He acts more like a stalker than the husband he's pretending to be, and their domesticity is really captivity. Starbuck's eyes are always shaded by the dark so Leoben can never be sure of what she's thinking or feeling. His is far from Six's idea of love; far from Sharon's unfailing belief in her own humanity. Leoben possesses the same calm, mildly curious outlook that he displayed in "Flesh and Bone," when Adama told Starbuck that she wouldn't understand the Cylon's plan until later.

While "Occupation" seems almost depressing in its scope, the ending provides the ultimate reset, which, with a note of hope, sets the resistance group's, *Galactica*'s, and our own spirits soaring. While that hope flickers, the devastation continues: Duck marches to his death, the suicide bombing futile in the extreme and devastating in its perceived necessity; Leoben unlocks the door to his home and invites Kara to his bed while his corpse lies on the floor behind them; Tigh covers his eye with a makeshift patch and continues to sound the drums of war.

"Occupation" tells a really disturbing story, and it turns all our preconceived notions around. None of the characters are doing what they seem to be. They're all creating order in the only way they can, and in some ways, that speaks to the double-entendre of the episode's title. The humans are trying to keep themselves occupied so that they can survive; without their various occupations, they're just a people that have been defeated, with nothing left to do but what the folks on *Galactica* are doing: waiting.

Headcount: There's no headcount given — Gaius and the Cylons are in power, and survivor count isn't one of their priorities. Instead we see that it's been 134 days since the Occupation began, 514 days since the Colonists settled.

Interesting Fact: It's hard to see exactly what Kara uses to stab Leoben through the neck because it happens too quickly and the stabbing is so flurried. Some fan theories included knitting needles and a fork with the middle tine filed out, but Ronald Moore says that it's actually chopsticks.

What's In a Name? Tigh's first name, Saul, most likely has its origins in the Bible, where Saul was recognized as the first king of ancient Israel. The Book of Samuel provides three distinct stories about how Saul became king: two of them involve some form of visionary appointment, while the third recounts that the Ammonite army laid siege to Jabesh-Gilead. When the city surrenders, the terms of their surrender dictate that the right eye of each person be removed as a sign of their entry into slavery. When the other tribes of Israel heard about the surrender, they gathered an army under Saul's leadership, and are led to victory against the Ammonites. In celebration and appreciation, the people proclaim Saul their king. The biblical story offers a number of similarities with Tigh's story in *BSG*. Both the king and Tigh are warriors fighting against a situation they believe is unjust, battling ceaselessly against an enemy that has already won the fight. In the same way the Ammonites had already won over Jabesh-Gilead, so too have the Cylons already taken over New Caprica; the only choice that remains in both cases is to fight back. There's also a clear and nasty reminder of the biblical story in the removal of Tigh's eye . . .

Did You Notice? Actress Kandyse McClure (Dee) is credited for the first — and so far, only — time as Candice McClure in this episode. She's credited as Candice in other projects (like the 2000 movie *Romeo Must Die*), but never before on *BSG*.

"I'll see you soon," Leoben gasps as he dies. That's a callback to the season 2 episode "Downloaded," where Six says to D'Anna just after she bashes her over the head with a rock, "See you again soon." The phrase is echoed by Duck's "See you soon, Nora" at the end of this episode, just before the bomb goes off.

The apartment room where Starbuck is being held is actually the set of Starbuck's home on Caprica, revamped. (We saw her place in season 2's "Valley of Darkness.")

So Say We All: HAVE HOPE.

WE'RE COMING FOR YOU.

302   Precipice

Original air date: October 6, 2006
Written by: Ronald D. Moore
Directed by: Sergio Mimica-Gezzan

The New Caprica Police starts cracking down on the Colonists after the suicide bombing. Adama comes up with a plan to rescue the Colonists.

"Precipice" starts with a meeting of past and present in the characters of Roslin and Gaius. Gaius's constant companions are the Cylons, a fact that's made all the more obvious here: he doesn't meet with Roslin in his office on *Colonial One*; instead, he announces his loyalties by coming to a Cylon detention cell to ask her to intervene with the Resistance. It's a reversal of Roslin meeting with him in Adama's quarters to request that they make a joint statement to the press regarding their mutual decision to table the issue of settlement on New Caprica. Shades of truth, lies, the pair's inability to communicate or come to any understanding — all of this is illustrated by the small gestures they perform. Gaius hands Roslin her glasses — he's in control. She puts them on — she's dignified and aware of the game he's playing. He tells her to look him "in the eyes" — but their eyes are separated by two sets of glasses. The message is clear: there can be no connection, no communication — no truth — between these two. The past is as set as stone between them, and there's no coming back from it. In her eyes, he's a two-time traitor; in his, she's a hypocritical fool. He grants her her freedom, but it comes at a cost: she has to accept something from him. She does it, unhappily; and she's even more unhappy that he's made a point. She *doesn't* believe that suicide bombing is the right thing to do, the good thing, and it's unimaginable to her that she and Gaius should be on the same side of any fence.

Over the first two seasons, Roslin has grown. She's much more willing now to listen to other sides of a story, while in the miniseries, for instance, she completely overrode Adama's "advice" to make the fight their first priority, rather than any potential survivors. Over the last year and a half, Roslin has changed her mind about a lot of things: the scriptures, Hera, Sharon, Adama, and she stands now on the edge of a precipice that, it seems, she doesn't fully recognize yet. Her mind is made up about Gaius — can it ever change? If she can't admit to him that she feels he's right about the suicide bombings, will she ever be willing to look at him differently?

Gaius is another character that's standing on a precipice — the difference is, he's always stood on one. He's been close to the edge for as long as we can remember; we've never been sure he's entirely mentally stable. He went from perfectly happy egocentric genius with a beautiful girlfriend to an "odd little man" with a mental version of a blow-up doll all in one episode. In "Precipice," Gaius knows signing the death warrant will change everything. He knows that by signing it, he's edging inexorably closer to that uncomfortable truth he suspects about himself — that he's not so much a victim as an out-and-out traitor. Suddenly, as if his hand never even traced the letters, the signature is there.

And look at the way the Cylons get him to sign the paper — they shoot Six: they *know* that he'll sign it, it's just a matter of pressing the right buttons, and because Gaius is such a predictable person, they know that Six is the one to push. And bam. She's gone, Six-in-a-red-dress reappears, and Gaius is one step closer to living back in his fantasy world. Later in the episode he appears disconnected from reality, staring blankly as Gaeta brandishes the execution order. Faced with the proof of his own actions, Gaius does what he always does, nothing. He suffers the loss of Six, and realizes his own unimportance on New Caprica — because for once, for *once*, he said no to something, but it didn't matter.

One of the overarching themes of these first few episodes of season 3 revolves around what it's possible to live with. How much guilt? How much responsibility? How much betrayal? How much twistedness can Starbuck endure, for instance, before she gives in to the warped quality of her life and starts to believe the lie? Hers is a nightmare existence, and it's about to become even more surreal with the appearance of Kacey. Kacey, the blonde cherub child who looks like she really could be Starbuck's. Like Doral, who saw Gaius's button and pulled the trigger on it, Leoben pushes Kara to the point of no return, taking the fear he saw in her back in "Flesh and Bone" and turning it on her so she has no choice but to fall over the edge. She's been standing on the edge of her own precipice for four months now — the calm, unconnected, glazed look of despair and rage on her face when she sat back down to her dinner, her hands soaked in Leoben's blood in "Occupation" is proof enough of that — and he shows her a child, confirms her worst fears of being a victim of medical rape, and *snap*. Her reality shifts, and she'll never be the same.

Ellen's another person standing on the edge; she doesn't appear much in this episode, but what time she *is* there is chilling. When she takes the map from Saul and leans over, pretending to throw it into the fire, the camera angle shifts suddenly. Ellen is seen on the other side of the fire, her hands up in an attempt to warm herself or ward off the abyss she sees opening before her. It looks like she's standing on the brink of hell: will she fall off? Jump? Fly? Poor Ellen — on *Galactica*, she was so easy to hate and look down on. She was an ambitious alcoholic determined to drag Saul along with her; now, she's flawed, made human by her love for Saul — and how ironic that Ellen is humanized, just as the Cylons are, through the need for love.

Those same issues are just as present back on *Galactica* as they are on the surface of the planet. In "Occupation," we wondered how long Adama could let guilt consume him before he was faced with a choice — let it win, or break himself loose of its shackles. In "Precipice," Adama's come into his own again: he knows what he has to do and he's willing to let his son think that he's off his rocker — for sending Sharon down to the surface, for reinstating her as an officer — because he has direction and focus, two things it seems he's been sorely lacking for quite some time.

So-called minor characters are nicely fleshed out here. Jammer's arc does make more sense if you've seen *The Resistance* Webisodes, as they provide more detail on why exactly he turns to the New Caprica Police to find his place in the struggle (see "The Resistance" chapter) but we still see enough of him to know that he's not clear with himself. Jammer hasn't been a big character over the last two seasons, but in *The Resistance*, he was shown to have good intentions — like he tells Chief here, he doesn't want the Cylons on the streets, policing the humans — but it's all about perspective: he's not comfortable with what he's doing. How much of that is his own conscience, however, and how much is his own projection of what Chief and Tigh will think of him? He only frees Cally because she's Chief's wife — what of the rest of the 200 people? Is it enough that he does what he can for one person, or should he do more, free more, prove himself definitively a member of the NCP or a member of the Resistance? He does what he has to, and does what he can — much like everyone else.

At the end of this episode, everything has changed. In a great example of "the enemy of my enemy is my friend," Roslin and Tom Zarek are allies — and they provide some of the only moments of levity in the entire episode. Gaius is staring down at the abyss. Starbuck is stuck in a dreamworld she's starting to believe is real. Ellen has stepped into hell. Lee is trapped in a life of his own making. While the situation hasn't changed much since the end of season 2, "Occupation"/"Precipice" changes everything we thought we knew about the characters — and the only question is: can we take it?

All of This Has Happened Before: Tigh absolutely rocks this episode to its core. His battle-weariness and Old Man of War attitude bring to mind the Norse god Odin — one of the foremost gods of Nordic mythology, and the god of wisdom, war, battle, and death. He's also known as the god of poetry, magic, prophecy, and the hunt — *and* he has only one eye. Odin sacrificed his eye to obtain wisdom, and is often said to have been an instigator of wars. Tigh's speeches in the first two episodes of season 3 — as well as the next couple of episodes — have a poetic ring to them, and he's definitely encouraging warlike mentalities and attitudes. He's also very much the center of the Resistance, despite having been imprisoned for a long period of time; Anders, Chief, Ellen all look to him as their leader, or god, in the art of war and resistance.

Numbers: There were 33 people killed in the suicide bomb attack; this is the second time the number 33 has been placed front and center in the series. The first episode of the series was called "33," and it has some pretty intricate numerological, historical, religious, and cultural significances. See page 58 for more on 33.

Interesting Fact: If you've ever wondered how Tricia Helfer — or Grace Park, or any of the actors who plays Cylons — cope with scenes featuring more than one model, wonder no more. Tricia laughed in a recent interview, "I think there have been a few times this season where everybody involved in the scene — from the director on down to the cast, crew, everybody — has just been at their wits' end, because there were four of my characters in one scene. There were a bunch of Cylons in the room, and it's really hard because in the end, you're talking to nothing."

Did You Notice? "Precipice" marks the first time that all seven known Cylon models have appeared in the same episode.

Even though we found out Gaeta's first name, Felix, back in "Final Cut," this episode is the first time it's been said out loud by another character.

The coded callout that Sharon yells out at the end of the episode, "C-Bucks rule!" is a callback to season 2's "Downloaded," in which we saw a car with a bumper sticker on it saying "C-Bucks rule."

It seems kind of strange that the Cylons are bitter about humanity's inability to value life the way the Cylons do, considering the fact that in season 1, a Doral model used the same suicide bomb tactics as the Resistance did in "Occupation." (See "Litmus.")

So Say We All: TIGH: I've sent men on suicide missions in two wars now, and let me tell you something. It don't make a godsdamn bit of difference whether they're riding in a Viper or walking out onto a parade ground. In the end, they're just as dead. So take your piety and your moralizing and your high-minded principles, and stick 'em somewhere safe until you're off this rock and you're sitting in your nice, cushy chair on *Colonial One* again. I've got a war to fight.

303   Exodus, Part 1

Original air date: October 13, 2006
Written by: Bradley Thompson, David Weddle
Directed by: Felix Enriquez Alcala

Sharon gets the launch codes that will allow the Colonists to escape New Caprica.

One of the most famous exoduses chronicled in human history is the one told in the Bible and Torah about the story of Moses. The exodus chronicled in this two-parter is much more a team effort. Each team plays a part in bringing the fleet back together, but it's not until the second part of "Exodus" that there'll be any sort of payoff for the jeopardy that grows throughout this episode. This is just the first part of the journey, when the preparations are made. The Resistance doesn't even know at this point if Sharon will be able to procure the launch codes that will allow them to leave the planet — if she can't, then all their planning is for naught. In some ways, this is the hardest part: the uncertainty and the preparations and the waiting. In four months of futile acts of war and anger, escape has never been so close.

The first surprising thing about "Exodus, Part 1" is the sudden jump backwards in time. The last episode of season 2 jumped forward a year, while "Occupation" skipped ahead four months, so with the story picking up so fast at the end of "Precipice," the step back in time is jolting. When the scene shifts to Sharon and her team landing on New Caprica and making their way to the meeting with Anders and the Resistance group, it's the first time that switch in point of view has been done on the show: in "Precipice," we saw those exact same events from Anders' perspective. It's an interesting way to show how the Centurions' attack was foiled: all we saw in the last episode was that they were under attack, and then they weren't, so seeing the "behind the scenes" of that event is very effective — most shows would just have Sharon telling Anders, "I set up a sharpshooter because it was a logical place for an ambush." Instead, we're right in the thick of the action.

Unfortunately, the Centurions' thwarted plan provides the ultimate proof of Ellen's treason, and it isn't looking too good for her when the episode ends. Saul is confronted with the undeniable truth. But here again, it's context that changes everything. She isn't a traitor in the same way that Jammer could be seen as a traitor, or Gaius could be seen as a traitor, or Starbuck could be seen as a

The grossest screen kiss ever — Starbuck and Leoben (CAROLE SEGAL/ © SCI-FI/COURTESY: EVERETT COLLECTION)

traitor for believing Leoben — or even the same way that Adama and Lee could be seen as traitors for jumping away when the Cylons arrived. Each treason is specific to the character's own set of beliefs: the worst possible treason they commit is their betrayal of their own values.

Two of the largest threads of this two-part episode are the quests of D'Anna and Six. D'Anna becomes a kind of visionary through her dreams (it's the first time we've seen a Cylon dreaming). Meanwhile Six is pursuing her own mission: to explore love. This version of Caprica-Six and Gaius seems to be picking up where they left off before the attack on the Colonies, but they've both seen, lied, and changed so much since then that, while their earlier escapades were filled with color and were vibrant with discovery and passion, now they're a cliché in the great book of lovers everywhere. In a wonderful reimagining of this scenario, Gaius, far from the traditional response of a man faced with his own impotence, doesn't feel guilty or think his virility is at stake. Instead, it's the impotence that surrounds the rest of his life that bothers him: his inability to stand up for the human race, his inability to stand up to the Cylons.

Are You an Insurgent Or a Resistant?

In the end of season 2, we see the Cylons arrive on the Colonists' new home, New Caprica. President Gaius Baltar immediately surrenders, and the final scene of the season is one of the Cylon Centurions marching into the settlement. Between seasons 2 and 3, ten Webisodes, collectively entitled *The Resistance*, aired, showing the birth and growth of a Resistance in New Caprica. The first four episodes of season 3 focused on the Resistance and the Cylons' reaction to the group's actions. One of the interesting things about those four episodes is the terminology used: while the members of the group refer to it as the Resistance, each time the Cylons talk about those members, they use the terms "insurgents" and "insurgency." So what's the difference? And does it make a difference?

Briefly, insurgents are those who engage in insurgency – that is, an armed revolt against an established political or civil authority. A Resistance movement, however, is a different thing entirely, because it's a group that is fighting against an occupying force. So it makes sense that Tigh, Chief, Anders, Barolay, etc., refer to themselves as a Resistance because, from the Colonists' perspective (at least, most of them), the Cylons are invaders. They came, they saw, they occupied, and they're still there, an unofficial but overshadowing force behind New Caprica's government. And those that are resisting their presence are just that – resistants.

To the Cylons, however, it's a different story, because they're there with the Colonial President's consent – even (with some twisted interpreting) at his invitation. So the Cylons think of themselves as an integral part of the government, a recognized authority, even though their decisions require the official approval of the President. From that perspective, the Resistance isn't resisting – they're rising up against an authorized government body. There's nothing to resist: Gaius surrendered unconditionally, and the Cylons are now *there*.

So are the resistants insurgents? Or are they really resistants? It all depends on your point of view – and it's not necessarily an easy question, because some of the Colonists believe that the Cylons and humans can live together, so in their mind, too, the Resistance is an insurgency. And there are similar diversions in beliefs amongst the Cylons too. The question is an important one, but there's no black-and-white answer.

Six's impotence is different. She lived on Caprica for two years, slept with Gaius for two years, lived as a human, worked as a human, felt as a human. Trapped in a Cylon's body, she feels like the ultimate pariah, belonging to neither race. The humans would execute her as happily as the Doral model did in the previous episode, and she knows it. She doesn't belong anywhere except with Gaius, and it's actually really difficult to watch her suffering. It's also interesting to compare her and Gaius to other couples on the show — Sharon and Helo are a loving, supportive, functional couple, while Starbuck and Leoben are a parody of a couple. Six and Gaius fall somewhere in between: the love they have for each other is real, but Six is just a little *off*, and Gaius is just a little *depressed*, and it's tempting to say that their relationship is just a little . . . *dysfunctional*. But it's not that easy, because as they sit on opposite sides of their bed, backs to one another, looking at the floor, both at a loss, they still seem to be looking for a way to connect.

Other characters feel impotent too: back on *Galactica*, Lee faces one of the biggest decisions of his life. He has to take all the threads that have been unraveling since the first attacks and make sense of them before he can figure out what he believes and what he wants to do. He believes at first that it's madness for Adama to attempt a rescue of the settlers, and that the only choice is to go on, leave behind any survivors and just *go*. And indeed that's what Anders expected Adama to do — in "Occupation" he angrily reminded Tigh that Anders and his group would never have gotten off Caprica if it had been left to Adama. It seems like the logical thing to do — cut their losses and make their way to Earth. But what Lee believes — or thinks he believes — doesn't really matter, because deep down, something's gnawing at him. He wonders whether it really *is* the same situation, whether this time it's the wrong choice to leave all those people down there. What if it's no longer just about the survival of the human race, but about the survival of the connections that they've made and the relationships? And ultimately, despite the fact that he's grown complacent and "lost his edge" (in Dee's words), Lee has to redefine himself as a pilot and an officer, and not just as the son of a pilot and an officer.

BSG has examined the idea of accessing the subconscious or the greater unknown through dreams (Laura), visions (Gaius, Lee), and prophecies (Leoben). In "Exodus, Part 1," it's D'Anna who's dreaming — of Hera. It's hard to say yet just what D'Anna's journey will be. Leoben seemed to be connected to some otherworldly presence — God, according to his theology — but D'Anna goes to see an oracle — a human oracle at that. Of all the Cylons, she's probably the most likely to look for answers outside the realm of the Cylon, simply because as a member of the fleet, she took on the role of reporter — someone who was interested in the different sides of a story. D'Anna's visit to Selloi points to the idea that not all Cylons are created equal in terms of their connection to God, otherwise D'Anna would have been able to see the future as Leoben said he could.

Another Cylon that's starting to fray around the edges is Brother Cavil. It's consistently hilarious that he's meant to be a man of the cloth, and yet he's pretty much the least sympathetic and empathetic Cylon model we've seen so far. He has a really cynical approach, laughing wonderingly at humans and Cylons alike, pointing out their flaws. Cavil chose to make himself die faster rather than suffer through the agony of a lingering death — but then again, he's the Cylon who's seemed the least interested in making himself more human, so perhaps that doesn't bother him.

Interesting Fact: The actor who plays Charlie Connor of the Resistance in this episode is Ryan Robbins. You might recognize him from the miniseries, where he played the Armistice officer who died in the very beginning, and who is presumed to be Boxey's father. He's also well known for his role on the sci-fi show *Stargate: Atlantis*, in which he plays the part of Ladon Radim, one of the leaders of an alien people.

Did You Notice? An oft-noted fact about this episode is that Chief has lost the beard he's sported since the end of season 2. Aaron Douglas shot the scenes for this episode long after he had shot scenes for other episodes and the producers felt a fake beard would look, well, fake.

There's a slight discrepancy between the end of "Precipice" and the beginning of "Exodus, Part 1": in the former, Cally is clearly seen running when the gunfire begins, while in the latter she's thrown to the ground before the shooting begins. The original sequence was probably done to build tension at the end of "Precipice."

The scene of Maya holding Hera/Isis has a very specific composition: it looks a lot like Pietà paintings and sculptures that depict the mother and child *par excellence* — Jesus as an infant held by His mother, Mary. The mother is nearly always portrayed as looking lovingly down at the child, and she's either holding Him cradled in her arms or poised on her lap. The pose is so specific that it can't be anything but a reference to that.

Classic *Battlestar Galactica*: A comic book by the same name as this episode was published in 1979 and followed the story line of the original series pilot episode "Saga of a Star World."

So Say We All: ADAMA: One day you will tell your children, and your grandchildren, that you served with such men and women as the universe has never seen, and together you accomplished a feat that will be told and retold down through the ages. And find immortality as only the Gods once knew.

304   Exodus, Part 2

Original air date: October 20, 2006
Written by: David Weddle, Bradley Thompson
Directed by: Felix Enriquez Alcala

Ellen and Saul face the consequences of Ellen's betrayal.

When "Exodus, Part 1" left off, things weren't looking so good for Ellen Tigh, and when her arc picks up again in this second part, her fate is sealed. On the official *BSG* forums, Kate Vernon, who plays Ellen, explained that Ellen knew about the poison in her cup: "Ellen absolutely knew what was in the cup. She spared her husband having to give her the poison. As much as she wanted him to knock it out of her hands and come up with a mercy plan, she knew her husband wouldn't go against the Resistance." Executive producer David Eick notes, "In the case of Ellen Tigh, there needed to be damage, measurable permanent damage to some of our people as a result of the events on New Caprica. We needed to have some consistency in how we treat the people we care about, in that they don't get off the hook just because we care about them."

Whatever your take on the scene, it's heartbreaking, and not only because Ellen is seen in a fully sympathetic light. As she bares her soul and confesses her sins — following the death rite practices of cultures the world over — Ellen becomes more than the libidinous alcoholic that first stepped foot on *Galactica* in "Tigh Me Up, Tigh Me Down." It's a beautiful, horrible scene, and it feels like we owe it to Tigh to watch Ellen die with the same devotion and courage that he exhibits. If he doesn't let himself look away, then how can *we* let ourselves? Ellen's not in any physical pain, but her emotional agony tears at the heart, because it's so easy to see how she got in to that situation. She wanted to save her husband, and she did it — whatever it took. She did what every member of the Resistance and the fleet is doing every day: whatever they have to to get what they need. It's horrible to watch also because Saul quite probably wouldn't have done the same for her: the fight is too important to him, and he wouldn't jeopardize that for anything — not even for the love of his life.

Ellen's death isn't the central point of this episode but it colors everything that occurs around it. When Tigh makes it back to the *Galactica*, he's a changed man, and his physical changes — the eye patch, the limp — are but the least of it. He climbs down the stairs onto the hangar deck and Adama's eyes soften and harden as he takes in what the four months have done to his friend. A divide appears between them as throngs of people gather on Adama, lifting him up to sing his praises as Tigh, the man who lost an eye, killed his wife,

Kate autographs an official piece of memorabilia (ALBERT L. ORTEGA)

fought the Cylons every day, walks away, lost and alone. What's interesting about that scene is that we've been rooting for Adama throughout both parts of the "Exodus" saga, and suddenly, as he's glorified, Tigh's bitterness and grief rise up, like the voices of the crowd and Adama himself on their shoulders, and threaten to overwhelm the scene.

One of the larger themes of this episode is the passing on of stories through the generations. In "Occupation," we saw that Laura's been keeping a journal of the time under the Gaius/Cylon rule; and in "Exodus, Part 1," Adama gave a rousing speech about the importance of the mission on which the *Galactica*'s crew was about to embark, saying that their story would be "told and retold down through the ages."

In many ways, *BSG* is constructed very much like an epic — Dee even talks about Adama like he's already a myth, saying "there'll be no one to remember a man named William Adama, or a battlestar named *Galactica*. That is our charge to keep." While the humans crave "immortality as only the Gods once knew," their Cylon counterparts are far more wary of the idea. In this episode, D'Anna confronts Gaius with her vision of the future, creating a world in which the humans continue to tell stories about the "evil Cylon" to their children and their children's children. Her spiel sounds partly like a rational projection of what human/Cylon relations could be like in the future, but it also sounds like she's afraid of the legacy the humans could pass on. While the humans crave a link to time — cherishing their bond with the past, fantasizing about the future — the Cylons exist pretty much entirely for the present moment. There is no real concept of past or present for them, despite the fact that their first attacks on the Colonies were the product of many years of rage and vengeful desires. For D'Anna, at least, the future is something to be feared, not embraced, and the link with time is something to be equally feared, not cherished.

"Exodus" finishes the arc that was opened with "Lay Down Your Burdens," bringing to a close the New Caprican era and Gaius's presidency. By the end of the episode, things have come full circle for the crew: the fleet is reunited, Lee and Adama have come to terms with their relationship once again, the halls of the *Galactica* are bustling with life and energy, in huge contrast to the beginning of "Occupation," when they echoed, hollow and empty, and Adama is shaving off his mustache. This two-parter has it all — drama, tragedy, excitement — and one of the best entrances of a starship into orbit ever seen. It looks like *Galactica* is going to drop like an anvil onto the surface of New Caprica, and she's never looked bulkier or less graceful! Apollo's last-minute sacrifice of the *Pegasus*, which swoops in to save Adama and his ship from destruction, adds even more. Apollo's is an act of sheer joy and ambition, and he walks more confidently, speaks more cleanly, and looks Adama in the eyes. If he hasn't found his war again, he's at least found some purpose — as has nearly everyone; aside from Starbuck and Tigh, who may have both survived, but at what cost?

Are You There, God? It's Me, Gaius. "[New Caprica will be] buried like the cities of old. Consumed by the wrath of God." Gaius has had a tough few episodes. He's made a total sham of his presidency, defied the Cylons enough so that *they*'re mad at him, betrayed the humans enough so that *they*'re mad at him, and now he's wandering the ruins of what he perceives as his city with just Six and a miracle child for company. In some ways, Gaius looks at New Caprica like his own creation, his vision for humanity — a way to redeem some of his past actions, perhaps. It may have started out as a political ploy but as he sat in his office on *Colonial One*, he managed to convince himself that he was building something. New Caprica stood in for his ego, his life — it was something good to come of all his treason, and now it lays dying.

Interesting Fact: According to Moore, "Exodus" was "originally written and shot to be a single episode but there was so much story material within it, so many things had to be accomplished that I knew fairly early on that we were probably going to be looking to split this sucker into two parts."

What's In a Name? Maya is the name of the adoptive mother of Hera (or Isis). In Hindu philosophy, maya is a fundamental concept that defines the force that creates the illusion that the material world is real. In simpler terms, maya is the phenomenal universe — that is, the universe that is perceivable in a material way. She has two main functions: she hides the Brahman, or supreme being, and she presents the material world instead of Brahman. In that sense, the *BSG* Maya is performing the same function, as she is both hiding Hera from the Cylon and human populations and holding up an illusion, Isis, in Hera's place. The duality of the baby is emphasized by the fact that Hera is "the shape of things to come" — a being that is more than human or Cylon, but a combination of both, and perhaps something more — while Isis, as Maya's daughter, is to everyone aside from Laura, Adama, and Dr. Cottle, just a baby. In Hindu philosophy, Maya is also seen as part of the Divine Mother concept of Hinduism, placing *BSG* Maya firmly in a maternal role.

In Greek mythology, Hera is best known as the wife of Zeus, but she is also the daughter of the Titan siblings Cronus and Rhea, and one of the most powerful of the Olympians. She was aligned especially with the lives of women, and also presided over marriage. In *BSG*, Hera is the result of a powerful marriage that broke traditional bonds, and she's a girl. Hera seems to be pointing to a new way to view things, both as a female and as a "hybrid" of a Cylon and a human. The Hera of Greek mythology was tremendously important to their literature, often acting as a foil against which plots would unfold, and *BSG*'s Hera seems to follow a similar function.

Dark happenings in "Collaborators"

Did You Notice? Before the *Pegasus* swoops in, *Galactica* is apparently facing four Cylon basestars, but when the *Pegasus* arrives on the scene, there are only three. Later, when one basestar has been destroyed, the DRADIS screen shows four basestars, where there should only be three.

When Saul is draped out over Ellen's laid-out body, it's a reversal of the traditional image of a woman bent over her husband's dead body that we see in a lot of tragedies.

Leoben's prophetic words from "Occupation" come true in this episode, but the context changes everything. Starbuck does indeed kiss him and tell him that she loves him, but it's all fake — and she ends the scene by planting a knife in his side. How's that for an imperfect vision?

The manoever that the Viper planes implement in this episode is the same one they bungled sixteen times in "Occupation." This time, though, they perform the move perfectly.

305   Collaborators

Original air date: October 27, 2006
Written by: Mark Verheiden
Directed by: Michael Rymer

The fleet might be reunited but the events on New Caprica have left a mark.

If this were another show, the events that occurred between "Occupation" and "Exodus, Part 2" might be simply pushed aside, the consequences forgotten, actions assumed to be forgiven. Not in *BSG*, where the exodus is only half the story and the rest is still unraveling. "Collaborators" is a dark episode. After the thrill of the rescue from New Caprica and the excitement of the fleet being reunited, it's a solemn atmosphere as everyone works through what has happened to them. Some — like Chief and Anders — work more quickly than others, but all of them have their own reasons for being angry about their time under the occupation. Tigh lost both Ellen and his eye, Starbuck was held captive by a creepy Cylon stalker who toyed with her mind, Connor's son was killed, Chief's wife was held for execution, and Anders' wife was missing and presumed dead. They all have their reasons, and they all take *something* from the Circle.

The teaser for "Collaborators" is chilling. Jammer was a familiar face in the slew of background characters on board *Galactica*, and it's hard to watch the major players act as judge, jury, and executioner for him. Jammer's execution — or is it murder? — suggests that everyone dies alone: there's not a friendly face in the group, and later we find out that a dozen others have been tried and punished in the same way, "taken care of" by people on other ships.

Anders is the first of the Circle to recognize that he's not getting what he needs from it, which makes sense. He and fifty-two other people survived in a postapocalyptic scenario because they were able to look at their situation and act accordingly. Anders didn't know that they'd ever be rescued, he just kept fighting. Then he *was* rescued, and he moved on from that experience and adapted, which is something he's really good at. Even as Starbuck lashes out and tells him she's not ready to pursue their marriage at the moment, he adapts. He says what he needs to, and moves on. If only everyone were that transparent!

While the title of this episode most obviously refers to those who collaborated with the Cylons, whatever their motivations, it also implicitly refers to the members of the Circle and Tom Zarek himself, who authorized the Circle's activities. Tigh, Barolay, Connor, Chief, Seelix, and Starbuck (and Anders, before he left) are all collaborating in the murders. It's interesting that Starbuck doesn't have any blood on her hands, really, because she comes in when Gaeta is being judged and his execution never occurs, but she of everyone exhibits the most vindictiveness. She's clearly not in the Circle for justice — she's in it for revenge. Starbuck seems unhinged, and while her usual MO would be to take to the bottle, given a flesh-and-blood target, she seizes that instead.

While Starbuck falls not-so-gently into a downward spiral, Apollo continues to work on himself, both physically and mentally. He's not in this episode much, but during the time he does spend on screen, he's calm and composed, very different from the Apollo we saw in "Occupation" and "Precipice," where he was practically frothing at the mouth at some of Adama's actions. Now he looks serene, as if he's finally made peace with the idea that he's a military officer and he's settled into his place in the grand scheme of things again. It can't be easy on him, though, considering he was the commander of a battlestar but has been demoted back to CAG. Apollo doesn't seem to bear any resentment about that state of affairs, and this could be due to the fact that sacrificing the *Pegasus* was his idea. Adama thought Lee and the fleet were far, far away; it was Apollo who decided to disobey orders and help with the rescue operation, so in all the ways that count, Apollo chose his own destiny, knowing full well that they wouldn't all survive the attacks and that he would likely not be commanding his own ship if he did survive.

A sharp contrast to the blinding anger and darkness covering the Circle and its actions is Laura Roslin and her speech at the end of the episode. Even the lighting in that scene is totally different from the lighting in the scenes revolving around the Circle: everyone is bathed in soft light that serves to emphasize the message of forgiveness that Roslin conveys. Laura is hoping that the TRC will let everyone be heard, without judgment or punishment, and pave the way to a more democratic and just society — a society everyone had been trying to build until the Cylons arrived.

Headcount: The headcount is back, and it's shocking: 41,435 survivors, compared to 49,550 from "Lay Down Your Burdens."

Interesting Fact: James Callis is really naked in his scenes in this episode. Lucy Lawless recalls in an interview her reaction to his nudity: "He was standing there holding his genitalia and the camera was on us, so it might've been on his back, I don't recall. It was over the shoulder on us, and at some point he took his hand away and fluttered his hands in the air. […] I think it was the only time ever that I have had to walk away from a scene because I was just flummoxed."

Did You Notice? Starbuck holds up the execution order signed by Gaius on New Caprica. Among the names we see are: Justin Singh (clerk), Dennis Moore (driver), Xander Zorost (mechanic), Laura Roslin (teacher), Lester Thoro (food services), Arimin Stahl (supply), Sally Menlo (facilitator), Kalan Pelham (administrator), Alex Lamere (office worker), Fore Ramone (office worker), Jane Seadle (mechanic), Jacob Morose (entertainer), Sue Emmanuel (doctor), Ali Mueller (botanist), and Tom Zarek (detainee).

If you were wondering how no one noticed an airlock being opened when Jammer was executed, you're not the only one — it's one of the show's most frequently mentioned nit-picks. Ryan Robbins, who plays Connor, said in an interview, "*Battlestar Galactica* really try super hard to pay attention to details. We have people, you know from NASA, […] technical people that get phone calls from time to time [asking] what would actually happen. There's a fine line between scientific fact and truth and dramatic effects for television so sometimes I think lines get a little bit fuzzy. But I'll bet somebody out there […] has a great reason why nobody notices that airlock being opened, but it ain't me."

306   Torn

Original air date: November 3, 2006
Written by: Anne Cofell Saunders
Directed by: Jean de Segonzac

A group of Cylons is infected by a beacon they believe the 13th Colonists placed to destroy the Cylon population. On Galactica, Starbuck and Tigh spread their own virus.

"Torn" is split into two main story lines that mirror each other: the discovery of the plague aboard the basestar, and the plague carried by Starbuck and Tigh, who contaminate the entire ship with their venom. The two arcs interweave to create a tapestry of misery. A couple of important things come out of this episode: we learn that the Cylons communicate through the "datastream" — that is actual water — that's connected to a Hybrid. We also learn that deep mystery surrounds the Final Five Cylon models — no one will talk about them, and no one's seen them. There are seven models so far, although not all have model numbers attached to them: Six, Sharon, Leoben, Doral, Simon, D'Anna, and Brother Cavil. This is the first time we've heard the term "the Final Five" (true to form, the Internet immediately leapt onto the alliterative wagon and renamed the original seven the "Significant Seven") and the use of the word "final," with its echoes of the "Final Solution," as well as the alliteration with the letter "f" makes these Cylon models seem all the more important.

When we learn the Cylons are also seeking Earth, it seems almost like the Cylons are *all* a little like Leoben — stalking the human race to the ends of the galaxy as Leoben did

Starbuck; former annihilators of humankind, they decided that the slaughter was a mistake and that they should live in harmony with their human brethren. But the Cylon idea of living in harmony was a bit peculiar: occupying a nation isn't the same as living together with its people. And now, with the humans gone from New Caprica, the Cylons have a new goal in mind: Earth.

In some ways the Cylons' new goal makes perfect sense. Each of the models that have played a major part in events up until now have felt a real need to look for *something*, whether it's love (Six), knowledge (D'Anna), or humanity (Sharon), they've been seeking out something that will make them feel more alive. From the first words we ever hear from them — "Are you alive?" — the quest has been a defining characteristic.

"Torn" continues the thread that was started in "Collaborators" — that of the hatred Starbuck and Tigh find increasingly hard to deal with. Their common MO comes up with a vengeance in this episode — they spend most of their time drinking. From the bottle, from shot glasses, it doesn't seem to matter as long as the alcohol obliterates any memories they have of what was done to them — and what they did — on New Caprica. Because it isn't just anger that's consuming them, there's also a fair amount of guilt. The cause of Saul's guilt is fairly obvious — he killed his wife — but Starbuck's is a little more complex. She killed a man (six times) but she spent four months held captive by him. Even though he's a Cylon, and even though he kidnapped her, toyed with her, and played on her weaknesses, she momentarily saw him as the person that gave her a chance to redeem her childhood. Then there was the betrayal, and she's back where she started. It's entirely possible she's not feeling guilty at all but is angry with herself for being taken in by his game, taking that anger out on Kacey and her mother early in the episode. Angry, too, that she spent four months locked up in what amounts to a jail cell, unable to fight back or have an impact on any part of the Resistance's movements — something that would sit very badly with someone as restless and action-prone as Starbuck is.

So "Torn" gives us Tigh and Starbuck, torn between what they know to be their duty — move on, do their job — and what they feel they need in order to exorcise their demons. And then Adama falls on them, the wrath of Zeus thunders down on them from above, as they sit in their chairs, insolent and uncaring. He stands above them as judge and executioner (he not only hands them a loaded gun, he also kicks the chair out from under Starbuck in a move similar to what one would make if one were hanging someone). It's a terrifying scene because it's so harsh, and while we've seen Adama's anger aimed at others before — Apollo, Chief, Sharon — this is the first time he's been frightening. He's enraged, in the most literal sense of the word — it's as if the wrath is exuding from him — and the viewers are themselves torn between wanting him to understand that the people he's yelling at aren't ready to hear him and knowing that it's a necessary step in their recovery. By the end of the episode, Starbuck's starting to forgive herself: she looks in the mirror, sees Kara staring out at her, the Kara that Leoben created, that Leoben wanted; the Kara that couldn't save herself, that resisted but, in the end, couldn't see through the lies he told her; and she grabs that person, symbolized by the long, extremely girly, extremely un-pilot-like hair, and makes the change back to someone she can recognize.

Tigh, however, hasn't moved on when "Torn" ends, and the unease that we first glimpsed at the end of "Exodus" when the Colonel wandered off alone while Adama was exulted by the crowd has clearly become a serious issue between them. Their discomfort with one another is palpable. They're stilted, both sad, both angry, but how do you tell your friend that you killed your wife, that you curl up with her clothes and hear her voice, see her in the corridors? It's a really tough situation for both men, because they're so close but still so distant. Theirs has been a relationship of things unsaid — they just *know* each other. But the four months of occupation changed everything, and Adama can't know why, and Tigh can't change it.

Headcount: There are 41,422 survivors at the beginning of the episode, down 13 from "Collaborators."

Are You There, God? It's Me, Gaius. The beginning of "Torn" shows that Gaius's mindscape has drastically changed from the Caprica house he's favored until now. On a secluded beach, Six by his side (in the ubiquitous red clothing — this time a bikini), Gaius seems in his element. Note, too, the presence of water in both mindscapes: while in his previous projections he was merely overlooking the water, safely ensconced in his bedroom, living room, or deck, now he and Six are on the shore, edging closer to the water. Given what we learn in this episode about how the Cylons communicate through water, it seems very telling that Gaius's mindscape has shifted so radically. No longer does he see himself and Six between the walls of a civilized house, with all the mod cons. Now they're much closer to nature, and he's as close as he can be to the water without actually swimming in it.

Interesting Fact: The beginning dialogue between Six and Gaius is not what was originally shot, and the actors' mouths have been covered with bright light in postproduction so that the dubbed dialogue could be aired over top of the filmed sequence.

What's In a Name? Sharon gets her new call sign in this episode: Athena. In Greek mythology, Athena was the goddess of war, wisdom, and practical reason. She was also known as the protector of the city. As Athena, Sharon is definitely warlike: she has every reason to be angry with both the Cylons and the humans, and she has the capacity — due to her personality *and* her programming — to perform her duties with great skill. She's lived as both a Cylon and a human, so she can see both sides of the war between the races; her double identity grants her particular insight and wisdom in that regard. As a palace goddess (not a household deity), Athena was supposedly inviolate. But Sharon was raped in season 2, which indicates a distinct difference between her namesake and her own experiences. That difference also points to the duality of the Cylons — they are near-immortal, suprahuman beings, but they mimic the human body and the human experience.

Did You Notice? Some of the names called out for Sharon's call sign include: Chrome Dome, Titania, Wind-up Toy, Raptor Adaptor, Microchip, Digital Dame, Mayflower, Carburetor, Tin Can, Toaster Babe, Transistor, Robopilot.

The director's name is misspelled in the credits — he's listed as "Jean de Segoznac."

The phrase "end of line" that the Hybrid uses could be a reference to the sci-fi movie *Tron* (itself an anagram of the episode title "Torn"), in which the control program finishes its sentences with the words "end of line." If so, it emphasizes the robotic, mechanical aspect of Cylon existence. "End of line" is also a computer coding term, but there's some debate as to whether the sequence indicates termination or separation of different lines of text.

Classic *Battlestar Galactica*: Sharon's new call sign is, though mythological in origin, also a reference to the original series, where Athena was Adama's daughter. She worked as a bridge officer aboard *Galactica* but also piloted a Viper in an episode in which many of the (male) pilots were infected with a deadly disease ("Lost Planet of the Gods"). Athena was played by Maren Jensen.

So Say We All: GAIUS: It's a bit of a coincidence, isn't it? That I could see such a vivid reality that I've created, and the Cylon projection experience seems to be so similar.

SIX: Is it a coincidence?

GAIUS: Well, what are you saying? There's a connection? What, because of my experiences with you . . . Am *I* a Cylon?!

307 A Measure of Salvation

Original air date: November 10, 2006
Written by: Michael Angeli
Directed by: Bill Eagles

The leaders of the fleet wrestle with the question of genocide of the Cylon population.

"The nature of the mind is to disconnect," Six says in this episode, which features the ultimate meeting of sex and violence as the Six in Gaius's mind passionately makes love to him while he's being tortured by D'Anna on board the Cylon basestar. It's a disturbing association, and the scenes are deliberately set up to mimic one another. The deck chair in the beach mindscape, for instance, is angled the same as the torture chair, so when Gaius switches from one locale to the next, his body is in the same position — it really is just the framework of his mind that changes.

One of the interesting things about the past two episodes has been watching Gaius wander through the Cylon ship in the same floundering, wondering way that he did on the *Galactica* back in the miniseries. As a scientist, he's endlessly curious about things, and although we're rarely shown Gaius asking questions — he's a genius, he figures things out by himself, or with the help of Six, or a helping "hand" from God — his face and body language at the beginning of the series screamed his need to understand what was going on. He was like a fish out of water, looking around him as if he didn't know where he was — and if he'd never stepped foot on a battlestar before, much less in the middle of an apocalypse, his confusion makes perfect sense.

When the episode begins, Gaius is in a strange place, both physically and mentally, and he spends the whole episode proving Six's words wrong: the nature of the mind is *not* to disconnect, but in fact to connect. Biochemically (and simply) speaking, the brain functions when neurons fire and connect with one another — without those connections, the brain can't work: it's the connections that create memories, that allow us to access memories, make us walk, talk, think, communicate — it's one of the things that makes us human. And the end of Gaius's torture session is ample proof of that: he connects with Six, tells her what she desperately needs to hear, that he believes in her. Their exchange is also a callback to a scene from "Torn" between the corporeal Six from the basestar and Gaius, when he found out the Six models were the only thing standing between him and summary execution, and he called out to her that she needed him — only realizing later that perhaps he needed her, too.

Gaius doesn't just connect with Six, though, but also with D'Anna, *through* the connection with Six. Just as his words to the Six in his mind in "Torn" were heard by the basestar's Six ("Am *I* a Cylon?!"), so too are his words here heard by D'Anna — although at least these ones were actually spoken. Despite the fact that there's an obvious schism between the mind and the body throughout "A Measure of Salvation" — one woman in charge of torturing the body while the other pleasures the mind — Gaius, Six, and D'Anna work to dispel that idea and connect to one another through each other.

The main thrust of this episode is the question of genocide, and it's interesting that we see the humans wrestle with the issue but we never saw the Cylons do so. The miniseries opens with the Cylons' attempted genocide of the human race, but how they got to that point is summed up in a few sparse lines of text. Here, the ethical fences are clearly defined, and no one has exactly the same stance. What's most surprising at first is that it's Apollo who comes up with the idea of obliterating the Cylon race. Still, looking back at his reactions to the Cylons over the last season and a half, it's actually not that surprising. When Helo and Sharon first rejoined the fleet in "Home, Part 1," Apollo pulled his gun on Sharon and thanked Starbuck for bringing home the "garbage"; in "Precipice," he was strongly against Adama's decision to reinstate Sharon as a Colonial officer and send her to the surface of New Caprica; and in this episode he again shows his distrust of her when they board the diseased Cylon basestar. Whether or not exterminating the Cylons is the best thing to do under the circumstances, the characters' reactions are interesting to watch. Helo in particular is interesting because the man has never disobeyed an order before — not even when his unborn child was about to be aborted ("Epiphanies"). And here, faced with a military and presidential decision, he does what he thinks is right and kills the Cylon prisoners in what amounts to a form of euthanasia. Again, this does fit in with Helo's character — he's a stand-up guy who wants to do what's right, if at all possible; it's just shocking in this episode because it's the first time we've seen him go against a direct order and do what he feels best *despite* the military.

This whole episode is pretty controversial stuff, and really pushes the boundaries of television serials. What other show talks about euthanasia and genocide, mixes torture and fairly explicit sex on a beach, all in the same episode? No wonder everyone's always so tired on the show — there are some hair-raising, exhausting things going on.

Among the threads that return in this episode is the idea of fate versus coincidence. Gaius tells D'Anna, "I had nothing to do with the virus. It was a coincidence," and she replies, "There's no such thing as coincidence. God wills the universe according to His design." This is a thread that's been ongoing since the miniseries when Six started talking about God's plan, and it was continued by Leoben in "Flesh and Bone," so we *know* that the Cylons believe in God and a divine plan of some kind. At least, most of them do — who knows what Brother Cavil believes? Gaius has gone through so many transformations in terms of his religious beliefs over the past two seasons — from atheist to convert to prophet — that his reconversion back to hard science here ("I'm a scientist, and as a scientist I believe that if God exists, our knowledge of Him is imperfect") just points to the idea that science is how he measures his salvation. It's his saving grace, his way out. Through an understanding of the processes of the body and the mind, he can manipulate his circumstances so that he's no longer in a torture chamber but having sex on a beach. But as he realizes at the end of his fugue, there's more to salvation than just science — because his words offer salvation to Six and to D'Anna for different reasons, and they also save him from continued torment.

Echoing the theme of "how much can one take" from "Precipice," "A Measure of Salvation" looks at how each person measures their own salvation. For Helo, he can't be saved unless he stops the genocide of the Cylons. Sharon can't be saved unless she's finally accepted into the fleet as one of them, no longer an outsider. Six, D'Anna, and Gaius are all, differently, saved through Gaius's faith. Starbuck measures her salvation by the fact that she's out there, a fighter pilot once more. And Tigh — he measures his salvation in a bottle. It's different for each person, but by the end of the episode, it's clear that salvation is an ongoing process. It's not enough for Gaius to say he believes in Six and D'Anna — now he'll have to make good on that; not enough for Tigh to drown himself in alcohol — because eventually he'll have to be sober again.

Headcount: There are 41,420 souls in the fleet as of this episode. That's two down from "Torn."

Interesting Fact: James Callis had a particularly hard time with Gaius's torture scenes. In an interview with *iF Magazine*, he said, "I know it's acting, but you are acting go[ing] through being tortured. It was not a happy day, and it went on and on and on. Challenges like that, I know people are being tortured as we are speaking right now around the world, and even though this may sound strange I can feel the path of their pain. When you are doing something like this you don't want to dwarf, diminish, or minimalize the real pain that people are going through. You can't afford to let those kinds of people down. In some way, who better to be tortured than Baltar, really? There's a certain feeling among people who watch the show that is, 'When are you going to get your just desserts pal?' [...] That's what makes this show so interesting is all of these strange dynamics that are trying to fit together. While you can say sooner or later push comes to shove, you made your bed and you'll have to lie in it, when you watch it happen, I would imagine [...] that it doesn't make you feel comfortable or happy and [...] your heart goes out to somebody."

Did You Notice? Helo's so tall he has to duck his head when he leaves *Colonial One*!

When "A Measure of Salvation" aired, it was preceded by a content warning. That's not the first time this season; the premiere "Occupation"/"Precipice" also carried such a warning.

When Helo tells Sharon that he can live with his actions even if they were a mistake, but he can't live without her, it has the same feel to it as in "Exodus, Part 2" when Ellen confesses her sins and love to Tigh.

The Cylon ships use a supply route known as the Region of NCD2539 Above/North.

The Cylons are sick with the disease lymphocytic encephalitis, which is caused by the pathogen lymphocytic choriomeningitis encephalitis. Unlike the Colonists, humans aren't immune to the disease, although it's not especially dangerous unless the immune system has been compromised.

So Say We All: ADAMA: Posterity really doesn't look too kindly on genocide.

ROSLIN: You're making the assumption that posterity will define this as genocide. If they do, at least there'll be someone alive to hate us for it.

308   Hero

Original air date: November 17, 2006
Written by: David Eick
Directed by: Michael Rymer

On the forty-fifth anniversary of Adama's entry into service, an old colleague escapes from the Cylons after having been held prisoner for three years.

"Hero" begins with a military-style musical accompaniment. Music is an important feature of this episode, the first of the season to break with the longer arc of the exodus from New Caprica. Various characters still feature heavily — Tigh's downward spiral is complete as he huddles up with his dead wife's lingerie in an uncomfortably fetishistic scene — but the episode focuses on a new character, Bulldog, who only appears once this season but who still makes a strong impression. He's a great example of a guest character — autonomous, fleshed out, interesting but not overdone. There's nothing about him that screams "very special guest star, pay attention!" but he holds the attention effortlessly — both Adama's and the audience's. Our first introduction to him is through his voice, so it's a surprise when we finally do see him, after five minutes of hearing only his pleas through a distorted radio, that he seems so bedraggled — nothing like a soldier, but dignified nonetheless.

Like "Scar," this episode looks sideways at the popular concept of heroism and the traditional definition of a hero. However, while "Scar" worked with Kat's perception of Starbuck as a hero, and the ways in which Starbuck conformed to and defied the conventions of heroism, "Hero" breaks the concept entirely, and Adama, Tigh, Bulldog — and the Cylons —

are left to wonder how to define themselves when their world has been turned upside down. They are all heroes in their own minds: Tigh and Adama both fought in the Cylon wars, and they're actively engaged in the salvation of the human race; Bulldog survived an ejection into outer space, as well as three years as a Cylon prisoner. But when Bulldog finds out that what he believed of his experience is in fact untrue — that Adama never came looking for him, and was in fact the one who shot him down in the first place — his past and present collide. He thought he was a hero, partly because he thought Adama and the admiralty considered him a hero, were searching for him and mourning him. So when he discovers that his version of the past is false, he's forced to challenge everything he thought he knew.

In a parallel scene, Lee is placed in the same situation when his father admits that it might have been his own actions years ago that caused the Cylons to launch the genocidal attacks against the Colonies. The scene switches from Tigh revealing the truth to Bulldog to Adama revealing the truth to Apollo, and in both cases, when the past is redefined, the present must be as well. Humanity's situation is unchanged, whether or not the mission Adama led caused the attacks, and Bulldog still spent years as a prisoner of the Cylons, whether it was they who shot him down or Adama, so what's changing here is the perception each character has of himself and of others.

"Hero" also continues another arc — that of the Cylons on the basestar, specifically D'Anna, who's been having dreams again. This time, she's being cornered onboard the *Galactica*, which might indicate that she feels like she's being pushed into a situation she can't escape from, an interpretation that's supported by the words "End of Line" etched on the hatch in her dream. In computer speak, "end of line" is used to mark the end of a line of code, but it's also considered to be a separator between continuous lines of code, so D'Anna's dream could be linked to the Hybrid in some way. The Hybrid is the one who utters those words in the series, and for the last eight episodes, D'Anna's clearly been looking for *something*. She turned first to the baby Hera ("Exodus, Part 2"), then to Gaius ("A Measure of Salvation"), and now, she turns to death to see what exactly is missing from her existence. The scene where the Centurion shoots her is shocking: it's brutal, and the mechanical, cold surroundings make it all the more affecting. It's surprising, too, because the Cylons have explicitly talked about the sin of suicide, and yet in "Exodus," a Brother Cavil model described at length how he scratched through his own skin to cut his carotid artery, and in "Torn," the diseased Six model begged Gaius to kill her. So D'Anna's suicide — couched as an execution of sorts — can't be an entirely unheard-of factor in Cylon existence. When she resurrects, she murmurs in awe, "There's something beautiful, miraculous between life and death," further highlighting the idea of separation rather than ending. Her face at her rebirth is enraptured, awed, with the same glint of fierce faith that she showed in "Downloaded" as she stared down the barrel of a gun at Anders and proclaimed loudly that God loved her. That same fervency is apparent here, but her attitude is different, she seems humbled, which just makes the mystery of the Final Five that much more intriguing — to her *and* to us. D'Anna is usually such a player — she always sports a little smirk that makes her seem like a cat toying with a mouse — so her scenes in "Hero" are chilling.

The Geneva Conventions

The articles that make up the Geneva Conventions were written between 1864 and 1949, and were last added to in 1977. Distraught by behavior he had witnessed during the Battle of Solferino in 1859, Henri Dunant – founder of the Red Cross – initiated the international discussions that would lead to the Conventions' creation. Their general aim is to improve the situation of war for both soldiers and civilians, and one of the most prominent clauses in the Conventions calls for the humane treatment of prisoners of war. This is the purpose of the Third Convention, of which Article 13 reads "Prisoners of war must at all times be humanely treated," while Article 17 reads, "No physical or mental torture, nor any other form of coercion, may be inflicted on prisoners of war to secure from them information of any kind whatever. Prisoners of war who refuse to answer may not be threatened, insulted, or exposed to unpleasant or disadvantageous treatment of any kind."

The Geneva Conventions have been frequently in the news lately because of some difficult international situations around the world. Of particular interest to the *BSG* world is the situation in Iraq, which made headlines in 2004 when a number of military personnel from the United States were accused of severely mistreating Iraqi prisoners at Abu Ghraib prison.

What does an international treaty have to do with the *BSG* universe? We've seen instances of torture used on Cylon prisoners throughout the series ("Flesh and Bone," for instance) because they're Cylons, machines – not human. But "Pegasus" was the first time we saw a Cylon who's survived the torture: we see for the first time the consequences of the inhumane treatment of a prisoner – regardless of their nature, Cylon or human. Whether or not the Colonists had some form of Geneva Conventions of their own, they're obviously not in use here, and it's left to the viewers to decide how they feel about that.

"Hero" ends with a redefining of the concept of hero, as well as the concept of penance. While Adama feels he should punish himself for his actions by resigning from the service, Roslin makes him realize that nothing he can do can change the fact that the present is as it is: the fleet is still running from the Cylons and they're still looking for Earth — and they still need someone to look up to — a leader, a hero. And so what Adama believes he should have done to conform to his idea of a hero doesn't matter, because to the fleet, he is still the same person he was before Bulldog came along. The past has changed Lee's and Bulldog's perception of him, but to everyone else, he's Admiral Adama — the man who'll lead them to Earth. To take that away would be like admitting that everything they had all gone through since the Cylon attacks was worth nothing. In the end, Adama's punishment is to recognize that he will never be able to reveal the guilt he feels about the attacks, because no one wants to hear it. He's got to shoulder that burden alone, just as Tigh has to "get up and walk out of [his] room" alone.

And it's interesting that the end of the episode shows Tigh preparing to tell Adama what happened to Ellen. Their relationship has taken some heavy hits in the last little while and their lines of communication have been closed — and like Adama said in "Collaborators," it's just *wrong* to not have Tigh in the command center. Tigh needs that purpose, that driving force of a solid position in the fleet behind him to help him keep an even keel; without it and without Ellen, he's lost. So it's touching that he would make good on his words, walk out of his room, and approach his friend, ready to bare his soul as Ellen bared hers before she died. And unlike "Torn," Adama offers no judgment when Tigh asks for a drink, just nods. As the liquor flows, the lines of communication are open, once again pointing to the idea of a liquid conduit — like the Cylons, who plunge their hands in altered water to communicate.

Headcount: We're up to 41,421 to account for Bulldog's appearance.

All of This Has Happened Before: In Norse mythology, the Valkyries are female deities who served Odin, the god of war and wisdom. Their purpose was to select the most heroic people who had died in battle and bring them to Valhalla, the hall of the gods. They're depicted in various ways throughout history, but many scholars now agree that they were originally Odin's priestesses and led sacrificial rites — sometimes sacrificing themselves. It certainly fits nicely that the *Valkyrie* sacrificed Novacek — and, to Adama's mind, led to the sacrifice of the human race.

Interesting Fact: The music in this episode is very particular, and it really works to highlight the different undercurrents at work between the different characters. Composer Bear McCreary wrote on his blog, "In general, I only write thematic material for characters who matter in the grand scheme of the series, in hopes that the character will return at a later point in the story. In rare cases I make an exception in order to give a guest star a particularly resonant musical voice. For example, Bill Duke's Phelan from season 2's 'Black Market' required his own theme, since all the events of the episode led up to his eventual standoff with Lee. 'Hero' was obviously another such case. Novacek's mysterious past drives nearly every scene in the entire show, and it was clear he required his own theme as well."

Did You Notice? The part of Adama's letter of resignation that we can see on screen reads: "Laura, It has been an honor and a privilege to serve and work . . . as commander of the *Galactica* and commander of the Colonial Fleet during these trying times. I apologize for not revealing to you the true nature of the . . . *Valkyrie*'s mission. My actions and decision during that . . . have weighed heavily on my heart for the past three years . . . Novacek's recent arrival and the revelation of his capture and imprisonment by the Cylons has confirmed something

that I can no longer deny even to myself. My violation of the Armistice Treaty during that mission has led directly to the devastating Cylon attacks on our Colonies. I can no longer in good conscience continue to serve. Therefore, it is with deep regret that I, Admiral William Adama, am resigning my commission, effective . . . I am naming Major Lee Adama to succeed me as commander of the fleet."

Eddie and Mary, without the weight of humanity's survival on their shoulders (ALBERT L. ORTEGA)

The invitation to Adama's ceremony reads, "William Adama, Our Admiral, Our Leader, Our Friend. Join the Presidential Anointing of the Medal of Distinction to William Adama for his 45 years of Courageous Service."

So Say We All: TIGH: I hear you got a medal.

ADAMA: Yeah. They're handing them out for everything these days. Good behavior. Attendance. Plays well with others.

309 Unfinished Business

Original air date: December 1, 2006
Written by: Michael Taylor
Directed by: Robert Young

A ship-wide boxing match allows Lee and Kara to work through their anger.

From the physical connectivity of a punch or of lovemaking, to the social connectivity of marriage and friendship and snuggling in an old river bed on a lost planet, "Unfinished Business" shows the importance of human connections. And even when it hurts so much they're bleeding from it, the crew has been so disconnected from their lives for so long that they crave the connection, because it ties them to reality and to each other in a way they haven't experienced for over two years.

Nine episodes after the rift between Apollo and Starbuck was first revealed ("Lay Down Your Burdens, Part 2"), it's finally explained. "Unfinished Business" takes the tensions that have been simmering in the background since the season premiere — and longer, in the case of Starbuck and Apollo — and ignites them. No more repression, no more resentment — this episode has everyone pounding out their rage on one another. In between scenes of Lee and Kara, we catch glimpses of what life could have been on New Caprica: Roslin and Adama are among those who are trying to move on with their lives, snuggled up in the alluvial deposits of what is to become home. In season 1, the tension between the two was attributed to the conflicting priorities of the military and of civilian life, but their relationship has gradually shifted to one where they can see each other as the parents of this newly rebirthed society — a society that they helped to create and that they guided through its darkest times. Lying on the foundations of Roslin's future home, they move toward each other in tiny increments. There are so many eyes on them — the eyes of the Colonials and the eyes of the past — that it must seem an unfathomable step that they take toward each other, but neither Laura nor William has ever allowed fear to control them, and while we've seen that determination in situations fraught with military and political tension, we've never seen it in operation on a personal level. Laura's always been more open with her feelings — she grieved more or less openly for Billy, she cried over her cancer, she expresses her fear, so her easy, carefree approach to the potential of her new life is less surprising than Adama's. He, unlike Laura, has been closed off emotionally since the series began, letting only glimmers of wild emotion free: anger (he sure throws a lot of stuff around!), his pride in Lee, his love for Starbuck. The seeds for Roslin and Adama's relationship were sown back in "Resurrection Ship, Part 2," but we never thought they'd actually get to a point where they could lay down their burdens and look at one another with civilian eyes.

Despite those casual glances in other directions, "Unfinished Business" focuses on Lee and Kara: the push-pull between these two has been obvious since the miniseries, but there's so much history between them that they've never had the guts, or perhaps the impetus, to do anything about it. Zak, Anders, Dee, their respective personalities — something has always stopped these two from going too far. Between bouts of bloody, vicious punching, their story unfolds, and it's tragic. The thing about living in a postapocalyptic society is that, even when things slow down and you start to make plans for building a house and giving up on being a fighter pilot, the world is still messed up and unprepared — there's just no room for crazy love. When Lee stands up and screams to the gods, to the sky, to anyone who'll listen, that he loves Kara, she watches him aghast and thrilled at the same time. It's like a Greek tragedy, like Apollo is defying the gods and daring them to do something about it: and she's pulled along with him, giddy with love and endorphins and liquor and rebelliousness. *This* she's wanted for years: *this* is joy. Except it's not what she wants: she wants safe. She wants to be able to drink her partner under the table. She wants to wear the figurative pants in the relationship. She doesn't want someone who challenges her, snipes at her in jealousy ("Kobol's Last Gleaming, Part 1"), makes her take responsibility for her actions. Anders accepts her, gets ridiculously drunk with her, loves her in her drunken lewdness, and doesn't want to control her. For all that Lee loves her, he won't let her get away with what Anders does — and she can't accept that kind of love. Part of her is still the child whose mother made her suffer, and that person won't be beholden to anyone. We see it in her eyes when Lee tells her to get up and proclaim her love: she wants to be out of control in the cockpit — but she can't be out of control in love.

Starbuck might want it, she might crave it, but she can't make herself take the step that Adama and Roslin allow themselves to take, that Lee's allowed himself to take. They're both so crazy and wide open in this scene, so connected and yet so distant. It's the first time we've seen them approach this aspect of their relationship since "Scar," but the feeling is very different: then they were desperate, angry, surrounded by metal and machinery; now, in a very romantic scenario, they're surrounded by nature, connected, softer, with fewer ragged edges showing. Those edges are still there, though, and even though Apollo and Starbuck allow their walls to fall at the end of the episode under the watchful eyes of their respective spouses, crazy, unrepentant love like that will always be unfinished business, because there's no room for it in a world where lines have to be drawn every day, and social niceties and connections must be maintained so that a new civilization can be built.

Headcount: There are 41,422 people on board, one more than "Hero."

Interesting Fact: A lot of fans hated the four-way "triangle" between Starbuck, Apollo, Anders, and Dee — and they're not the only ones. Katee Sackhoff has gone on record as hating that story line with a vengeance: "I actually hate the triangle. I think it's ridiculous. I wish she would just be with one of them and call it a day. But then that wouldn't be dramatic, now would it?"

Did You Notice? When Chief steps into the ring, he's wearing his dog tags, but by the time he's lying on his back, they've vanished and remain missing for the rest of the fight.

The fights shown are as follows (winner's name comes first): Helo versus Apollo, Starbuck versus Hotdog, Kat versus unknown, Chief versus Adama, Starbuck versus Apollo (draw), Sergeant Fischer versus unknown. Fischer is portrayed by mixed martial arts specialist Paul Lazenby.

So Say We All: ROSLIN: Didn't expect to find you playing in the sand.

ADAMA: It's not sand; it's alluvial deposits. This used to be the river mouth.

ROSLIN: And you just *had* to take off your shoes and play in the alluvial deposits.

Luciana Carro (Louanne "Kat" Katraine)

··

Date of birth: March 23, 1981

Did you know? Luciana first got into acting as a child because she was so shy: her parents encouraged her to act to overcome the shyness.

On deciding to pursue an acting career: "My high school drama teacher was Gerry Campbell [actress Neve Campbell's father]. I'll never forget it. It was my last year of high school, I was in history class and somehow he found out that I had decided that after I graduated I was thinking of going to beauty school and becoming a hairstylist. He dragged me out of class by the collar of my shirt into the hall, and told me if I didn't at least try to pursue an acting career I would break his heart. He wanted me to go to theater school. So I did and that's where it all started for me. My love affair with the theater and the camera continues to this day."

On shooting the season 2 episode "Final Cut": "I had to turn down something like two or three *BSG* episodes in season 2 because it conflicted with my *Dr. Dolittle 3* shooting schedule. I was so heartbroken. Then they offered me the 'Final Cut' episode and when I read the script I told my agent, 'You gotta make it happen!!!' And she did. *Dolittle* gave me one day off. I shot all my scenes in 'Final Cut' in one day. That day was pretty intense let me tell you! But it was worth it."

310   The Passage

Original air date: December 8, 2006
Written by: Jane Espenson
Directed by: Michael Nankin

When the fleet's food supply is contaminated, they have to figure out how to pass through a heavy radiation field to find more food.

The passage in this title is literal and metaphorical, referring to the fleet's passage through the nebula, Kat's transformation from drug runner to CAG of the Colonial fleet, and her passage from life into death. Although a standard storytelling technique, the use of pathos and a "deep dark secret" to make Kat's death more poignant seems almost like a cheat. Kat is interesting regardless of what happened before we met her. We know that. Adama knows that. Even Starbuck realizes that. So why the backstory? The only person who seems to need it is Kat herself. In that sense, "The Passage" tells the story of Kat's acceptance and redemption — not by her peers but by herself. In a storytelling technique that we've seen in episodes from earlier seasons ("The Captain's Hand," "Water"), the personal story is interwoven with a larger tale of survival and scarce resources. In fact, "The Passage" feels like a remake of "The Captain's Hand," with the same use of death as a form of retribution, only this time, the character has been fleshed out enough that we're more involved in the process of her death. The fact that she's been given the rank of CAG again, if taken at face value, is probably meant to be heartwarming, but it rings false. She's been flying for only two years, and she's really going to take over from Lee, who's had way more experience in terms of both flying and leadership? The gesture seems like just that, a gesture made to a dying pilot — and in that sense, it *is* heartwarming because Adama can be deeply generous when he wants to be, and it really speaks to his own skills as a leader that he can see what Kat yearns for — the acceptance and the respect that go hand-in-hand with a command position — and without a second's hesitation gives it to her.

And a long process it's been, too, one whose beginnings can be traced all the way back to "Scar," when she started vying for hotshot pilot status with Starbuck. She was less ready to die than Starbuck was in that episode, but in this episode she sees herself distorted and cracked in a charred window, and realizes that the journey she wanted to make is complete. She reinvented herself — reimagined herself, in fact, in the same way that this *Battlestar Galactica* has been reimagined — and in redefining herself, she's come full circle. Like Adama in "Hero," Kat comes face to face with her past, represented in the character of Enzo, and she manages not only to stand up to it, but to regard it as a form of salvation. Although Kat approaches Enzo for sex immediately after the confrontation with Starbuck, making it seem like an act of fear or rebellion, it feels more like an act of peace, as if she's done fighting: she's come so far from who she was before the attacks that it's only who she is now that matters. And that person has completed her journey. The fact that she has sex with him is seen only in flashback, as if the act was a rite of passage for her, sacred until it had fulfilled its purpose in allowing her to take that last step into death.

Kat's death is neither painless nor fast, and there's a parallel wrought between her demise and the repeated deaths that D'Anna puts herself through back on the Cylon basestar. While both are suicides (Kat deliberately switches radiation badges with Helo, after all), Kat lingers in agony, visited by people who have grown to like and respect her. In contrast, D'Anna dies quickly, painlessly, and alone except for a Centurion she's programmed to kill her. Even the environments in which the two women die are different — compare the sick bay, with its overtones of gray infirmity and suffering to the Cylon basestar, which gleams, sterile and mechanical. It seems again like a callback to Starbuck's words in "Flesh and Bone": "Human beings have to suffer and cry and scream and endure."

In a twisted version of the usual addictive substances that are passed around the fleet (see Starbuck's and Tigh's frequent intake of alcohol, for two dozen instances), it's a Cylon who's addicted, this time to death. Or rather, the "space between life and death," which raises a bunch of questions about how the Cylons experience death. Sharon said in season 2 that death is a learning experience ("Scar"). D'Anna does seem to be intent on learning *something*, and her motives closely resemble the human quest to understand what happens to the soul after death. The approach she takes is simultaneously so human in its longing and intensity and yet so robotic in its implementation.

Some of the best scenes in this episode are Adama's. From his breakout into hysteria with Tigh (their relationship seems be right back on track) — which is in such bad taste, but so funny — to his patience and gentleness with Kat as he pulls out a chair and sits with her to keep her company as she makes that final transition, he is both leader and father, friend and comrade.

Headcount: We're back to 41,420 again in this episode. Seems someone's always dying or being born off screen these days . . .

Are You There, God? It's Me, Gaius. One of the strongest threads of this episode is Gaius's continued journey into self-discovery. He's turned from science to God, and now he's turning to the Cylons as an answer to his identity. He asks D'Anna, "Have you seen my face?" and his voice is frantic, anguished. In "Torn," Six taunted him, saying, "And if you're really a Cylon . . . then wouldn't you rather just get it over with and die?" But in this episode, Gaius seems to almost *want* to be a Cylon. Which makes sense in the arc of his character because he's ridiculously incapable of taking any kind of responsibility for his actions, so if he were a Cylon, he would nicely evade any kind of guilt that he might feel about humanity's fate.

Interesting Fact: Jane Espenson said of writing this episode, "This show is so rich, the world is so full, and there are emotions along every axis between every pairing of characters, that it's incredibly easy to find things that you just *have* to explore. This is part of what gives the series such a great voyeuristic quality . . . as a viewer you just *know* that there are scenes that have played out between these people that you have never seen, and you get to infer what they must've been. I like that the edit of this episode hints at the things unseen."

Did You Notice? With Kat's death, of the three nuggets that were first introduced in season 1's "Act of Contrition," only Hotdog survives.

Gaeta doesn't applaud when Tigh walks into the CIC. It's likely he's harboring some resentment over how Tigh treated him after the exodus from New Caprica.

A note on the memorial wall reads "God rest your souls." The show is usually really good at changing all mentions of a singular "god" to the plural "gods" ("godsdamn," for instance).

In a nice bit of continuity, Starbuck places Kat's photo next to the picture that Kat herself placed of Reilly's girlfriend back in "Scar."

Classic *Battlestar Galactica*: The plot of this episode seems to be based on the pilot episode of the original series, "Saga of a Star World." In that episode, Viper pilots Boomer, Apollo, and Starbuck volunteer to guide the fleet's ships through a nebula that contains a mine field with extremely dangerous levels of radiation so they can resupply the ships with food.

311   The Eye of Jupiter

Original air date: December 15, 2006
Written by: Mark Verheiden

Directed by: Michael Rymer

The Cylons and the humans converge at the Temple of Five.

   This episode, with its emphasis on "eye," immediately brings to mind the concept of viewership, and the issues raised here further develop the idea: what is being viewed, who is viewing it, how is the view — and the act of viewing itself — expected to change? "The Eye of Jupiter" is an episode that works both for and against passive viewers, and for and against more engaged viewers, because it neither tells a complete story nor unfolds in the way the viewer expects it to.

   One of the big changes wrought in this episode is in how the war is waged. In the first two seasons and the first half of this season, the war was fought using military strategy; now the warfare has turned psychological as the two parties, intent on the same goal — Earth — look in the same spots and try to outmaneuver each another. Anders and Lee turn to untried guerilla tactics to stop the Cylons, and D'Anna changes the Cylons' strategy without even telling anyone. "The Eye of Jupiter" examines three main concepts related to vision: perception, prophecy, and blindness, and each character and their story plays with components of each. Chief, for instance, is blind to the reason why he was drawn to the Temple of Five but understands that something in him was able to see past what he perceived with his eyes. In the same way, Anders has his eyes wide open to his wife's flaws, but he has apparently turned a blind eye to her cheating until now, when faced with a situation he perceives as threatening. Starbuck has willingly blinded herself to her own hypocrisy: in her mind, it's acceptable to cheat but unthinkable to divorce. She and Lee seem to lack any form of foresight into the consequences of their actions, which is ironic when contrasted to the rest of an episode that focuses so clearly on the idea of prophecy and destiny.

   For Gaius, the stalemate between the Cylons and the humans can be solved with a few well-chosen words to the right people: he places himself in the position of mediator and diplomat, and when he boards *Galactica*, the pull he's obviously feeling toward humanity bodes ill. He wants so badly to be accepted. He's even dressed for the part — he looks downright classy and elegant, seemingly a fitting companion for the President of the Colonies and the commander of the Colonial Fleet. However well he presents himself, however, Roslin in particular perceives him as a threat, a willful and corrupt traitor, and walks out without even listening to him. She blinds herself to anything but her projected image of him.

   The main thrust of this episode is the fulfillment of one phase of Pythian prophecies, which have been used as a map for humanity's quest since season 1. The entire first half of this two-parter plays like a prophecy in itself: the music is foreboding, the situation gradually escalates, tensions between parties reach crisis points, and when the words "To be continued" scroll along the screen, there's a definite feel of impending revelation. At the same time, we feel certain that none of this can end well. We *know* that Lee won't order Anders shot, just as we know that Starbuck is alive, that Dee will have to rescue her, and that the festering wound between the four characters will have to be ripped open before it can be healed. As with all oracles, however, our vision is incomplete as we cannot see the details of what will occur — we just know the outcome.

The Cylon camp is experiencing similar problems. They are working with the same prophecy as are the humans, but the way in which events are unfolding could never have been predicted. The warning signs for D'Anna's growing self-involvement have been there, foreboding, since the beginning of the season. And Six even mentions that everything is not okay in the world of the Cylons — but they blind themselves to the fact that D'Anna has managed to separate herself entirely from the consensus of the group, even breaking up with Six on both her and Gaius's behalf.

The most obvious source of prophecy in this episode, aside from the Scrolls of Pythia, is the Hybrid. It's interesting to note that the humans are relying on a written legacy that has been passed down throughout the centuries, while the Cylons are basing their experience of the universe on a Hybrid who is intimately tied to the here and now — a direct link to the universe as it exists in the present moment. This ties in to previous episodes, which looked at the differing views of legacy and the relation to time ("Exodus, Part 2"). The Hybrid's speech patterns are reminiscent of apocalyptic and ecstatic revelations, where the language is cloaked in ambiguity. She mentions the "five lights of the apocalypse" (perhaps similar to the Bible's Four Horsemen of the apocalypse), and advises that Gaius — *not* D'Anna — "look into the eye to know" himself. What's interesting here is that, while both Cylons and humans believe the Temple of Five to be a stepping stone to Earth, which in turn represents their new beginning, the prophetic words of the Hybrid seem to be pointing to the idea that the Temple of Five houses the Final Five — who might very well be the harbingers of the apocalypse. Beginnings and endings, life and death: all very mandala-like, all very circular, much like an eye.

Headcount: There are 41,402 people left, making the losses from the passage through the nebula about eighteen, barring any births in the fleet.
Interesting Fact: In real life, the Jupiter Eye is known as the Great Red Spot. It's a real part of the surface of Jupiter — and it looks a lot like an eye. It's not just a spot, either: it's a hurricane that scientists believe has been raging for more than 300 years, and it's the largest storm system in the solar system. Its coloring and shape are not set, but change, for unknown reasons.

"The Eye of Jupiter" was the last episode to air on Friday nights. As of the next episode, *BSG* began to air on Sunday nights.
Did You Notice? This is the first time the Cylons have used their "human" names to refer to one another: Six refers to Three as "D'Anna," while D'Anna refers to Cavil as "Cavil." Until now, they've always referred to each other by their numbers, or simply talked directly to each other without using names.

If the Temple of Five looks vaguely familiar, it's because it's the same set that was used for Ragnor Anchorage in the miniseries. It's actually an abandoned factory.

Some of the guns used in the battle sequences were loaded with balls of dust that helped to create the feel of a real battle when fired.

According to the podcast, the very distinctive landscape was scouted out especially for this episode. "The Eye of Jupiter" was filmed in Kamloops, British Columbia (Canada); Moore explains, "We had kind of shot out almost all the locations that were easily accessible to us in Vancouver. [...] You've seen a lot of the same forest. You've seen a lot of that one rock quarry where we built the New Caprica settlement, and we didn't have a lot of other choices, and [...] it was antithetical to the idea of the algae planet, to go to a planet and harvest the algae, if you were in the deep dark forest. [...] This is as close to barren as we could conceivably get."

312   Rapture

Original air date: January 21, 2006
Written by: David Weddle, Bradley Thompson
Directed by: Michael Rymer

While Dee tries to rescue Starbuck, D'Anna and Gaius struggle to find the truth about the Final Five.

In religious terminology, a rapture occurs when someone is transported by God to a state that approximates a state of heavenly bliss. It's a moment of pure *nowness*, and one that we've seen only in Cylons so far — perhaps because their relation to time is so different than the humans'. In "The Eye of Jupiter," Six rebukes Gaius and D'Anna, saying that they have "transcended the barriers that separate people," which works well with her character, because she's always been about the rapture of love and passion. Six *is* the definition of passion (the etymology of "passion" means "pain"): unlike D'Anna, who searches for her rapture in the faces of the Final Five, Six looks for rapture in its physical embodiment, in Gaius — in the sharing of experiences with another.

Gaius twists that definition of rapture, however, moving it out of the personal ("You mustn't misunderstand, it's not personal," he says) and into a realm that more closely parallels what D'Anna is looking for. The irony there is that although Gaius denies Six's personal rapture, his own quest is deeply personal: he wants to see the Final Five, but only because he needs to know if he is one of them. In some ways, Gaius's rapture would be to find out that he *is* a Cylon, because if he's not, then he's a traitor to the human race — and he can't cope with that idea. He can't "suffer and endure" the way Starbuck said humans must ("Flesh and Bone") and he wants the option of turning it off, of turning his back once and for all on humanity. The problem is that his humanity leaks through everything he does, and in "The Eye of Jupiter" he even mentions how much he misses living on *Galactica*. Rapture has the potential to transform him, but he can't get that far — no one can get that far — without first dying.

Gaius reveals himself to be just as self-centered as ever. "Did you see my face?" he begs D'Anna as she lies dying, in an echo of his words in "The Passage." He doesn't care about her rapture, because for both him and D'Anna, rapture is an intensely individualistic experience that *can't* be shared, that is not about connection with another. It's one reason that they both reject Six's definition and experience of rapture; they aren't interested in rapture for its connections, they're in it for their own personal gain. Whereas Six wants to bond, to be at one with them (she's forever touching Gaius, creating a physical link with him), D'Anna and Gaius don't want unity. They want the knowledge that will separate them from their people.

The end of the episode leans heavily on the fact that Gaius's quest is ultimately leading him to separate himself from everyone else — both Cylons and humans — and from his own rapture: when he's brought back aboard the *Galactica*, he's in a body bag. The overt symbolism of him being dead to the rest of the fleet for his actions on New Caprica and his new treason for leading the Cylons to Earth is obvious, but it's also a sad testimony to the idea that with D'Anna permanently dead, Gaius's link to the rapture of knowledge and a sure identity is also permanently gone.

Although Brother Cavil is one of the least sympathetic characters to appear so far — next to him, Gaius looks positively nice — it's interesting to note that the Cylons all have their preset roles, and they stick to them. It's Brother Cavil who is present when D'Anna is boxed, who performs the last rites, so to speak, before she's permanently killed — he's fulfilling a role typically held by a person of the cloth, as befits his title.

So far, season 3 has been something of a downer — and that's saying something with this show. But while seasons 1 and 2 had glimmers of hope and exuberance coming from *without* — the birth of the first baby, the shout-out-loud glee at shooting helpless Cylon Raiders — season 3 has so far emphasized the need for *inner* hope and transformation. No longer can external circumstances move these people to rapture; for them to move, they must first change. A good example is Starbuck and Lee: in the first two seasons, they shared many an irreverent moment, from the cute little Viper jiggle in "You Can't Go Home Again" to the over-the-top "Lee Adama loves me" in "Home." That irreverence is nowhere to be seen in season 3.

Headcount: 41,401 survivors are counted in this episode, a net loss of one since "The Eye of Jupiter."

Interesting Fact: Ronald Moore didn't know that Gaius would be brought back to the ship in a body bag until someone from Universal Studios called him and asked him about it. He bluffed, then called director Michael Rymer, who explained it to him. Moore notes, "I got a call from the studio, from the head of production at Universal. He called me and said, 'Are you aware that Baltar comes back to *Galactica* in a body bag?' And I said, 'Yeah, we talked about that, it was a complicated decision. We'll talk about that more later,' and then I hung up on him. 'Baltar comes back . . . What the frak are they doing down on the set!?' And then I called Rymer, and [. . .] he explained it to me, and I said, 'Oh. Well that's smart.'"

Roslin and Gaius's conversation and shouting match deserve their own callout because it's the first time we've seen Gaius really called to the carpet about his actions, and the first time we've seen Roslin lose control in any real way (chamalla-taking instances aside).

ROSLIN: I just wondered if you recognized even one of these faces. Did any image get through to you on the rare occasion when you ventured out . . .

GAIUS: I am not responsible for the occupation any more than I am for the genocide.

ROSLIN: . . . from behind your sandbags and your razor wire to see what was happening to your people?! Your people! *(she's enraged and screaming; he's nearly in tears)* I need to know! Now! Colonel Tigh, get in here! Get this man out of here . . .

GAIUS: This is not about uncovering any legitimate threat . . .

ROSLIN: *(makes a sudden hand gesture)* He's not going to talk. I want you to take him, I want you to toss him out the nearest airlock.

GAIUS: This is about exacting your pound of flesh.

ROSLIN: Guards! Get in here now! Get rid of him!

GAIUS: What happened to my fair trial?

ROSLIN: Take him out of here!

GAIUS: *(as the guards take hold)* Get your hands off me. Get your motherfrakking hands off me! I demand a fair trial! I am a citizen of the Colonies, and I demand a fair trial! A fair trial!

Did You Notice? When Boomer threatens to snap Hera's neck, the scene directly echoes the scene from the miniseries when Caprica-Six snapped the baby's neck in the market. The scene also caused similar problems with the networks, who weren't convinced that threatening a baby would make for good viewing.

This is the third time we've seen the opera house set. The first was in season 1 ("Kobol's Last Gleaming, Part 2"), and the second was D'Anna's experience of the space "between life and death" in "Hero."

313 *Taking a Break From All Your Worries*

Original air date: January 28, 2007
Written by: Michael Taylor
Directed by: Edward James Olmos

While Gaius is tortured for information regarding what the Cylons know about the location of Earth, Apollo and Starbuck try to figure out their respective relationships.

A dark moment for Lieutenant Gaeta (Alessandro Juliani), but a typically manipulative one for Gaius (CAROLE SEGAL/ © SCI-FI/COURTESY: EVERETT COLLECTION)

Like season 1's offering, "Lay Down Your Burdens," this episode takes a phrase that rings with clichés and reimagines it. In the *Battlestar Galactica* universe, one of the motifs that's returned to again and again is the need for fresh perspective, or else our world becomes rigid and codified — little better than a machine. Although the two episodes work the same way, "Lay Down Your Burdens" had a much more formal tone, but it explored the informal ways in which we lay things down to ease our way through life. In contrast, this episode's title strikes a colloquial chord with us but it investigates much darker and more formal material than it initially suggests.

The first indication we have of this inversion between title and subject matter is the figure of Gaius — never has Gaius looked less like himself than he does in this episode. There are strong parallels here to both religion and politics: whether a Jesus figure or a Saddam figure, Gaius is a palpable presence, even though ironically he looks the gauntest and most fragile he has in a while. On board the Cylon resurrection ship surrounded by Cylons he looked positively glowy with health, while on the *Galactica* he looks anemic and in serious need of some vitamin D. Because Gaius is still vacillating between being a Cylon savior and a human traitor, his physical appearance again opens up the questions that *BSG* has looked at in other episodes such as "Hero" and "Scar," namely, that it is just as important *who* is seeing as *what* is seen.

Added to that idea is another big subject: free will. Six says to Gaius, "Without free will, what are you?" At the beginning of the episode it seems as though Gaius is choosing to commit suicide — but how much of his choice was dictated by the effects of sleep deprivation? Both Anders and Dee give their respective partners free choice to stay or go, but what other choice did they have? Keeping someone you love regardless of the cost, as Ellen Tigh did, ended her life — is that the measure of love and free will? Without free will humanity is little more than a program, a code that repeats itself over and over; but free will interrupts lives and just as often as saving them, it allows for decisions that are even worse than making no decision at all. All of these questions roll uncomfortably through the episode, making ripples through all the scenes. Gaius's torture feels very satisfying on some levels — that bastard has done some really evil things! — but as he himself said, he did not *willingly collude* with the Cylons. This is different than saying he didn't have anything to do with the holocaust and the destruction of mankind. That's something the Gaius of season 1 might have said, but not this Gaius. This Gaius is, in effect, exercising his free will and accepting that he had some responsibility in what had happened. It may be a very small step, but, like Six's turning away and D'Anna's death wish, doesn't it point to his empathy and suffering — to his humanity?

While "Lay Down Your Burdens" offers a sense of finality, since the end of it was also the end of a season, "Taking a Break" seems more like a short reprieve. Gaius attempts suicide, Apollo and Dee talk about ending their marriage as do Starbuck and Anders, and Adama's "break" from the light duties of commanding the military involves torturing a prisoner and never again being able to say he hasn't directly affected Gaius's life. Roslin takes a break from her duties as president, first to lie to Gaius and then to assist in his torture. Gaeta's break from a sleepless night ultimately ends up with him trying to kill a man, something he has thus far been able to avoid — strange in a television series where bloodshed is rampant. In an echo of season 1 we are reminded that the postholocaust landscape does not allow for short reprieves; the difference is that in this season the reprieves are as much psychological as physical. Gaius's statement from the very first episode also echoes here, as there is only so much the human mind can endure.

The parallels of Gaius's torture scene in the series with the Guantanamo prison in real life may or may not be too contentious, but the episode itself certainly has some parallels to another episode: "A Measure of Salvation." Gaius being tortured on board the *Galactica* by Adama and Roslin is very reminiscent of Gaius being tortured on board the resurrection ship by D'Anna and Six. Both Six and Roslin seem initially favorable to extracting information by any means possible, but when the actual process starts, both women become incredibly uncomfortable and turn away. Six turns away because she loves Gaius, while Roslin turns away because she hates the hypocrisy of her position. Both of them have been pushed to the limits of what they can endure. Interestingly, it is Gaius who makes it through the episode: is it a coincidence that he is the only character seen in water? Everyone else is dry throughout the episode — in fact, besides Starbuck's ever-present bottle there is no liquid at all.

Notice that name on the credits? It may have flown by, but the director for this episode was one Edward James Olmos, so it's an even more delicious moment than usual when Adama is musing over which torture tactic to use on Gaius. The camera pans from a view of Gaius, face up, to Adama, who is holding a flashlight, the proverbial bringer of light in an apocalyptic sense as well as a little nudge to his role as the god behind the camera, the director.

Headcount: The credits show 41,403 survivors for this episode. We saw one person die in "Rapture," but Gaius and Hera both returned to *Galactica*, along with Six, which makes three extra people.

Interesting Fact: What *does* Gaius say to set Gaeta off? There was a whole subplot over several episodes revolving around the deaths of a number of Sagittarons — an incident that Gaius was involved in. When the two men are in the cell together, Gaius is telling Gaeta that he'll quite happily implicate *him* in the scandal, too, which is why Gaeta is so upset. The Sagittaron arc was written out late in the game — not until the finale was being written — and Moore feels that some of the mid-season episodes suffered as a result.

What's In a Name? The secret of Six's name is out . . . only, not really. In a deleted scene from this episode, Roslin asks Six if she will be a witness in Gaius's trial, and asks her name. The answer? Caprica. So she really *is* Caprica-Six — but it remains to be seen whether that's her name or just a handy descriptor to differentiate her from the other Six models. Whatever the case, it's interesting that this particular character's name would be tied so inextricably to the Colonies, to an idea of home, and to the events that took place on that home. Six — or Caprica — has been the most volatile of the Cylon models so far (although they're all a little creepy in their unique ways), emotional and passionate about Gaius and God. Her name links her to her experience of humanity in a way that no other Cylon is linked, aside from Sharon.

Did You Notice? The title of this episode is taken from the lyrics to the theme song of the popular television series *Cheers*. An interesting link considering the fact that there's a new bar on *Galactica*, and, more importantly, that the lyrics then go on to talk about how "sometimes you want to go where everybody knows your name."

There's an obvious callback to the beginning of season 3 ("Precipice") when Roslin slowly hands Gaius his glasses. He did the same to her back in that episode, when their roles were reversed and she was the one being interrogated.

This is the second episode to be directed by Edward James Olmos, after "Tigh Me Up, Tigh Me Down."

The scene where Gaeta stabs Gaius in the neck with his own pen is a reference to the *R. Tam Sessions*, a series of five videos based in the *Serenity* universe and released on the Internet by creator Joss Whedon. In one such Webisode, character River Tam stabs her interviewer in the neck with his pen.

So Say We All: STARBUCK: Kara Thrace and Her Special Destiny? Sounds more like a bad cover band, Sam.

314   The Woman King

Original air date: February 11, 2007
Written by: Michael Angeli
Directed by: Michael Rymer

When a disease sweeps through the refugees on Galactica, Helo discovers that a civilian doctor might be killing off specific people.

This episode feels uncomfortable, and the out-of-place feeling starts right with the title. Immediately there's a sort of "huh?" feeling: is this an episode about a woman who's crowned, a feminist retelling of a classic tale of power, a funny episode, some combination of all those things? The title doesn't sit well with any one of these subjects, because it doesn't really fit all the way around it, leaving us to wonder where exactly we're starting from.

Basically, our notion of kings, kingship, ruling, and rights get tossed into the grinder much as our notion of heroism did in "Hero." "The Woman King" looks at the scarcity of resources, and again it slips in the human

Tahmoh and Katee — friends on- and off-screen (Tahmoh, *GQ* will call you!)
(ALBERT L. ORTEGA)

aspect. On the surface it seems to be about a scarcity of living space, as the various refugees from New Caprica have to adjust yet again to holocaust and displacement. Medical supplies are becoming increasingly important, both to the survivors of the human race and to the story line itself. *BSG* does a great job making these components of science fiction and apocalyptic science fiction seem natural. Unlike some sci-fi series which could devolve to a sort of "problem planet of the week," *Battlestar Galactica* uses real-life situations as ongoing elements in its plot in order to add layers to its science fiction backdrop. A constantly moving refugee population *will* have medical supply issues, and it doesn't matter if they're in Afghanistan or in space — people die. Add to that the moral and ethical problems of religious observances, and you've got one tense situation that never has to leave its originating set. Much of the action is set up in the first shots of Helo, in a small, cramped space, surrounded by people, slowly coming to realize that while he wants to do the right thing, to provide leadership and benign rule to these people regardless of their personal differences, that ideal may not be possible.

That uncomfortable feeling translates well visually, too, with Helo's tall body like a beacon of hope: every time there is a crowd scene we scan the tops of heads until we see him towering over everyone. There's a sly sense of emasculation as regards Helo in this episode: the joking comments of Racetrack and the other pilots, Helo's little throne of an office, his having to battle the entire episode just to reveal the true intentions of Dr. Robert. And in some ways this emasculation is unfair. Helo does the right thing and at the end of the episode, sees his tenacity rewarded, but do we need to have a "nice guys finish first" subject so heavily emphasized? Add to that the fact that Helo is definitely *not* the pinnacle of righteousness: who killed five Cylons in a horrific way by asphyxiating them in their own cell? Who murdered an officer of his own fleet? Who defied a direct order from his commander? Helo may have strong morals regarding the sanctity of life and equality for all beings, but he's definitely not above doing the dirty work if that's what it takes to accomplish whatever he strongly believes in.

Another unfortunate parallel to draw here is that Dr. Robert could be perceived as an emasculated type of ruler. Doctors have the power of life and death, and to yoke this idea to that of a sovereign ruler and then throw the word "woman" into the mix makes it look like . . . well, it looks bad. The most obvious parallel here, Mrs. King, is seen as the most ineffectual character, but she simultaneously has the most integrity. However, most characters seem to have integrity if they're not looked at closely, but we're not given a chance to explore her circumstances — she may turn out to be more like Helo than we thought.

This episode got people talking on forums and at the proverbial watercooler. The episode seemed tailored to deliberately make us uncomfortable, with the endless shots of drudgery, and the cramped, despairing feeling, from the living quarters of the refugees to the tiny, claustrophobic box from which Helo issued orders. It also came on the heels of an unpopular story line between Starbuck and Lee, and focused on secondary and minor characters: even Dr. Robert managed to look both washed out and cramped at the same time. Finally, it dealt with an uncomfortable subject for a supposedly post-Marxist society: class. Until now class has been absent from this postapocalyptic story, and perhaps another reason the episode sits so awkwardly with us is because its sudden insertion into the story seems forced, and, like Mrs. King, ineffectual.

Headcount: There are two fewer survivors from the last episode, giving us a total of 41,401 souls. Although no one died onscreen in "Taking a Break from All Your Worries," it could be that cramped living conditions and ill-health are making their way through the refugee population, accounting for the two losses.

Interesting Fact: Tahmoh Penikett says he's waited "three years for [this episode]," and he was especially glad that it occurred when it did, in the middle of the third season, because the beginning of the season wasn't all that Helo-centric. In an interview with *Starburst*, he noted that over the last three years, he's grown as much as his character has, saying, "I'm definitely not as green as I used to be. We're filming twenty episodes a year now, which means more time on set and watching seasoned pros like Eddie Olmos, Mary McDonnell, and Michael Hogan do their thing. Talk about an eye-opener. They've taught me to be more focused and present as an actor, and that allows me to enjoy the creative process even more."

What's In a Name? Karl "Helo" Agathon is yet another character whose name is rooted in Greek history or mythology. In the first century BCE, Agathon was a celebrated tragic poet from Athens. According to Aristotle, Agathon's writing was known for two things: he created characters from his own imagination, not from Greek myths, and he used the choral lyrics in his plays as musical interludes rather than commentaries on the action. Plato describes Agathon as a hospitable, polite, handsome man, but other texts say that his writing was filled with mannerisms, and that he always tried to surprise the audience with unexpected revelations and developments. Helo is also a refined, handsome character, who seems to be the voice of reason whenever he's in a scene. He's in touch with his emotions, but he's also rational and at ease in his role as a military man and as Sharon's lover. He's not necessarily comfortable, but he's forthright in his decision to not give up on either facet of his life. Penikett says of his character's development, "Helo has been thrust into adulthood and become a man who is set in his moral values and knows the difference between right and wrong. He truly has come into his own and established himself as a very capable individual who, quite possibly, could one day become a leader."

Did You Notice? In the scene where Sharon is folding laundry, Hera's crib can be seen in the background: it looks like her mobile has two Imperial Star Destroyers from *Star Wars* hanging from it.

It's the first time anyone has called Racetrack by her given name, Margaret (which was revealed in "Final Cut"). She doesn't seem to like the name much, given her reaction to Connor when he refers to her as "Marge."

The game the gang is playing at Joe's Bar (appearance number two for the ship's new meeting place, replacing the pilots' lounge) is called "Pyramid X."

315   A Day in the Life

Original air date: February 18, 2007
Written by: Mark Verheiden
Directed by: Rod Hardy

It's Adama's wedding anniversary, and Cally and Chief are trapped in a malfunctioning airlock.

BSG often plays with the idea that a substance may have certain properties that can be clarifying or distorting, depending on the circumstances. Water, for instance, has been used in that capacity from season 1 on. But starting in season 2, we see another substance that exhibits those same properties — glass. Recently we've seen it in the glasses trade-off between Gaius and Roslin, and before that, in scenes with Sharon and Helo aboard *Galactica* that involved them being separated by glass. "A Day in the Life" adds more glass in the form of the barrier between Cally and Chief and the rest of the fleet.

Throughout season 3, *BSG* has moved away from large-scale confrontations — be they space wars or elections — and focused on the day-to-day life of a postapocalyptic society.

"The Woman King," "A Day in the Life," and "Dirty Hands" zero in on the domestic. One ironic thing about these episodes, and this one in particular, is that even though the focus is on the moment-to-moment fluid action that is not part of the vast arc of the show, the camera is fixed and stationary. In contrast to the very chaotic feel of the documentary-style camerawork that has been used in other episodes, this stationary style lends a solidity to the story lines and emphasizes the idea that a day in the life never *is* the stationary, boring phrase that the title purports it to be. The consequences of the holocaust continue to make themselves apparent as Chief and Cally tackle the schism between their service life and their married life.

Galactica is an old ship, and was about to be decommissioned prior to the attacks, it's been in several battles, and has probably made more FTL jumps in the last year than it did during its entire fleet career. The fact that it has held together as long as it has is something of a minor miracle. One day, *this* day, something was going to break.

This same metaphor of something just waiting to break is also applied to Admiral Adama. We're so used to seeing him under control that the scenes with his dead wife are surprising but not worrying, because as usual, Adama seems to know exactly how to act. A gentle tone, a slightly sad but ultimately loving and reasonable interaction with her, reassures us that things are as we expect them to be. It takes a while to realize that Adama's relationship with Carolanne is eerily like Gaius's relationship with Six — right down to the blonde hair (that's four blonde women, if you're counting, and zero blonde men). The image of the ship and the image of the marriage intertwine and mix within the character of Adama. He too was thinking of retiring, and he too has fought long past what could reasonably have been expected of him, and lives constantly now in a state of wartime tension. His cracks, unlike the ship's, stem from trying to hold on to something too tightly, because that psychic armor is what keeps him together, keeps him functioning — which is, ironically, the same thing he warned Lee about in "Kobol's Last Gleaming." Like Chief, Adama was always looking to his career for the next excitement, never acknowledging that things in his personal life had changed. Unlike Tyrol, however, Adama either never had or never took the chance to rethink his marriage. His days were uniformed and uniformly set — and he liked it that way. Now, with the stress of so much war and strife, with all the changes in his life (from leading the remnants of humanity to safety to acknowledging a romantic interest in someone), he too must either look at himself clearly and stop patching things up so that he can continue as if nothing has changed, or risk annihilating himself from the inside out, venting all the ragged pieces of his life at once.

While the parallels between Cally and the Chief's and Adama and his wife's situations are clear, they don't necessarily match up. The rescue mission for the two trapped crew members doesn't feel as important as it should be, and only really comes into focus later in the episode when it's drawn into parallel with Adama's own story. This episode echoes "Flight of the Phoenix," both in the use of the vessel as a metaphor and in the use of a malfunctioning airlock to provide jeopardy (in the season 2 episode, it was Starbuck, Lee, and Hotdog).

Always a terribly uneven character, Cally suffers from being compared to a raging, abusive alcoholic. Her strongest moments are in the hangar when she's talking with her commanding officer. Knowing that she's being overheard as well as seen through the clear glass that separates her from life, Cally is unconcerned about the distorting effects the glass may have: the reality is that every day in some marriages there is strife and compromise, and Cally is not going to let a distorted view get in the way of making sure her child is looked after. On the other side of the glass, Adama overhears Cally's situation, and the intimacy that it forces into the open works as a catalyst for his own demons — even if he doesn't know it.

Headcount: There's a loss of four in this episode, possibly the Sagittarons from the last episode. The survivor count is now at 41,398.

Interesting Fact: In a recent interview, Nicki Clyne talked about the show in general, as well as the challenges of working with a baby. "When we filmed the miniseries, I really had no concept of where the show was headed, if anywhere. [...] Now I feel as if I'm part of something much bigger. I think *Battlestar* can be a powerful initiator for people to ask questions about the way the world operates — if we're open to the discussion, of course. I'm also very supportive of using current technology to further integrate viewers' participation and access. [...] The Webisodes were very quick and low-budget which, while stressful at times, also allowed for some more flexibility and experimentation. [...] I think the most challenging so far has been working with the baby. Not only has he grown exponentially in size but his temperament can be rather unpredictable. Having said that, I usually find these scenes the most

enjoyable because it forces Aaron [Douglas] and I to stay very present in order to work with whatever the baby comes up with, whether it's laughs, cries, regurgitated food, et cetera. Definitely keeps us on our toes, and sometimes at work very late."

Did You Notice? This is the first time we've seen Carolanne since the flashback to Zak's funeral from the miniseries. She's a bit more fleshed out, as it were, in this episode, but she's still an elusive figure at best by the episode's end.

In a wonderful parallel to the season 1 episode "Water," Roslin lends Adama a book entitled *Blood Runs at Midnight*. Each time they give each other a book, or return it, their relationship seems to shift in some way. The first shift involved them trying to bridge the military/political divide immediately after the apocalypse; when she returned the book, she was preparing for her "final journey" toward death. Now, they're venturing into unknown territory again and starting to act a bit more flirtatiously.

Aaron is a real joker, and the fans love it even though he doesn't get to show much humor as Chief Tyrol

(CHRISTINA RADISH)

In the final scene when Chief holds Nicky up to the pressure chamber that holds Cally, you can see "Baby Gap" on the baby's socks . . . Now that's some distribution network.

This is the forty-ninth day since the last Cylon attack: that's the longest they've been without a sighting since the first attacks on the Colonies, except for the time on New Caprica.

Chief uses the word "FUBAR" to denote the current situation in the airlock. That's an acronym usually attributed to the U.S. Army that means, "Fucked Up Beyond All Recognition." (Other variations exist — "Beyond All Repair" is one.)

So Say We All: ROSLIN: This is very difficult for me to say, but I'm going to go to the gym.

ADAMA: Prepare yourself. On its best days, it smells like the inside of a shoe.

316   Dirty Hands

Original air date: February 25, 2007
Written by: Jane Espenson, Anne Cofell Saunders
Directed by: Wayne Rose

Strife rips through the fleet when Chief realizes how bad the working conditions are and calls a general strike.

Following on "The Woman King," "Dirty Hands" takes a look at the mechanisms that drive the fleet. Although the main tension of the story involves the tylium workers and their plight, there is another thread that speaks to the problem of blindly following a tradition. We saw this in the "The Woman King," but instead of the subject being looked at from a religious point of view, this time it's a political one, and Chief follows it up specifically when he confronts Adama and Roslin with the inequities between those who fly the Vipers, and those who fix them.

What's boldly asserted in this episode is that everyone's hands are dirty in one way or another. The *BSG* universe often uses the physical body as a way to talk about ideas. In three seasons we have seen episode titles like "The Hand of God" "The Captain's Hand," and now this episode. Tracing the image from season 1 on there is a distinct hierarchy being followed. While season 1's episode focused on direction from outside humanity, season 2's entry showed authority inside humanity, and season 3's episode widens the focus to include not just one person but everyone. Each member of humanity must take responsibility for their actions, from Seelix to President Roslin, and just as important, each person should have the ability to become the best that they can be.

There is an emphasis placed in this episode on writing. Gaius's smuggled book is part Marxist economics, part megalomaniac memoir. Does Gaius think he has dirty hands? His book says no, because he clearly states, "I wash my hands of the phony democracy," but Gaius's culpability makes his hands just as dirty as the rest of humanity's. Throughout season 3, Gaius' position has been fluid — sometimes he's good, sometimes bad. He's also moving continuously between a chaste redemptive man and libertine — a male version of the Madonna/whore figure.

The written word is an interesting subject in *BSG* — once you get over wondering where in the heck they get all the trees out there in space — and we've seen it from "Occupation" onward gaining momentum as a way to "talk." Until now much of the communication we've seen has been wireless. But newspapers, presidential orders, leaflets, and books have been passed around. Unlike wireless transmissions, paper still has a sustainability and longevity that oral or programmed communication doesn't.

The clearest parallel between the title and the story is the tylium workers. They really have terrible working conditions, and even Roslin's sentiments about the fleet having many dirty and unrewarding jobs that need to be done rings hollow. The tylium workers' plight is also an excellent way for *BSG* to look at one of their important subjects, immediacy. If humanity is to move forward at all, not only do they need to broaden their definition and include the Cylons, they also must take responsibility for the present and stop always looking to the future. Humanity must be *maintained*, not just expanded. The intimation that humanity is a machine that needs maintenance is a subtly ironic one, but it's something that *BSG* continues to look at. Humanity, and what defines it, is as much a function of language as it is of feeling. The various writings we see in the show are a nudge to that idea. Compare Laura Roslin's memoirs at the beginning of the season, as she writes down for posterity the things she sees and feels, to Gaius's memoirs. Gaius defines humanity over and over again, each time defining it to best suit his immediate needs, and at the moment he needs to rant. So he writes a polemical book that happens to be in the right place at the right time. Suddenly he's a hero again. Both memoirs reveal an aspect of humanity, but they don't speak to its totality.

Regardless of how many books are written, though, the fact is that the workers on board the tylium ship have been relegated to a dark corner and unless they are seen to be as important as the Viper pilots, humanity is going nowhere fast. The scenes with the workers on the line doing the actual refining are a clear illustration of inequity. Jumping into a Viper and going up against Raiders can get you killed, but so can pushing an ore cart along an assembly line: why the difference in how we see them? Neither one works without the other, and the episode does a great job of reimagining our idea of the hierarchical value of work, instead placing them side by side and giving them equal visibility and equal weight. The tylium workers cannot just strike because they feel like it. Yes they have real problems, and yes those problems need to be dealt with, but their work is integral to maintaining humanity. The scenes between the deckhands and the pilots also highlight a difficulty that's been a part of fleet life since the miniseries — the difference between military operations (where the pilots do as they're told) and civilian operations (which operate on consensus). To the military, there's no such thing as a strike — it would be called mutiny. How are those conflicting ideas put together so that things can continue? "Dirty Hands" calls everyone to account for their actions and continues to resist a simplified view of both the fleet or the people it carries.

Headcount: There are two more people on board this episode: 41,400.

Interesting Fact: The scene when Roslin takes Gaius's papers from him was originally written to be even more humiliating for Gaius but was changed on set because the actors felt it wasn't true to their characters. Moore explains, "In the draft, I was quite adamant that they actually did strip Baltar. That they stripped him completely, and he was totally naked and the pages fell out. [...] That there was a humiliation factor involved with the fact that she was going to strip him completely naked. And that he was going to make her do it. The actors did not share my view on this scene, and felt quite strongly that actually he would preserve his dignity at a certain point, and that Laura would not push it beyond a certain point. [...] There is still a part of me that wishes that she had humiliated him to that level, that the end of the scene was her realization that she had humiliated him to that level and [her] regret, and that Baltar was defiant and felt victory, and yet felt shame. I like the conflicting agendas of those two things. But I don't have to do it on the set. They know the characters, on some level, better than I do, and I acquiesced to their take on the scene."

Did You Notice? Seelix is given a first name — Diana, who, in Roman mythology, was the virgin goddess of the hunt. She was the twin sister of Apollo (he's both a Greek and a Roman god), and was associated with wild animals and nature.

This is the first time the issue of the fleet's tylium supply has been looked at in any real depth since the season 1 episode "The Hand of God." In that episode, Gaius was in a very different position as vice president and main advisor in all things Cylon, and the decisions were being made by the "upper class" echelons. In this episode, they're being made by the so-called little people.

Gaius reveals that he's originally from Aerelon: that answers the question that was raised back in "Flesh and Bone" when he told Boomer that he thought he detected a slight Aerelon accent in her voice, as to how familiar he was with the Aerelon accent.

Some kudos for Eddie and Katee
(ALBERT L. ORTEGA)

317   Maelstrom

Original air date: February 25, 2007
Written by: David Weddle
Directed by: Michael Nankin

When Starbuck starts having strange dreams about Leoben, Apollo and Adama try to figure out if she's still fit for duty.

"Maelstrom" is a departure in more ways than one from the last three episodes, which focused on more minor characters like Chief, Cally, and Helo. For months before this episode aired, the Internet was rife with rumors about a major cast member suddenly going missing from the opening credits, and producers and writers noted in advance that "Maelstrom" would change the entire framework of the series.

"Maelstrom" is a peculiar title for an episode that's built on slow moments of connectivity: between Starbuck and Socrata, Lee, Adama. What "Maelstrom" does is provide closure for Starbuck. Like Kat in "The Passage," once the character's journey is complete and has come full circle to find the truth about who they are and what they're afraid of, they have to move on or risk stagnating. Interwoven with scenes of child abuse that are shockingly cruel are moments of tenderness in the present moment that help Starbuck move on from what she's been so afraid of her entire life. When Lee offers to take second (that's a huge thing in the piloting world), it's like their entire perspective shifts: Kara looks at him and sees not *Lee the lover* but *Apollo the friend*, and she's able to let go of everything she's been holding on to, that whole messy affair, their mutual grief about Zak, and see what's in front of her. Kara's always been one to look for what she hasn't got: when Anders wasn't there, she wanted him, but when he *was* there, she cheated on him. When Apollo was with Dee, she wanted him, but when she had him, she went and married Anders. In "Maelstrom," she finally sees what she has, and she doesn't go looking for more. It's a huge moment for the character, and the bittersweet edge to the conversation with Lee is fitting because it's a departure and a goodbye for Starbuck.

Later, when Lee's swooping madly through the storm system, there's an edge of panic in his face and voice that echoes the season 2 episode "Flight of the Phoenix" — except this time, Starbuck isn't fooling around with a stealth ship, she's pretty much committing suicide. There's been a string of suicides on *BSG* over the last season: Duck ("Occupation"), D'Anna, Kat ("The Passage"), Gaius (attempted), and now Starbuck. Over the last three seasons, everyone on the *Galactica* has been through so much, and this third season hasn't been kind to anyone. A modern-day Persephone, Kara was kidnapped by Leoben, a modern-day Hades, who whisked her away to his Underworld, where she became his queen, until she was rescued by Anders. But in true mythological fashion, she never really left the Underworld, just as part of her never really left her mother's house that day when she walked out on Socrata, and she's been returning there, time and again, ever since. Kara's pattern of staying in her past is something we saw in "Unfinished Business," when she walked away from Lee to go with the man she could control, and it's not until the end of "Maelstrom" that Kara finally closes her eyes and lets the universe take over, lays down her burdens, takes a break from all her worries, and breaks apart, in the most awful way imaginable.

"Maelstrom" plays like one long preparation for death. The solemn tone to the episode, the ticking of the clock that just stops, Kara's conversation with Lee about where she wants her photo placed on the memorial wall, and the crazy cinematography all work towards a death ritual that Kara makes her way through, slowly and with more than a tinge of the absurd. Her whole life — the important parts, anyway — doesn't so much flash before her eyes as walk procedurally and purposefully, as if to ensure that she look at them with the same purpose. The lighting throughout the episode is washed out, pointing to the idea that Starbuck is just done, broken. In every scene, her face is semi-veiled with shade or spots of darkness: she's never wholly illuminated until the very end, when light washes over her, visually indicating the "space between life and death" that she explodes into.

The moment of her death is a mix of auditory and visual shock: colors explode over the screen at the same time as a moment of silence descends, shroud-like, over the CIC and Lee's Viper plane. How hard would it have been for him to tell Adama not to bother sending out a rescue team? But at the same time, in the back of his mind, in the back of all their minds, is that thought: *we knew it was going to happen some day.* Not because Starbuck was inherently suicidal, but because as a Viper pilot in a time of war, her life expectancy — the life expectancy of every single pilot — is dramatically reduced.

This episode marks a shift in direction whether or not you're a fan of Starbuck, because her very absence will mean that everything she touched has to change. Love her or hate her, like she said about Admiral Cain in "Resurrection Ship, Part 2," the fleet was a lot safer with her than they will be without her.

Headcount: There are 41,400 survivors at the start of the episode; there's one less by the end.

Interesting Fact: The destruction that Edward James Olmos wreaks on the model ship at the end of "Maelstrom" was completely unscripted and unplanned — and one of the most expensive scenes of the entire series, because it's actually not a model ship but a museum quality ship that the props people had rented. Edward didn't know it was genuine, and in the moment lashed out in emotion.

What's In a Name? We've already looked at the name "Starbuck," but the pilot's first name is also an interesting choice. In Norse mythology, Kara was one of the Valkyries, warrior maidens who selected the best of the warriors slain in combat to go to Valhalla. Valkyries were also known as "swan maidens" as they were thought to turn into swans with the help of a feathered cloak. (See "Hero" for more on the Valkyries.) One day, while flying low as a swan, the myth says that Kara impaled herself on her husband's upraised sword while trying to prevent a battle from breaking out. Some similarities with Starbuck's arc in this episode are obvious: Starbuck *is* a warrior, she *was* trying to stop the Heavy Raider she (thought she) saw before it attacked the fleet, and she *was* flying low into the storm system.

Did You Notice? When Socrata tells Kara that she knows she'll do fine "because [she's her] daughter," it's a callback to a scene in season 1's "The Hand of God" when Adama and Apollo have much the same conversation. Apollo asks Adama how he can be so sure that he, Apollo, will be successful on the mission, and Adama answers, "Because you're my son."

The return of the model ship: it's been seen throughout the series, most noticeably in "Home, Part 1," when it was used in part to symbolize the fleet, family, and the need to build solid foundations. This is the first (and last) time we've seen it finished.

This is the third time Starbuck and Adama have exchanged the lines about the rain and "bringing in the cat."

The last time we heard the words "good hunting" was in "Exodus, Part 2."

Even though it looks like Apollo can see the Cylon Heavy Raider when he locks in on Starbuck's Viper, official word has it that he *didn't* see it, leaving the question of whether it was really there or all in Starbuck's head unanswered.

Classic *Battlestar Galactica*: In the original series, Apollo was the straitlaced officer and Starbuck his hotshot pilot best friend, and it's that relationship that Moore wanted to pay homage to in the scene between Lee and Kara in this episode, when they lay their differences to rest and make peace with who they are to one another.

318. The Son Also Rises

Original air date: March 11, 2007
Written by: Michael Angeli
Directed by: Robert Young

When Apollo takes over as head of security for Gaius's attorney, he rethinks the course of his life.

"Hey James, you look better in a beard than I do!" (DAVID DOWLING/ SHOOTING STAR)

"The Son Also Rises" is a play on the title of Ernest Hemingway's first major novel, *The Sun Also Rises*, and it's also a callback to a biblical passage in Ecclesiastes, which reads, "the sun also ariseth." Two things are clear in this episode: first, that the loss of Starbuck has affected the crew of *Galactica*, and in unexpected ways; and second, that the common conception of family and duty are colliding in equally unexpected ways. Lee and Gaius are placed side by side in this episode, both physically (as we see them in numerous shots together, although nearly always placed opposite one another to denote their different viewpoints) and emotionally (as Gaius prepares himself for a drawn-out trial, Apollo struggles with his life and who he has become). The long periods of inactivity between Cylon sightings have had one sure consequence: life has had to go on. And without the Cylons around, what *is* this ragtag fleet, what is left of humanity besides the sum of its survivors? Can nothing else be salvaged from the wreckage of the Colonies? What of society, what of civilization, what of laws and rights and life outside of surviving?

In that sense, "The Son Also Rises" fits in with the season's other socially minded episodes like "Dirty Hands" and "The Woman King" — episodes that go back to the roots of season 1 and ask questions about the reimagining of civic life and community. One of the main shifts in this episode is in the way that Gaius is now viewed. Until now, Gaius has been seen nearly exclusively from an interior point of view — and almost always his own. Whenever the Six from his subconscious is in the room, we're seeing things from his perspective, for instance, and because Gaius has, for the last season or so, been seen mainly in the same scene as Cylons rather than humans, we're used to that perspective. All of a sudden in this episode, we're seeing Gaius through the eyes of his attorney, through Lee's eyes, through the fleet's eyes. Suddenly, he's not the misunderstood genius or the slightly eccentric "odd little man": he's a man convicted of horrendous crimes, on trial for his life, and being judged by every single person in the fleet. The external viewpoint serves to emphasize the sense of judgment that's being carried.

So while Gaius is gaining in infamy, Apollo is realizing that perhaps the existential crisis he had at the beginning of the season wasn't as cleanly resolved as he thought it was. Perhaps the dreams that were cut short, which he mentioned in "Dirty Hands," are more important to him than he thought. And if the fleet is going to be looking for Earth for the foreseeable future, then he — then everyone — has the opportunity to change their lives, in the same way the workers tried to do in "Dirty Hands." Apollo has the chance to do what he wants with his life — that's got to be like a breath of fresh air, and after Starbuck's death and its lesson about letting go, maybe piloting doesn't make as much sense as it used to. He never wanted to be in the military long-term anyway, so there's a certain sense of "why not?" in his attitude in this episode. This is Lee's big opportunity to move away from the choices he's made and abided by, but hasn't always believed in wholeheartedly. Does duty always come first, or is there a point when, as Kat did and Kara discovered, it's time to let go and move on?

What "The Son Also Rises" shows is that, sometimes, myths aren't always written down: Lampkin steals Gaius's pen, telling Lee that Gaius will gain favor in the fleet if they think he's been "silenced." Far from letting Gaius's story tell itself, Lampkin is actively engaged in the construction of the myth of Gaius as a martyr, laying the foundations for a reimagined story. Gaius takes on the role of victim in the rewriting of his own life — which fits in well with what he's tried to believe of himself since the miniseries. His story has epic, mythical qualities to it — and now it's time for Lampkin to make the man fit the story.

The episode ends on a note of sadness that simultaneously offers closure and hope: the hope of a new day intrinsically linked to the dying of the old day. In a move that echoes Starbuck's placement of Kat's photo on the memorial wall, Lee takes the photo he's been carrying around out of his pocket and places Starbuck, reverently and lovingly, where she belongs: in the past, with the rest of the heroes who have gone on. Everything is breaking — from the purely physical break of Anders' leg to the psychic break of Six's resolve to testify against Gaius — especially Apollo's vision of his own life. He finally breaks with his father, breaks with the military, and picks up the broken threads of the life he dreamed of before the attacks. And while Gaius's attorney views Lee's break in a negative light (his note to Gaius reads like a portent of doom targeting Admiral Adama), it's ultimately a hopeful sign: the son is coming out of the shadow of his father, and as he walks away, his back is straight, his eyes dead center, his head high, as if he's finally coming into his own — something he's been yearning to do since the miniseries. He doesn't yell at Adama, doesn't make a scene. Instead, he gently places his wings on the desk and firmly tells his father who he wants to be. Like Kat and Kara before him, he dies to find the space between his old life and his new dream.

Headcount: There are 41,399 survivors in this episode, marking Starbuck's death.

Did You Notice: This is the first time a major cast member (in this case Katee Sackhoff)

Rekha Sharma (Tory Foster)

Date of birth: unknown

Did you know? A Canadian actor with Indian heritage, Rekha Shanti Sharma is, aside from her role as Roslin's aide, probably best known for her repeat guest appearance on Canadian drama *Da Vinci's City Hall*, in which she played Constable Cindy Winters. Rekha appeared in the blockbuster movie *The Core* alongside Hilary Swank. Some of her other screen names are: Reika Sharma, Rékha Sharma, and Rékha Sharms. Under the first, she guest starred in the pilot of the hit TV show *House M.D.* in 2004.

has been missing from the credits. Although cast members have been missing in episodes before, their names have always appeared.

This is the first time since season 2 that any member of the talk show "The Colonial Gang" has been seen: this marks the reappearance of Playa Palacios.

Kara's personnel folder includes a combat citation with a field commendation for valor and bravery, a pilot performance decrement, a disciplinary notice for assault on a superior officer (Tigh, perhaps), another disciplinary notice, and a record of disciplinary proceedings.

You can clearly see the ship Adama destroyed at the end of "Maelstrom" when Lee and he are talking: its mast looks askew, as if it sustained some permanent damage.

Lee places Starbuck's photo next to Kat's, exactly where she requested it in "Maelstrom."

319, 320 Crossroads, Parts 1 & 2

Original air dates: March 18 & 25, 2007
Written by: Michael Taylor (Part 1), Mark Verheiden (Part 2)
Directed by: Michael Rymer

Gaius's trial finally begins and a schism appears in the fleet. And all along the watchtower, princes keep the view.

One thing you can say about *BSG* is that it knows how to do endings. "Crossroads" is such a huge, landmark episode, and so many different threads are brought together that it's impossible to discuss Part 1 without referring to Part 2. At the end of the season, the wind howls, hurtling us towards Earth, the camera swoops and swerves and with a sudden switch in angle, turns everything we thought we had understood over the last three years upside down. Again. Everything has changed: four people we, and the fleet, have grown to love and trust are Cylons, Starbuck is alive — maybe — and the Cylons are on the verge of an all-out attack.

"Crossroads" looks at the journey that each character has traveled since the Cylons first attacked; years have now passed, and things are so different but simultaneously so much the same. The fleet is still running, they're still looking for Earth, they're still fighting the Cylons, they're still struggling with resources, internal schisms, religion, and class. They're still figuring out who they can trust. Love, loss, faith, hope, conflict, hatred, anger — all these emotions that we call human and that have been defining the survivors since the attacks become the starting point for a whole new adventure as relationships are redefined and lives redrawn.

The finales for seasons 1 and 2 focused on a fragmented fleet, full of people with personal conflicts that made the large-scale conflict with the Cylons all the more intense. In this season 3 finale, the fleet is more united than ever with the reappearance of Starbuck, the end of Gaius's trial, and Apollo taking to the cockpit again. As united as the fleet might be, however, it's a superficial unity because underlying this finale is the knowledge that Tigh, Chief, Anders, and Tory are all Cylons — and for all their purposefulness, who's to say that they might not, like Boomer in season 1, suddenly fall under the influence of their programming?

"Crossroads" opens on an opera house, immediately framing the events as a form of spectacle, a voyeurism that's further highlighted by the courtroom drama of the finale. The lack of music throughout the episode only emphasizes the absurdity of the pop song, and heightens the drama of the courtroom scenes. And the title provides the best entry into the stories because pretty much every character is at a crossroads of one kind of another. The only one who seems to be on pretty certain ground is Starbuck — kind of ironic considering the fact that she was floundering throughout most of the season.

Many season finales tend to close some doors and open others; "Crossroads" doesn't close a single door — instead, it bursts everything open wider than it was before. The image of a crossroads is twofold: first, that there is no closure — it's open-ended and offers four different directions; second, what happens from that point on is all a matter of choice. Just as Tigh chooses in the beginning of Part 1 to drink and testify while drunk, so too does he decide at the end of Part 2 that, even though he's a Cylon, his identity is not written in stone, or code — he is Saul Tigh, he is the XO of the *Galactica*, and he is choosing that identity, every day.

In the same way, Lee chooses in every moment of this finale who he wants to be. What he comes to realize is that his identity is fluid and entirely up to him. He can be the ruthless lawyer, he can be the passionate witness for humanity, and he can be the Viper pilot Apollo — and none cancels out any of the others. He's come so far since season 2, when Roslin and Zarek asked him to publicly denounce Adama over the radio when Roslin was planning the jump to Kobol. Although Lee ultimately makes the same decision in this episode when Lampkin places him on the stand, he doesn't merely not testify against his father; instead, he makes an impassioned argument for the difference between guilt and culpability, accomplishing the next phase of his transformation into the defender of cities and civil liberties — a transformation he began in "Bastille Day."

Other threads come full circle, too, among them Roslin's cancer and her hatred for Gaius. For the first two seasons, Roslin was portrayed as one of the most sensible and sensitive people in the fleet — that she was the official representative for their people was just icing on the cake, so to speak. But over the last season, she's hardened. Her time on New Caprica, her guilt over what happened on the planet, her realization that she hasn't always made the best decisions (hiding Hera and not informing Adama, for instance) have forced her into a corner. It's a corner that she's been fairly adept at avoiding until now, but Lee backs her into it and her sorrowful recollection of their first moment of bonding from the miniseries ("Captain Apollo") makes her seem fragile in a way that we've not seen in a long time. In a nice callback to the beginning and middle of the season ("Precipice" and "Taking a Break From All Your Worries"), glasses are used symbolically: Roslin puts them on as a form of armor, to protect herself from Lee's questioning, and removes them when she exposes her cancer and lays herself bare. It's interesting that both her and Lee's displays of courage occur at the same time and seem to operate at cross-purposes: while Lee proves Adama wrong by questioning Roslin himself, shouldering the burden of responsibility for her suffering rather than delegating it to Lampkin, Roslin steels herself and reveals a personal issue, and one that must be all the more devastating to her because she thought she had beaten it.

What happens in this season finale though is that, despite the fact that the fleet is operating as one in a way it hasn't in a while — with no trial to distract it, there is nothing but the single-minded purpose of finding Earth and beating back the Cylons in the last ten minutes — everyone stands alone. Apollo burns his bridges with Adama, watches Dee leave him, loses Roslin's affection and respect — and though he joins the fight, he's alone in the Viper plane — alone, that is, until Starbuck shows up. Although it's been officially stated that Starbuck is real, and not a hallucination, "Crossroads" places Lee and Gaius in parallel positions as pariahs among their people — and all of a sudden Lee, too, has a blonde woman hanging around . . .

But despite the focus on Lee and Gaius's trial, "Crossroads" reveals itself to be all about the four people who discover they aren't who they thought they were. "All along the watchtower, princes kept the view." The lyrics to the song are chilling, because they apply so well to Tigh, Chief, Anders, and Tory. Tigh is Adama's right-hand man, someone in whom Adama has complete faith. "You never embarrass me," Adama tells Tigh in Part 1. Would he still say that if he knew Tigh were a Cylon? Would it not be the ultimate embarrassment to realize that the man you've known for forty-odd years has been a Cylon all along? Chief is in charge of all the equipment that's necessary for the fight against the Cylons — and in the last few episodes, he's also become a spokesperson for the "lower class" so he holds a lot more power than he did when we first met him. Tory is Roslin's right-hand woman, the power behind the throne, so to speak. Anders is a civilian leader: he's commanded three resistance groups (on Caprica, New Caprica, and the algae planet) and he's the link between the military and the civilians. Each one holds massive strategic power, and the final words

"All Along the Watchtower"

The song was originally written by Bob Dylan, but it's often covered by other bands. Probably the most famous cover is by Jimi Hendrix — in fact, his cover of the song is so famous many people think Hendrix wrote it! It's also been done by U2, the Dave Matthews Band, Prince, and the Kronos Quartet (one of their members, Philip Glass, is the same Philip Glass whose music is heard in the season 2 episode "Valley of Darkness"). The folksong was written and sung in reverse order, so the conversation of the joker and the thief actually comes after the rider approaches the castle. For the *BSG* version, composer Bear McCreary enlisted the help of his brother for the vocals. Tigh, Tory, Anders, and Chief repeat the lines from the opening verse throughout the episode.

in the CIC are absolutely terrifying: "You can count on me," says Tigh, while Tory reassures the President of the Colonies, "I'm here if you need me."

Throughout the finale, the camera works to emphasize the changes that are afoot, serving as a sort of visual foreshadower and prophetic voice: there are a number of strange shots on hands and various body parts that offer a distorted view of the character. In the courtroom, for instance, the camera focuses foremost on Tigh's hand, making his face seem out of proportion to the rest of his body and twisting the viewing angle so we're not really sure how we're seeing him — or how he's seeing himself. His reality is shifting; the reality of the show is shifting; and from here on in, nothing will ever be the same. And if the conventions of apocalyptic science fiction are reimagined in this finale, with its emphasis on courtroom procedures and Apollo's reinjection of a moral responsibility, so too are the characters reimagined, from Tigh to Tory, from Apollo to Starbuck, from Lampkin to Gaius.

The song's prophetic overtones and its casually dismissive relation to time (it's actually best understood when the lyrics are read in reverse) add a visionary quality to the finale. The absurdity of the music (a far cry from the orchestral or classical overtones that usually accompany *BSG*) combined with the strange lyrics offer an imagistic and archetypal reading of the finale. Figures like the joker, the thief, the princes, and the riders converge at the crossroads, ready to choose a path. The future, past, and present are spread out wide before these characters, like so many different directions. They clearly feel that humanity is worth choosing, so it must be worth saving: Tigh, Chief, Anders, and Tory are children of humanity, brought up amongst humans, believing they are humans, caring about human

Some of the cast and crew get together for one of the largest fan conventions in the United States — Comic Con (ALBERT L. ORTEGA)

issues, and acting like humans even when their lives have been turned around.

Funnily enough, the prophetic lyrics actually seem more anti-prophetic, as they even include the words "this is not our fate" and they're contrasted to the casual foresight that's peppered throughout — from Helo's "smell it in the air" to Roslin's "feeling" about Six. How they — and we — expect the story to turn out is just not how it *will* turn out, because prophets can foresee all they want, but without context, they will never know the truth.

As Tory raises her eyes toward the end of the episode, they seem shrouded, cloaked in shadow, and they meet Tigh's one eye — the other missing, concealed — it's as if time stands still and the entire future of the fleet flashes before *our* eyes. It's made even worse by the fact that neither Roslin nor Adama realize that anything has happened — Adama doesn't even look at Tigh, and Roslin just distractedly glances at Tory — but everything has changed. The princes are keeping watch over the tower — but the princes aren't who we thought they were . . . so are we safe? Is humanity safe? And if identity and humanity is a choice, as Sharon's experience seems to argue, then has anything really changed at all?

Headcount: The final episode features no survivor count. We do learn, however, that 5,197 people died under the Cylon occupation of New Caprica or in the exodus from the planet. **Are You There, God? It's Me, Gaius.** Gaius makes his final transition from atheist to savior figure in the finale, but unlike earlier seasons, when he adopted a Christ-like attitude and pose ("The Hand of God," for instance), now he proclaims, loud and clear, "I'm not God." Ironically, the denial of deity status is one of the hallmarks of actually being a god figure (Jesus denied he was God; the Buddha said he was only enlightened, not a god) and for the first time, Gaius is unaware of his own status. It could come from his isolation: in his cell, away from the rest of humanity, he has to define himself — and without others to validate whatever view of himself he holds, it's likely that he's had to regain a bit of humility. That isolation and self-reliance is highlighted by his wide-eyed wandering through the corridors of the *Galactica* after he has been declared innocent and left to his own devices by Lampkin and Apollo. For a minute, it almost looks like he'll have to make his own way in the world — but then, salvation arrives (in the form of a woman, echoing the appearance of Six in his subconscious in the miniseries). This time, the woman is human, and flesh and blood — but as the rest of the episode proves, that might not make any difference, after all.

Interesting Fact: When Ronald Moore first decided on the end of "Maelstrom," he told only Katee that he would be bringing her back for the season finale, but when it came time to film "Maelstrom," the cast was absolutely incensed, and the atmosphere on set was described as almost mutinous. Edward James Olmos and Mary McDonnell were particularly upset, and Moore decided to tell the cast what was going on in the finale.

Did You Notice? Over the radio, a message is heard, other than the song "All Along the Watchtower." The message is, "Houston, the Eagle has landed," which were Neil Armstrong's words after the first human-made machine had landed on the moon.

Susan Hogan, who played the tribunal judge Captain Franks, is the wife of actor Michael Hogan who plays Tigh.

The show's usual title sequence was not aired for either part of the series finale; the names of the main stars were simply placed on-screen during the teaser.

Helo says, "A storm is coming." His words echo Sharon's words in "Lay Down Your Burdens, Part 2," when she told him that "Something dark is coming."

The opera house from the dream sequences in this episode is the same opera house from Kobol that we've seen throughout the series (starting from "Kobol's Last Gleaming, Part 2") and most frequently in this season, through the dreams of D'Anna.

There are three groupings of three people in the second part of the finale (three being a perfect, sacred number): three women (Sharon, Roslin, and Six), three men (Gaius, Lee, and Lampkin), and three Cylons (Chief, Anders, and Tory).

Gaeta has a really strange relationship with the truth: he lied for Dee in "Resistance," exposed the truth about the elections ("Lay Down Your Burdens, Part 2"), and now he decides to lie on the stand.

Adama has another shaving scene in this episode but it's very different from the one in "Exodus, Part 2." There it was a sign of a fresh start; here, it's a sign of rage and frustration.

This is probably the first time since "Pegasus" that we've seen Adama actually drink: he's always on the verge of pouring a drink, but he never gets as far as drinking it.

"I have a feeling . . ." Roslin's words are an echo of her words in "Lay Down Your Burdens, Part 2" where she said that she felt it in her gut that Gaius being president would be a very bad thing.

Tigh's speech, "I would do anything, say anything," is a lot like Ellen's speech in "Exodus, Part 2" when she was confessing to Saul. She said, "I'd do anything, frak anyone."

The fact that Saul lost his eye is darkly ironic now, since the Centurions from both the original and the reimagined series have only one (red, moving) eye.

With Chief now revealed as a Cylon, his and Cally's son is now the second human/Cylon hybrid — provided Cally isn't the final model, of course.

So Say We All: ROSLIN: Yell at me. I want to get out of bed. […]

ADAMA: Get your fat, lazy ass out of that rack, Roslin!

The *BSG* Timeline

Following is an approximate timeline for the last half century or so of Colonial history, gathered from the show itself as well as other resources — the best one being the Battlestar Wiki entry on the reimagined series' timeline. The years aren't always exact, and there are some discrepancies, but it should provide a fairly easy "at a glance" framework for the series. Everything above the Cylon nuclear attacks from the miniseries is considered to have taken place Before Day Zero, or BDZ; those that occur after do not carry an acronym after the year.

Year 69 BDZ:	Saul Tigh born
Year 64 BDZ:	William Adama born
Year 52 BDZ:	Cylon Wars begin
Year 50 BDZ:	*Galactica* enters service
Year 45 BDZ:	Adama enters service
Year 40 BDZ:	Cylon Wars end with the signing of an Armistice
Year 34 BDZ:	Adama takes leave of absence from the service
Year 20 BDZ:	Tom Zarek imprisoned for terrorism or freedom fighting
	Adama and Tigh meet
Year 17 BDZ:	Adama reinstated
Year 15 BDZ:	Tigh reinstated by Adama
Year 11 BDZ:	Laura Roslin enters politics
Year 5 BDZ:	Galen Tyrol (Chief) assigned to serve under Adama
Year 4 BDZ:	Kara Thrace (Starbuck) graduates from Fleet Academy
Year 2 BDZ:	Caprica-Six starts to live on Caprica, meets Gaius Baltar
	Zak Adama dies
	Kara assigned to *Galactica*
Year 1 BDZ:	Adama, Tigh, Gaeta, Chief assigned to *Galactica*
Day Zero:	Cylons destroy the 12 Colonies
Day 6:	*Olympic Carrier* destroyed
Day 10:	*Galactica*'s water tanks sabotaged

	Boomer begins to suspect she's a Cylon
Day 12:	Prisoner uprising on *Astral Queen*
Day 14-15:	Starbuck goes missing and finds a Cylon Raider
Day 17:	Doral model sets off suicide bomb on *Galactica*
Day 24:	Sharon and Helo have sex for the first time on Caprica
Day 25:	Leoben Conoy model discovered and executed
	First mention of Starbuck's "destiny"
Day 28:	Ellen Tigh arrives on board
Day 46-49:	First session of the new Quorum of Twelve
	Gaius elected vice president
Day 50:	Kobol discovered
Day 51:	Raptor One crashes on Kobol
	Adama arrests Roslin
	Starbuck finds Helo on Caprica
	Boomer shoots Adama
Day 51:	Group on Kobol rejoins the fleet
Day 53:	Tigh establishes martial law
	Starbuck and Helo meet Samuel Anders and the resistance group
	Cally Henderson kills Boomer
Day 54:	Roslin escapes from prison
Day 61:	Adama takes back command of the fleet
Day 62:	Starbuck, Helo, and Sharon leave for Kobol
Day 64:	Roslin and group begin searching for Tomb of Athena on Kobol
Day 65:	Adama reunites the fleet
	Tomb of Athena and map to Earth found
	Roslin becomes president again

From here on, things get a bit fuzzy, and there's an officially recognized timeline problem spanning two months. The timeline affects season 2 episodes from "Flight of the Phoenix" to "Epiphanies."

Day 189:	Roslin's cancer cured
Day 270:	Hera Agathon born and adopted by Maya
	Planet known as New Caprica discovered
	Starbuck and group land on Caprica to rescue resistance group
Day 283:	Gaius Baltar elected president
Day 284:	*Cloud 9* destroyed by nuclear warhead

We'll be assuming that settlement of New Caprica began about five days later, around Day 290.

Day 411:	Starbuck and Lee have sex
Day 412:	Starbuck marries Anders
Day 650:	Cylon forces arrive on New Caprica
	Starbuck kidnapped by Leoben
Day 784:	Tigh released from detention center
Day 785:	*Galactica* Raptor and New Caprica Resistance make contact
Day 787:	Ellen Tigh dies
Day 789:	*Pegasus* destroyed
	New Caprica evacuated and fleet reunited
	Hera taken by the Cylons
Day 795:	Roslin takes over as president with Zarek as VP
Day 925:	Bulldog rescued

From there, the timeline gets fuzzier still, with fewer markers. What we do know is that "A Day In the Life" takes place forty-nine days after "Rapture"; that when the events of "The Son Also Rises" occur, three years have not yet passed since the Day Zero attacks; and some time in between then, Starbuck dies.

Online Resources

In writing this book, a lot of different online sources were consulted, both official and unofficial. Official sites are sites that the person or company in question owns, maintains, or actively endorses, while unofficial sites are usually run by fans. Each site listed here offers something special, and it's far from an exhaustive list. If you take these as your starting point, you're sure to find *something* interesting.

The Show

SciFi Channel
www.scifi.com/battlestar
The official site for *Battlestar Galactica*. Web site hosted by the SciFi Channel, features quizzes, episode summaries, Ronald Moore's blog, and a huge forum section, among others.

BattlestarGalactica.com
www.battlestargalactica.com
A huge site devoted to *Battlestar Galactica*, both old and new. Features reviews, interviews, episode summaries, articles and merchandise. Unofficial.

Battlestar Wiki
en.battlestarwiki.org/wiki/Main_Page
BSG had such a huge presence on the peer-contributed Wikipedia that an offshoot was set up entirely devoted to the show. Probably the largest collection of information on every aspect of the show that is available on the Web.

Twiz TV
www.twiztv.com/scripts/battlestar
Transcripts of all episodes of the reimagined *BSG* from the miniseries through to season 2. Unofficial.

The Sad Geezer's Guide

www.sadgeezer.com

Click on the *BSG* banner for another comprehensive site that deals with many aspects of the show, has transcripts for all seasons including 3. Unofficial.

Television Without Pity

www.televisionwithoutpity.com/articles/category_1188.html

Not really a "resource" per se, but a fun site that gives great episode blow-by-blows, and often hilarious or moving commentary. Definitely unofficial (but it's got street cred).

Space

www.spacecast.com/bsg

The Canadian science fiction channel that airs the series. Includes behind-the-scenes footage, synopses, bios, and forums.

Sky One

www.skyone.co.uk/programme/pgeProgramme.aspx?pid=3

The UK's sci-fi station, boasting a fan forum, overviews, photo galleries, and cast info.

The Cast/Crew

Jamie Bamber

www.jamiebamber.co.uk

Jamie Bamber, this is your Web site! Pretty much the unofficial official Web site for Jamie Bamber. He's even posted there. Includes biography, news, pictures, a *vast* collection of articles dating back to his *Hornblower* years, and a fan section.

James Callis

www.jamescallis.com

In the words of the webmaster, "Although this Web site is not endorsed by James or his agents, James does occasionally pop in and leave updates on the messageboard."

Aaron Douglas

www.aarondouglas.biz

Fan-run official site on which Aaron posts a blog. Includes, filmography, forum, images, news, and a biography of the actor. Official.

Tricia Helfer

www.triciahelfer.com

Good promotional site for this model/actor with photos and a question/answer section. And yep, Tricia answers all the questions.

Bear McCreary

www.bearmccreary.com/html/blog/blogmain.htm

Music is a huge part of the *BSG* experience, and the composer for the show has a site that includes online demos, photo gallery, and blog that he posts to fairly often. Official.

Mary McDonnell

www.socket-52.com/marymcdonnell/mainpage.html

A fairly comprehensive site of this hardworking actor. Includes news, biography, information on stage, film, and television appearances, a photo gallery, interviews starting in the 1970s, and merchandise. Unofficial.

Edward James Olmos

hometown.aol.com/mbeve10258/EddieOlmos.html

It's really ugly, but it gives a great overview of this actor and activist. Includes information on his community service, lectures, and speeches, as well as all his work in film and television. Official.

Grace Park

(at the time of this writing) None! Grace! Where are you?

Katee Sackhoff

www.katee-sackhoff.org

A pretty site that needs (free) membership for photo access. Includes biography, quotes, pics, and fan creations, as well as an address to send her fan mail. Unofficial.

Basic Sources

www.tv.com
blog.scifi.com/battlestar/
www.imdb.com
scifi.about.com
www.pantheon.org
www.britannica.com

Bibliography

Aeolus. "Helo Hath No Fury: An Interview with Tahmoh Penikett." Online. July 3, 2006.

"Alessandro Juliani." www.battlestar-galactica.fr. Online. Accessed May 11, 2006.

"Aviator Call Sign." en.wikipedia.org. Online. Accessed May 11, 2006.

Commander Taggart. "From a Visitor to the Cylon Alliance: An Interview with Richard Hatch." Online. July 12, 2004.

Damen, Marcel. "Nicki Clyne Fan Site Interview." November 3, 2006.

Davies, Philip John. Ed. *Science Fiction, Social Conflict, and War.* Manchester: Manchester University Press. 1991.

Dawkins, Richard. *The Selfish Gene.* Second ed. Oxford: Oxford University Press. 1989.

Dylan, Bob. "All Along the Watchtower."

"Ecological Footprint." www.earthday.net. Online. Accessed December 21, 2006.

Egnor, Mike. "Aaron Douglas Galactica.tv Interview." Online. October 12, 2006.

Elliott, Sean. "Exclusive Interview: *Battlestar Galactica*'s President, Mary McDonnell." *iF Magazine.* Online. March 15, 2006.

Eramo, Steven. "Saul Survivor." *TV Zone* #195. October 13, 2005.

Gold, Kenn. "*Battlestar Galactica*'s Paul Campbell: Life after Billy." Media Blvd. Online. April 21, 2006.

Good, Marcie. "Actor Follows in Parents' Footsteps." *Vancouver Courier Online.* Online. August 5, 2004.

Gordon, Carole. "Hail to the Chief." *Eclipse Magazine.* Online. July 22, 2006.

Grendy. Interview with Kate Vernon. Online. October 6, 2006.

Gunn, James. Ed. *The Road to Science Fiction.* Maryland: Scarecrow Press. 2003.

Holman, Hugh & Harmon, William. Eds. *Handbook to Literature.* Fifth edition. New York: MacMillan. 1986.

HyperEpos. "Basic Definitions of the Epic." Online. Accessed May 11, 2007.

"Interview with Donnelly Rhodes." *Vancouver Magazine.* March 1988.

Lewis, James. *Doomsday Prophecies.* New York: Prometheus Books. 1999.

"Luciana Carro Q&A." GalacticaBS. Online. Accessed May 11, 2007.

"Lucy Lawless Sheds Light on *Battlestar Galactica*." Scifi.about.com. Online. Accessed May 11, 2007.

Mendel, Arthur P. *Vision and Violence*. Michigan: University of Michigan Press. 1992.

"Questions for Michael Trucco." MediaBlvd Forums. Online. Accessed May 11, 2007.

"Pilot Call Signs." www.f-16.net. Online. Accessed May 1, 2007.

Rabkin, Eric; Greenberg, Martin; Olander, Joseph. Eds. *The End Of the World*. Carbondale, IL: Southern Illinois University Press. 1983.

Radish, Christina. "She's Back and Ready to Entertain." *She Magazine*. February, 2007.

Reddish, Mitchell. Ed. *Apocalyptic Literature: A Reader*. Peabody, MA: Hendrickson Publishers. 1995.

Ryan, Maureen. "Ron Moore Talks About Friday's *Battlestar Galactica* and Prepares Fans For 'a Pretty Big Loss': 'You'll Be Pretty Shocked.'" *Chicago Tribune*. Online. December 13, 2006.

Seed, David. Ed. *Imagining Apocalypse: Studies in Cultural Crisis*. New York: Palgrave MacMillan. 1999.

Shelley, Mary. *Frankenstein*. New York: Penguin. 2003.

Stevenson, Jim. "The History of the Rank Insignia Chart for *Battlestar Galactica* 2003." Online. November 1, 2006.

Stevenson, Mark. "Evidence May Back Human Sacrifice Claims." *Associated Press*. Online. January 23, 2005.

"Virtual Water Trade Research Programme." UNESCO-IHE. www.unesco-ihe.org. Online. Access May 11, 2007.

"Water Footprint Concept." www.waterfootprint.org. Online. Accessed May 11, 2007.

Weber, Eugen. *Apocalypses: Prophecies, Cults, and Millennial Beliefs Through the Ages*. Cambridge, MA: Harvard University Press. 1999.

Weiss, Allan. Interview with the author. December, 2006.

Weiten, Wayne. *Psychology: Themes and Variations*. Sixth edition. Thomson: Wadsworth. 2005.

Whyte, Jason. "Nicki Clyne, Actress — Profile Interview Series Vol. 5." October 17, 2004. Online. Accessed May 11, 2007.

Biographies

"*Battlestar Galactica* Chat with Jamie Bamber." www.scifi.com. Online. Accessed May 11, 2007.

Breen, Matthew. "Rocket Man." *Out Magazine*. Online. August 2006.

Donnelly, G.J. "Mary McDonnell Previews *Galactica*'s Trial and Tribulations." *TV Guide Magazine*. Online. March 2, 2007.

—. "Mary McDonnell: Will *Galactica*'s Prez Get Emmy Vote?" *TV Guide Magazine*. Online. March 22, 2007.

Doorly, Sean. "Mary McDonnell Dishes About All-New *Battlestar Galactica*." *The TV Tattler*. Online. January 3, 2007.

Eden, Jenny. "What Katee Did." *TV Zone*, Special #66. October 27, 2005.

"Edward James Olmos." *Hispanic American Biography*. U-X-L. 1995.

"Edward James Olmos on Adama and *Battlestar Galactica*." www.scifi.about.com. Online. Accessed May 11, 2007.

"Edward James Olmos." *U-X-L Biographies 2.0 CD-Rom*. U-X-L. 1998.

—. "Exclusive Interview: James Callis Bears All for *Battlestar Galactica*." *iF Magazine*. Online. September 14, 2006.

Elliott, Sean. "Exclusive Profile: *Battlestar Galactica*'s President — Mary McDonnell." *iF Magazine*. Online. March 15, 2006.

Ellis, James. "60 Seconds Extra: James Callis." *Metro*. October 13, 2004.

Faraci, Devin. "Exclusive Interview: James Callis (*Battlestar Galactica*)." Interview for Chud.com. Online. February 28, 2007.

Glotz, Peter. "Caprica City's Exclusive Interview with Jamie Bamber." March 5, 2006. Online. Accessed May 11, 2007.

—. "*IGN* Exclusive Interview: *Battlestar Galactica*'s Katee Sackhoff." tv.ign.com. Online. October 5, 2006.

Goldman, Eric. "*IGN* Interviews Grace Park." tv.ign.com. Online. March 10, 2006.

"Grace Park." *Maxim Magazine* #85. March, 2005.

"Grace Park: Boomer Gets Ready to Rumble." scifi.about.com. Online. Accessed May 11, 2007.

"Hail the King." *Western Daily Press*. October 10, 2002.

"Interview with Edward James Olmos." *New York*. September 29, 1986.

"Interview with Katee Sackhoff." *Wizard Magazine* #166. June, 2005.

"Jamie Bamber on Apollo and *Battlestar Galactica*." scifi.about.com. Online. Accessed May 11, 2007.

Juba, Scott. "Jamie Bamber: *Battle*-tested." *The Trades*. Online. July 6, 2006.

"Katee Sackhoff Bio." www.kateesackhoff-fans.com. Online. Accessed May 11, 2007.

Kim, Lee Ann. "Grace Park Is More Human than Human." San Diego Asian Film Festival. Online. October 13, 2006.

Kroll, Jack. "Interview with Edward James Olmos." *Newsweek*. March 20, 1992.

Kuhn, Sarah. "Event Horizon: *Battlestar Galactica*." Online. December 20, 2006.

Lee, John. "Interview with Grace Park." Interview for Ktown213.com. Online. Accessed May 11, 2006.

Lynn, Sean. "Lovely James Callis." *B Magazine*. May 2001.

Madrigal, Patrick. "Edward James Olmos Interview." *What's Up! College Edition*. October 16, 2002.

"Mary McDonnell/President Roslin Ready to Preside on *Battlestar Galactica*." scifi.about.com. Online. Accessed May 11, 2007.

McFarland, Melanie. "Sackhoff on the Flak She's Gotten for her Strong, Sexy Starbuck: Frack [*sic*] It." *Seattle Post-Intelligencer*. Online. January 19, 2006.

Nuytens, Gilles. "Interview with Grace Park." Interview for The SciFi World. Online. January 24, 2006.

—. "Interview with Katee Sackhoff." The SciFi World. Online. Feburary 25, 2007.

Reynolds, Julia. "Olmos on Fire." *El Andar*. Winter 1998.

Rotten Tomatoes. "*White Noise 2* Set Visit: Katee Sackhoff Talks *Battlestar*, *The Last Sentinel*, and *Indy 4*." Online. April 25, 2006.

Rozemberg, Hernán. "The Other Side of the Debate Now Is Busy Making Itself Heard." www.mysanantonio.com. Online. February 4, 2006.

Ryan, Maureen. "Interview with Jamie Bamber (Lee 'Apollo' Adama)." *Chicago Tribune*. Online. June 17, 2005.

Scott, Harriet. "A Girl's Best Friend — James Is a Real Diamond." *Cosmopolitan Magazine*. May 2001.

Shewey, Don. "The Metabolism of Mary McDonnell." *Village Voice*. September 20, 1983.

Small, Jonathan. "Programmed for Pleasure." Online. March 8, 2005.

"Soldier, Sailor." *The Saturday Express*. April 21, 2001.

Tricia Helfer. Official Web site. Online. Accessed May 11, 2007.

Wiebe, Sheldon. "And Now, Direct from *Battlestar Galactica* — Boomer Talks to *EM*!" *Eclipse Magazine*. Online. February 1, 2005.

"William Adama: Edward James Olmos." www.scifi.com. Online. Accessed May 11, 2007.

Episode Guide

Aeolus. "Adorably Dangerous: An Interview with Nicki Clyne." Online. July 3, 2006.

Bear McCreary Web site. www.bearmccreary.com. Online. Accessed May 11, 2007.

Cairns, Brian. "Olmos There." *Cult Times* #138. February 21, 2007.

Craddock, Linda. "Ryan Robbins Interview." The SciFi World. Online. December 20, 2006.

Craddock, Linda & Nuytens, Gilles. "Bodie Olmos Interview." The SciFi World. Online. January 20, 2007.

Cullen, Ian M. "Sackhoff Admits to Hating the Viper Scenes." *SciFi Pulse*. Online. January 30, 2007.

Elliott, Sean. "Exclusive Interview: *Battlestar Galactica* Producer David Eick Loves Lucy, Lawless That Is." *iF Magazine*. Online. April 4, 2006.

—. "Exclusive Interview: Executive Producer David Eick Gives *iF* the Scoop about *Battlestar Galactica*." *iF Magazine*. Online. April 19, 2006.

—. "Exclusive Interview: James Callis Bears All for *Battlestar Galactica*." *iF Magazine*. Online. September 14, 2006.

—. "*iF Magazine* Gets Probed by Friendly Cylon and Former Warrior Princess." Online. November 28, 2006.

Eramo, Steven. "Jamie Bamber: A Man for all Seasons." *Starburst*, Special #71. August 11, 2005.

—. "More Bang for Your Buck." *Cult Times* #124. December 21, 2005.

—. "Moral Compass." *Starbust*, Special #79. January 24, 2007.

—. "Question of Authority." *TV Zone* #198. January 4, 2006.

—. "Saul Survivor." *TV Zone* #195. October 13, 2005.

Feraci, Devin. "Exclusive Interview: Brad Thompson and David Weddle (*Battlestar Galactica*)." Interview for Chud.com. Online. October 2, 2006.

Gold, Kenn. "*Battlestar Galactica*'s Paul Campbell: Life after Billy." Media Blvd. Online. April 21, 2006.

Goldman, Eric. "*IGN* Exclusive Interview: *Battlestar Galactica*'s Katee Sackhoff." Online. October 5, 2006.

—. "*IGN* Interview: *Battlestar Galactica*'s Tricia Helfer." Online. January 18, 2007.

Guare, John. *Six Degrees of Separation*. New York: Dramatists Play Service. 1995.

http://forums.scifi.com

"Katie [sic] Sackhoff Dishes on *Galactica*." *Wizard Magazine*. July 13, 2005.

Kuhn, Sarah. "Event Horizon: *Battlestar Galactica*." Online. December 20, 2006.

Moore, Ronald D. Podcasts for *Battlestar Galactica*. Transcribed by en.battlestar.wiki.org.

Navy Historical Center Web site. www.history.navy.mil/index.html. Online. Accessed May 11, 2007.

Nuytens, Gilles. "Grace Park Interview." The SciFi World. Online. January 24, 2006,

OMac Shaun. "Interview with Leah Cairns." Online. September 27, 2005.

Perenson, Melissa. "Interviews." *SciFi Weekly*. Online. October 4, 2006.

Phillips, Mark. "Spirited Mechanic." *Starlog Magazine* #348. August, 2006.

PinkRaygun.com. "PinkRaygun Interviews: Nicki Clyne." Online. April 20, 2007.

SciFi.com. "Behind the Scenes: Interview with Jamie Bamber." Online. July 12, 2005.

Small, Jonathan. "Programmed for Pleasure." Online. March 8, 2005.

The Holy Bible. King James Version. New York: American Bible Society. 2000.

Woodward, Bob. *Bush At War*. New York: Simon and Schuster. 2002.